Classroom Management
for Elementary Teachers

Classroom Management for Elementary Teachers

FOURTH EDITION

Carolyn M. Evertson
Peabody College, Vanderbilt University

Edmund T. Emmer
The University of Texas, Austin

Barbara S. Clements
Council of Chief State School Officers, Washington, D.C.

Murray E. Worsham
Northeast Independent School District, San Antonio, Texas

ALLYN AND BACON
Boston • London • Toronto • Sydney • Tokyo • Singapore

Publisher, Education: Nancy Forsyth
Editorial Assistant: Kate Wagstaffe
Senior Marketing Manager: Kris Farnsworth
Editorial-Production Administrator: Donna Simons
Editorial-Production Service: Matrix Productions Inc.
Composition and Prepress Buyer: Linda Cox
Manufacturing Buyer: Megan Cochran
Cover Administrator: Linda Knowles
Text Designer: Barbara Bert

Library of Congress Cataloging-in-Publication Data

Classroom management for elementary teachers / Carolyn M. Evertson . . .
   [et al.]. — 4th ed.
      p.   cm.
   Includes bibliographical references (p.   ) and index.
   ISBN 0-205-20006-0
   1. Classroom management.   2. Education, Elementary.   I. Evertson,
Carolyn M.
LB3013.C528   1996
371.1′024—dc20   96–20072
                                                                      CIP

Printed in the United States of America

10   9   8   7   6   5   4   3   2   01   00   99   98   97

Contents

CHAPTER 3   Managing Student Work   43

CHAPTER 4   Getting Off to a Good Start   59

CHAPTER **7** ## Communication Skills for Teaching   135

CHAPTER **8** ## Managing Problem Behaviors   159

Preface

The conventional wisdom about good classroom management is that no one notices it unless it's missing. Although everyone recognizes it as one of the most important foundations of good instruction, effective classroom management doesn't just happen. Smoothly running classrooms where students are highly involved exist because teachers have clear ideas of the types of classroom conditions and student behaviors necessary for a healthy learning environment. They not only have clear ideas, but they work very hard to create these conditions. This book describes what *you* can do to create a well-managed classroom. The process is described as teachers encounter it: first by planning in several key areas before the school year begins; then, by implementing the plan and establishing good management at the beginning of the year; and finally, by maintaining the management procedures throughout the year. We have tried to make the materials as useful and practical as possible by providing checklists to help you organize your planning. Several case studies and problem-solving scenarios are also provided that focus on critical areas that need special attention. We hope you will find much here that is helpful as you plan and organize for your own classroom.

This edition retains the same structure and many of the topics as the original edition. We have, however, made substantial additions and revisions to reflect current research and practice. Chapter 7 on communication skills for teaching was added in the second edition and is retained in this edition. Chapter 8, "Managing Problem Behavior," was added in the third edition and also has been retained. In addition, we have increased our coverage of the management of group-based learning activities and other approaches designed to accommodate greater diversity in student populations. Accordingly, we added case studies on classroom management in cooperative learning and inclusion classrooms. Finally, we have added several annotated readings at the end of each chapter that focus on applications and research. In addition to stimulating independent study, these readings, along with the case studies, may be useful for individual reports or group discussions.

In making these revisions, we have been influenced by our own experiences as teachers. However, most of our knowledge about classroom management derives from research and observation, both our own and others'. Our research program on classroom management extends over twenty years and has included observational studies and field experiments involving more than 500 elementary and secondary classrooms. Data collected in this research are a major source of suggestions, guidelines, and case studies in this book. We therefore gratefully acknowledge our debt to many teachers who permitted us to learn from them. Without this base of reality, this book would not exist.

We also wish to thank the following reviewers: Jennifer Humphries, Ashland University; Jane McHaney, Kennesaw State College; and Ralph Shibley, University of Rio Grande.

We are grateful to Catherine H. Randolph, who helped edit the third edition, for her editorial help on the revisions in this edition. She, Susan B. Talwalkar, Kristen W. Weeks, and Kay J. McClain, all teachers, made major contributions to the case studies through their critical analyses, suggestions for revisions, and by keeping us in the "real world." As always, we appreciate the contributions of the many observers, school administrators, and other researchers who both assisted and enlightened us.

Organizing Your Classroom and Supplies

Arranging the physical setting for teaching is a logical starting point for classroom management because it is a task that all teachers face before the school year begins. Many teachers find it easier to plan other aspects of classroom management after they have a clear idea of how the physical features of the classroom will be organized.

The number of things that must be considered in arranging the typical elementary school classroom is amazing! Of course, there is furniture—the teacher's and the students' desks, bookcases, computers, filing cabinets, chairs, and a table or two. In addition, there may be audiovisual equipment such as an overhead projector, tape recorder, record player, and television. Visual aids such as bulletin boards

Reprinted by permission: Tribune Media Services.

must be prepared; charts, globes, and maps must be displayed; and storage for materials must be provided. Finally, there are the personal touches that teachers often bring to a classroom—perhaps plants, an aquarium, or animal cages for hamsters. When you arrange these physical features, you will need to make many decisions. How should desks be arranged? Where should your desk be located? Where will groups meet with you? Where will cooperative groups work? What areas of the room will you use for presentations? How will you and the students obtain materials and supplies?

FOR REFLECTION

Before you begin to arrange your classroom, give some thought to the following questions. The answers will help you decide what physical features need special attention. Before you look at your classroom, think about the kinds of learning you would most like to see there:

◆ What will be your main types of instructional activities (e.g., small groups, whole-class discussions, teacher presentations, student presentations, individual assignments, group projects)? What physical arrangements will best support these activities?

◆ Will students be making extensive use of equipment (e.g., video monitors, tape recorders, computers) or materials (e.g., science or math manipulatives)? Will these need to be shared among individuals or groups?

◆ How much movement around the room will be necessary during the day? What areas of the room will be involved? Will students get their own materials, or will you distribute them?

◆ To what kinds of reference, research tools, or trade books will students need access?

◆ How flexible or permanent will the arrangement be? Will you need to change it during a single day, for each new unit, or will it stay the same for months? ∎

The decisions you make will have important consequences for the success of your instructional activities. Your room arrangement also affects how smoothly your day can proceed. For example, if areas for storing materials are poorly placed, bottlenecks may occur when students get supplies or return them, which could slow down the activities or waste time getting them started. The location for your meetings with individuals and small groups must be chosen carefully, or you may have difficulty watching the rest of the class. The positioning of desks is important because a poor arrangement may interfere with visibility of chalkboards or other instructional areas, increase distractions during instruction, or make it difficult for you and your students to move around the room. Your room arrangement communicates to students how you expect them to participate in your class. Desks arranged in groups imply that interaction and collaboration among students are expected at least for some activities. Desks in rows indicate that the focus of the classroom is the teacher, the chalkboard, or some other central point. Your room arrangement should reflect your philosophy of teaching and learning.

This chapter will help you make these and other decisions about room arrangement, equipment, and basic supplies. Each component is described, and guidelines and examples are given to help you plan. In addition, a checklist of room arrangement items is provided. Use it to organize your efforts in this important task and to be certain your classroom is ready for the beginning of school.

FOUR KEYS TO GOOD ROOM ARRANGEMENT

Remember that the classroom is the learning environment for both you and your students. It is not a very large area for up to thirty people interacting for long periods of time—as much as seven hours in a day. Furthermore, you and your students will be engaging in a variety of activities and using different areas of the room. You will facilitate these activities if you arrange your room to permit orderly movement, keep distractions to a minimum, and make efficient use of available space. Depending on your instructional approach, you may need different arrangements for different activities (e.g., whole-class, small group). The following four keys will be helpful as guidelines for making decisions about your room's arrangements:

1. **Keep high traffic areas free of congestion.** Areas where many students gather and areas that receive constant use can be sites for distraction and disruption. High traffic areas include group work areas, pencil sharpener, trash can, water fountain, certain book shelves and storage areas, computer stations, students' desks, and the teacher's desk. These areas should be widely separated from each other, have plenty of space, and be easy to get to. Also, if students are going to be working at computers or in various parts of the room during a single lesson, make sure they can move easily from place to place.

2. **Be sure students can be seen easily by the teacher.** Careful monitoring of students is a major management task. Your success in monitoring will depend on your ability to see all students at all times. Therefore, be sure there are

clear lines of sight between instructional areas, your desk, students' desks, and all student work areas. Be especially conscious of the placement of bookcases, file cabinets, and other pieces of furniture and equipment that can block your line of vision. Try standing in different parts of the room and checking for blind spots.

3. **Keep frequently used teaching materials and student supplies readily accessible.** Keeping materials accessible not only minimizes time spent getting ready and cleaning up, it also helps to avoid distracting slowdowns and breaks in the lesson flow. If you or your students must stop to locate needed materials and supplies, you run the risk of losing student attention and engagement. Time is lost as you must refocus attention to the lesson. (The idea of lesson flow will be discussed further in Chapter 5.)

4. **Be certain students can easily see whole-class presentations and displays.** When you plan where you and your students will be for whole-class presentations and discussion, be sure that the seating arrangement will allow students to see the overhead projector screen or chalkboard without moving their chairs, turning their desks around, or craning their necks. Also, don't plan to conduct whole-class activities in a far corner of the room away from a substantial number of students. Such conditions do not encourage students to pay attention, and they make it more difficult for you to keep all students involved. You may wish to check out how well your students can see by sitting for a moment at desks in different parts of the room.

Applying each of the above four keys will help you design good room arrangements. The specific components that will lead to this goal are described below. By attending to these areas, you will address all of the important aspects of room arrangement. You can be confident that you will have designed a physical setting that is efficient and conducive to student learning.

SUGGESTIONS FOR ARRANGING YOUR CLASSROOM

Wall and Ceiling Space

Wall space and bulletin boards provide areas to display student work, instructionally relevant material, decorative items, assignments, rules, schedules, a clock, and other items of interest. Ceiling space can also be used to hang mobiles, decorations, and student work. The following points should be considered when preparing these areas:

1. At the start of school, you should have at least the following displays for walls and chalkboards:

- ◆ Class rules (to be discussed in Chapter 2)
- ◆ A place for listing daily assignments or the daily schedule
- ◆ Some decorative display to catch your students' interest, such as a bulletin board with a "Welcome Back to School" motif, or a display that includes the name of each child in the room
- ◆ Calendar

2. Other displays that many teachers find useful include an example of the correct paper heading to be used in your class and a content-relevant display, such as one highlighting a soon-to-be-taught topic. Many teachers also provide posters of useful strategies for content areas, such as reading, and informational charts on the steps of the writing process.

3. You will probably want to cover large bulletin board areas with colored paper, burlap, or other fabric. This paper comes on large rolls and is often kept in the school office or a supply room. You can trim the bulletin boards with an edging or border of corrugated paper. If you can't find this item in your supply room, you can spend a few dollars for the materials at a school supply center or other store. You can also find books of bulletin board ideas for sale at such stores.

4. If you need ideas for decorating your room or for setting up displays, borrow hints from other teachers. A look in some other rooms will probably give you several new ideas.

5. Don't spend a lot of time decorating your room. You will have many other more important things to do to get ready for the beginning of school. A few

"Do you sometimes get the feeling that this classroom was designed for older students?"

Reprinted courtesy of James Estes/*Phi Delta Kappan.*

bare bulletin boards won't bother anybody. Leave one or two empty and add displays later or allow children to decorate a blank space for an art project or as part of a science or social studies unit. Also don't overdecorate. Wall space cluttered with detail can distract students and make a room seem smaller. Hanging mobiles and decorations from the ceiling can also be overdone. Your room will seem small enough when your twenty-five to thirty students are in it.

Floor Space

Arrange your furniture and equipment so that you can easily observe students from all areas of the room in which you will work. Students should be able to see you, the overhead projector screen, the main chalkboard, and any other area that will be used for presentations to the whole class. Of course, you will have to adjust to whatever constraints exist in your assigned classroom. Common problems are a classroom that is too small or that has inadequate or poorly placed chalkboard space or electrical outlets. You should assess your space and determine whatever feasible changes can be effected within the existing constraints. For example, if the classroom is small, be sure to remove unnecessary student desks, other furniture, or equipment; if you have inadequate storage, perhaps you can locate an extra file or supply cabinet.

A good starting point for your floor plan is to determine where you will conduct whole-class instruction. Examine the room and identify where you will stand or work when you address the entire class to give instructions. You can usually identify this area of the room by the location of a large chalkboard or the overhead projector screen. This area should also have room for a table or desk where you can place items needed in presentations and an electrical outlet for the overhead projector. If you prefer to have your students gather on the floor for whole-class instruction, allow adequate space when arranging the classroom furniture. You may also want to provide a large rug for this area.

As you begin to plan your floor space, you may want to make a scaled drawing of the classroom and templates for different furnishings (e.g., student desks, your desk, bookshelves, computer stations, etc.). This will decrease the number of times you have to move the heavy furniture in your classroom and will be a more efficient use of your planning time. When you start arranging furniture, have extension cords in hand. They are easier to plug in before a heavy bookcase is standing in front of the electrical outlet.

As you read the following items, refer to Figure 1–1, which shows an example of a well-designed floor plan for an elementary school classroom. Note how each item has been addressed. Of course, this is just one of many possible alternatives. The location of desks, the small-group area, and other physical features of the classroom will depend on the size and shape of the room and how different parts of the room will be used.

ARRANGEMENT OF STUDENT DESKS

Many arrangements of student desks are possible, but the key to their arrangement lies in what kinds of activities will be occurring in your classroom. If most instruction is whole-group, desks should be arranged so that all students can look at the instructional area without having to get out of their seats or having to sit with their backs to the area. If the majority of your instruction is teacher-led, you may prefer to arrange student desks in rows. If students will work in small groups frequently, you may want to arrange their desks in groups with students facing one another. If you arrange desks in groups, you will need to decide how many students to include in each group. You will also need to determine if your seating arrangement will vary according to the types of classroom activities or if it will be permanent. After you have established the seating arrangement, decide if you will assign students to their seats or if they can choose where they will sit.

Note that in the classroom shown in Figure 1–1, the student desks are arranged in clusters rather than in rows; however, no student is seated with his or her back to the major instructional area. If the teacher displays material on the overhead projector screen, all the students can see it by turning slightly in their seats.

◆ It is important to keep high traffic areas clear, so don't put desks or other furniture in front of doors, water fountains, sinks, the pencil sharpener, or other traffic centers. Also, try to avoid having your whole-class arrangement face potential sources of distraction, such as windows, the small-group area,

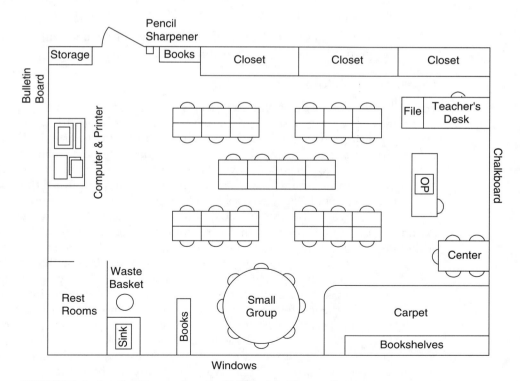

FIGURE 1–1   An Example of a Workable Room Arrangement

animals, or other eye-catching displays. Make sure that computer stations are accessible but not distracting.

◆ Leave enough room around student desks so that you can monitor them easily or give them help during seatwork activities.

◆ Some classrooms are equipped with tables and chairs for student seating instead of student desks. Table seating presents special room arrangement problems, especially in grade levels higher than first and second grades. If students are seated on all sides of tables, some will have their backs to instructional presentation areas. If you have enough space and tables, this visibility problem can be avoided by seating students on only three sides of the tables. An additional problem that can be troublesome is storage of students' supplies such as paper, notebooks, textbooks, crayons, and scissors. If there are no individual storage spaces under tables, tote trays (boxes or plastic dish tubs) may be used for students' materials. These must be stored on easily accessible shelves or carts. If you want to promote sharing among students, "community" tote trays can be shared. This also cuts down on the need for each student to have a full set of supplies. Plan the location of this storage area or areas carefully, for it will be used frequently and often by many students at once. Give thorough consideration to traffic patterns around and near tote tray storage areas.

◆ Count the desks or chairs and make sure you have enough. Replace damaged furniture or have it repaired.

COOPERATIVE GROUP AREA

You will need an area where you can meet with small groups of students, when you are brainstorming with a small group, when you are helping with a group project, or when you are working with individuals. This area should be arranged so that you can observe the rest of the class from your position within the small group. Thus, your chair should be placed so that you face the whole class. Note the position of the small-group area in Figure 1–1. If you are seated facing out toward the room, you can monitor the whole class even when working with the small group. In contrast, if you were seated in the opposite chair with your back to the class, you could not see unless you turned around. Note also that there is a table in this small-group area. Although it is not required for a reading group, a table does allow this area to be used for small-group activities that include writing or working with materials.

When a table (or extra chairs) is not available, students may be asked to carry their chairs and place them in a circle (or to sit on a rug) for group instruction. An alternative is for the teacher to assign seats so that students can remain at their desks or tables for small-group instruction while the teacher moves from group to group.

If many small groups will be working in your classroom at once (e.g., cooperative groups, small group research projects, literature discussion groups, or writing process groups), you will need to provide areas where they can meet. For instance, groups can meet on the floor, at student desks, or at the small group table.

If several small groups are meeting while other students are doing independent work at their desks, the small groups should be located so that they do not disturb the other students.

COMPUTER WORKSTATIONS

You may also have one or more computers in your classroom. If so, they can greatly expand the learning opportunities available to students, but getting the most from this resource means planning where they will be as well as how, when, and by whom they will be used. Your location choices may be limited because of the need for wall outlets and a phone line, so consider placing the computer workstations first and then arranging other centers and activity areas. If you plan to let students work as partners, you will need to allow plenty of space for access. If you also have a printer, you will need space for paper storage and a tray for paper output as well as storage for software, ribbons, or ink cartridges. You may also want to get plastic covers for the computers and printer when they are not in use.

THE TEACHER'S DESK, FILING CABINET, OVERHEAD PROJECTOR, AND OTHER EQUIPMENT

Your desk needs to be placed where it is functional. If you intend to use your desk to store instructional materials, it should be adjacent to the whole-class instructional area and preferably near any other major instructional area. If you plan to work at your desk at any time during the day, you will need to position your desk to facilitate monitoring of students. Use the same principle here as with placing the small-group area: Sit facing the students and be sure you can observe all of them from your seat. It is not necessary that students be able to see you from their seats, and some teachers prefer placing their desk at the back of the room rather than the front. If you plan to work with individual students at your desk, you will have to consider traffic patterns near your desk. Student desks should not be so close that students would be distracted by individuals approaching your desk or working with you there.

You will also need to consider students' access to materials on your desk. If students can use materials stored on your desk, such as a stapler or extra crayons, you will need to think about procedures for obtaining these supplies. For example, may students get these supplies whenever they are necessary, or do they need to ask your permission?

Other furniture items, such as the filing cabinet and storage cabinets, also need to be where they are functional. Seldom used supplies can be safely tucked away in a corner or hidden out of view. Furniture that contains items that will be used frequently must be near the area in which they will be used.

BOOKCASES

Bookcases should be placed where they will neither hinder your monitoring nor obstruct students' ability to see chalkboards or relevant displays. If the bookcases contain items used frequently, such as dictionaries or the classroom library, the

"Miss Marpole, I need to talk to you about your seating arrangement."

Reprinted by permission of George Abbott/*Phi Delta Kappan*.

bookcases need to be convenient and easily monitored. A bookcase for seldom used items should be in an out-of-the-way place. If you have only one bookcase, try to store unneeded items in a cabinet so that the bookcase can be used for the necessary materials. Consider using a rolling cart rather than bookcases for materials that may need to move from group to group, such as resources for a particular research topic.

Centers

A center is an area where students come to work on a special activity or to study some topic. Often a center will have special equipment such as a tape recorder with headphones for individual students. Other centers may be built around a special thematic study topic in science or social studies or around skill areas in a particular subject such as arithmetic or reading. Examples of types of centers in elementary classrooms include: classroom libraries, listening centers, writing centers, science discovery centers, computer workstations, math centers, art centers, and dramatic play areas. The number and type of centers will vary according to grade levels.

If you decide to have centers in your classroom, you will need to consider carefully the locations for each. For instance, if the center is to be a separate area of your room such as the classroom library, consider dividing the area from the rest of the class with a low bookshelf or table so you can easily monitor students. Also, if you anticipate increased noise or activity at a center, locate it so as not to disturb other students. If any of your centers require electrical outlets or phone lines, arrange them first. Also be certain that all necessary materials and equipment at the center are available and functioning properly. Post instructions for equipment use and cleaning up the center.

Pets, Plants, Aquariums, and Special Items

These can add a personal touch to a room as well as provide learning experiences for children. However, the first week of school is already quite exciting for students, so it is not necessary to introduce these special features immediately. When you do bring in such items, place them where they won't distract students, especially during whole-class activities. Of course, they should be placed where they will neither impede movement about the room nor interfere with activities of individual students.

Storage Space and Supplies

Once you have decided on your wall and bulletin board displays and have organized space within the classroom, you can concentrate on obtaining supplies and providing for their storage. Some supplies will be used frequently and should be readily accessible. Other items will be seasonal or infrequently used and thus can go into deeper storage.

TEXTBOOKS AND OTHER INSTRUCTIONAL MATERIALS

You need to identify the textbooks and other materials available for use in your class. Other instructional materials may include dictionaries, encyclopedias, magazines, newspapers, maps, globes, and math manipulatives. Determine which books the students are allowed to keep at their desks or take home and which must remain in the room for all students to use. Then find easily accessible shelves in a bookcase for those everyday books and materials that will not be kept in student desks. If you don't know what supplemental materials are available or what the school policies are regarding these items, check with the school principal, media specialist, or another teacher.

STUDENTS' WORK

If students do not have space to store their folders and journals, or if you prefer to keep them in a central location, make sure this area is easily accessible. For example, if students are seated at tables, you may want to place a basket or milk crate in the center of the table. The basket or crate can contain a hanging file for each student at that table, and the student can keep his folders, journal, and work in progress in the hanging file. If students are not seated at tables, or the tables are too small for the basket or crate, you can place baskets around the room for easy access. Also, if students will be developing portfolios and will have input in their assessment, place their portfolios in an accessible location.

FREQUENTLY USED CLASSROOM MATERIALS

These are supplies the children will use. Items included in a basic set are paper in varying sizes and colors, water-soluble markers, rulers, assorted pens and chalk for art projects, transparent tape and masking tape, stapler, and glue. These and any other supplies that are used daily—science materials, math manipulatives, calculators—should be kept in a readily accessible place such as on a work table or shelves. Students are usually expected to supply certain materials such as pencils, erasers, pens, crayons, scissors, and notebook paper or tablets. Because you cannot count on all students bringing these materials at the beginning of the year, make sure you have an ample supply of these items. It is also a good idea to give parents a list of supplies each child will need in your class.

TEACHER'S SUPPLIES

You will receive some materials from the school office for your own use. These items may include pencils and pens, paper, a large, lined display tablet, chalk and erasers, overhead transparency sheets, scissors, transparent tape, ruler, stapler, paper clips, and thumbtacks. In addition, you should have a grade book, a lesson plan book, and teacher's editions for all textbooks. Ask about other supplementary books such as thematic resources or math or science standards. These items can usually be stored in your desk.

OTHER MATERIALS

A number of other supplies will come in handy. If your room does not have a clock and a calendar, obtain these now. Both should be large enough to be seen from all areas of the room. You may wish to buy a desk bell or a timer if you are going to use these as signals for starting or stopping activities. You should also add the following items: tissues, rags or paper towels, soap, bandages, and extra lunch money for emergencies. Some teachers like to keep a few basic tools such as a hammer, pliers, and screwdriver in case a minor repair needs to be made.

STUDENT BELONGINGS

In addition to supplies that students store in their desks or in tote trays, you need storage available for items such as lunch boxes, book bags, outdoor clothing, lost-and-found items, and show-and-tell materials. Leave spaces for these items as you prepare your classroom. You might wish to prepare signs designating the use to which each space will be put. Planning for student storage will help keep your classroom from becoming cluttered and will help avoid the problem of misplaced belongings.

EQUIPMENT

Check all equipment, including the computer, TV, VCR, overhead projector, record player, tape recorder, headphones, and pencil sharpener to make sure they are in working order. Get any necessary extension cords or adapter plugs and store these with the equipment or in a handy place.

SEASONAL OR INFREQUENTLY USED ITEMS

This category includes holiday and seasonal decorations, bulletin board displays, and special project materials. Also included are instructional materials used only on some occasions: for example, calculators, protractors, templates, special art project materials, and science equipment. Because you do not need to have ready access to these materials, you can store them at the back of closets, in boxes on top of cabinets, or even out of the room if you have access to outside storage space.

To organize and keep track of your activities as you arrange your room and get your equipment and supplies ready, you will find it helpful to use Checklist 1 at the end of this chapter. Each aspect of room arrangement has been listed, and space has been provided for noting what has to be done and for checking off the area once you have it ready.

 ## FURTHER READING

Goodman, K. S. (1991). Yippie-aye-ay: Planning and organizing holistically. In Y. M. Goodman, W. J. Hood, & K. S. Goodman (Eds.), *Organizing for Whole Language* (pp. 3–17). Portsmouth, NH: Heinemann.

The author describes a process of planning for whole-language teaching that he calls "ecological." He advises teachers to start by determining who and what must be present in a given class, grade, or school. He also recommends attention to others, such as parents, community boards, and cultural groups, whose interests may influence the classroom setting.

Lambert, N. M. (1994). Seating arrangements in classrooms. *The International Encyclopedia of Education* (2nd ed.), Vol. 9, 5355–5359.

This article provides a summary of research on classroom seating arrangements. Although student seating is only one factor in the way the teacher arranges the classroom, it can have an important influence on a variety of student behaviors.

Rosenfield, P., Lambert, N. M., & Black, A. (1985). Desk arrangement effects on pupil classroom behavior. *Journal of Educational Psychology, 77,* 101–108.

The authors conducted an experiment comparing student behavior during discussion activities using different seating arrangements. Circle and cluster formations promoted more on-task behavior during discussions than did seating students in rows. The results suggest the importance of considering instructional and behavioral goals while planning the classroom's organization.

Schwarz, S., & Pollishuke, M. (1991). *Creating the child-centered classroom.* Katonah, NY: Richard Owen Publishers. Chapter 2: The physical set-up of the classroom.

This book has useful and practical information on room arrangements, planning varied activities, group work, creating learning centers, and creating an effective learning atmosphere. It includes blackline masters for teacher or student use.

Weinstein, C. S. (1979). The physical environment of the school: A review of research. *Review of Educational Research, 49,* 577–610.

This article reviews research on the influence of classroom environments on student behavior, attitudes, and achievement. Of particular interest is the first section, which examines studies of six environmental variables: seating position, classroom design, density, privacy, noise, and the presence or absence of windows.

SUGGESTED ACTIVITIES

The following activities will help you plan and organize your classroom space. Do as many of them as you have time for.

1. Figure 1–2 shows how one teacher arranged a classroom. There are quite a few potential problems with this room arrangement. See how many you can find and suggest one or more ways to correct each problem. (A key for this activity is provided in the Appendix.)

2. **a.** Examine Figure 1–3. Based on the room arrangement, what activities would you expect to be common in this classroom? What kinds of participation will be expected from students?
   b. Picture yourself as a student in the classrooms depicted in Figures 1–2 and 1–3. Place yourself in various areas of the room. Can you see what you need to see? Now place yourself as a teacher in the rooms. Can you see all students? Can you circulate freely among desks and work areas?

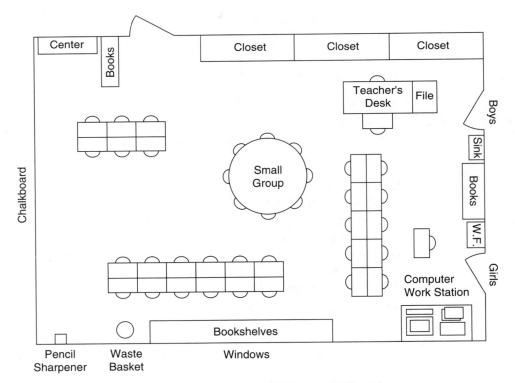

FIGURE 1–2 A Room Arrangement with Potential Problems

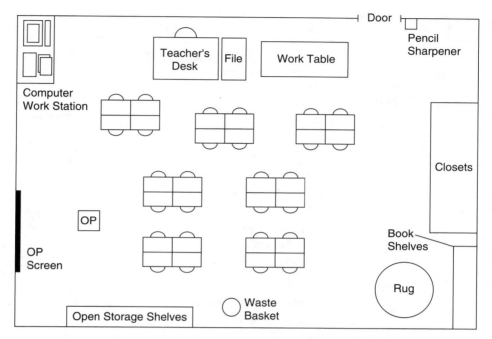

FIGURE 1–3   One Teacher's Planned Room Arrangement

    c. The teacher whose classroom is depicted in Figure 1–3 has anticipated having twenty-eight students in her class. She has just learned that she will have at least thirty-three at the beginning of the year. How can she rearrange her room to accommodate the five additional students without losing the advantages of the arrangement she has designed?

3. Visit other teachers' classrooms and examine their room arrangements. Use the items in Checklist 1 at the end of the chapter and the four keys to room arrangement (pp. 3–4) to guide your observation and analysis. If you are having a specific problem, ask several teachers for suggestions and look to see how they may have coped with a similar problem.

✓ **4. a.** Make a scale drawing of your room, as in Figure 1–1. Use it to experiment with different furniture arrangements and the organization of space on paper, a much simpler task than pushing the furniture around yourself. Evaluate your arrangement using the four keys to successful room arrangement.

    b. After you have arranged the furniture in your room, test the traffic patterns from a teacher and student perspective, keeping in mind the recommendations in this chapter.

✓ CHECKLIST I

ROOM PREPARATION

Check When Complete	Subject	Notes
☐	A. Bulletin Boards and Walls	_____
	B. Floor Space	
☐	1. Student desks/tables	_____
☐	2. Small-group area	_____
☐	3. Teacher's desk and equipment	_____
☐	4. Bookcases	_____
☐	5. Centers	_____
☐	6. Pets and plants area(s)	_____
☐	7. Traffic patterns	_____
☐	8. Computer workstation(s)	_____
☐	9. Classroom library	_____
	C. Storage Space and Supplies	
☐	1. Textbooks and trade books	_____
☐	2. Students' work	_____
☐	3. Portfolio files	_____
☐	4. Frequently used instructional materials	_____
☐	5. Teacher's supplies	_____
☐	6. Student belongings	_____
☐	7. Equipment	_____
☐	8. Seasonal or infrequently used items	_____

C H A P T E R 2

Choosing Rules and Procedures

Good classroom management is based on students' understanding of the behaviors expected of them. A carefully planned system of rules and procedures makes it easier for you to communicate your expectations to your students, and it helps ensure that the procedures you set up will be workable and appropriate. The goal of this chapter is to help you develop a sound system of rules and procedures for your class.

WHY ALL KINDS OF CLASSROOMS NEED RULES AND PROCEDURES

The rules and procedures you design will depend on the kind of classroom community you want to develop. For example, different rules and, especially, procedures will be necessary in a classroom where most instruction is teacher-led than in one where students work largely independently or in small groups. The important point is that no classroom operates smoothly without rules and procedures that are carefully planned and taught.

Rules and procedures vary in different classrooms, but we do not find effectively managed classrooms operating without them. It is simply not possible for a teacher to conduct instruction or for students to work productively if they have no guidelines for how to behave, when to move about the room, and where to sit, or if they interrupt the teacher frequently and make whatever amount of noise pleases them. Furthermore, inefficient procedures and the absence of routines for such common aspects of classroom life as entering and leaving the room, turning in materials, participating in discussions, or checking work can waste large amounts of time and cause students' attention and interest to wane. A brief example of a classroom with major problems in the area of rules and procedures is presented below.

At 8 A.M. when the beginning-of-school bell rings, twenty-one of Ms. Smith's twenty-six fourth-grade students are in the classroom. Most are not at their desks but are milling about the room and talking noisily. Ms. Smith calls out above the din, "Everyone, sit down!" With much effort, she succeeds in getting most of the children in their seats; however, three students are still standing and talking. The teacher goes to the front of the room and tries to begin a discussion of the previous day's field trip, but few children are listening. A few students straggle in at 8:06. Two others leave their seats. The teacher asks the children what they liked about their field trip. Only a few students respond. There is already some evidence of inattention: Several students are not facing the teacher, and others are quietly conversing among themselves. The teacher abandons the discussion and asks a girl to pass out papers. At 8:09, students are sitting with nothing to do while the teacher talks with children who have walked up to her desk. At 8:10, the teacher goes to the front of the class and announces that today she will show them something new. Two students are talking loudly, but the teacher ignores them. Three other students leave their seats: One goes to the drinking fountain, one to the pencil sharpener, and one to visit with another student. The teacher tells students to prepare for journal writing. Immediately, two students leave their seats to borrow paper, and the noise level in the room increases. About half the students get out notebooks. The students by the far wall are quiet, but they seem to be ignoring the teacher. One student goes to the closet, another to the pencil sharpener. Ms. Smith calls out, "Everyone, be quiet and get out your journals!" Several students call out, "What for?"

Observers of this classroom might criticize Ms. Smith for allowing students to get away with so much misbehavior. "Be stricter," they might say, "Punish the misbehaving students." Or, "Develop more interesting lessons to capture student interest." Some might even suggest that Ms. Smith set up a reward system to encourage good behavior. Although these suggestions could be helpful under some circumstances, they do not address the fundamental problem in this classroom: The students have not learned the behaviors that are expected of them. Furthermore, the teacher has not established procedures to guide student behavior. Problems are evident in several areas: the beginning-of-day routine, bringing materials for class, talking when the teacher is leading the class, out-of-seat behavior, attending to the teacher, and responding to questions.

Of course, even if the students know what is appropriate, they will not necessarily behave as they should. (For that reason, this book will not end with the present chapter!) However, giving the students a clear set of expectations for what is appropriate will be a major start toward establishing a positive classroom environment.

Keep in mind that the unique setting created by elementary school organization makes it essential to have a good set of classroom procedures. You will work with twenty-five to thirty students every day. Although your students will leave the room for lunch, recess, and perhaps some instruction, you will generally be confined to a single room with limited space and materials. You will be responsible for teaching many cognitive skills to a diverse population of students, and at the same time you will have to handle administrative tasks, arrange for appropriate materials and supplies, and evaluate students. In order to do these things well, you and your students need an orderly environment with minimal disruption and wasted time, leaving everyone free to concentrate on the critical tasks of learning. Carefully planned procedures help create this environment.

FOR REFLECTION

As you plan your routines and rules, consider what role students will play in choosing and implementing them. Some teachers prefer students to participate extensively by helping formulate rules, by discussing their rationales, and by offering alternatives in some cases. Other teachers prefer a more traditional, teacher-led system of rules and procedures. Still others prefer a blending of teacher and students working together. Consider which approach you prefer, why you prefer it, and how you would implement it. ■

RY CONSIDERATIONS

Definition of Terms

Rules and *procedures* each refer to stated expectations regarding behavior. A rule identifies general expectations or standards for behavior. For example, the rule "Respect other persons and their property" covers a large set of behaviors that should always be practiced. Rules may indicate unacceptable behavior as well as expected, appropriate behavior, although teachers sometimes manage to write rules that are only positively stated (for example, "We ask permission before talking in class"). In addition to general rules, many teachers will have a rule or two governing a specific behavior that could become an issue or that they want to prevent (for example, "Gum chewing is allowed," or "Gum chewing is not allowed").

Procedures also communicate expectations for behavior. They are usually applied in a specific activity, and they are usually directed at accomplishing something rather than prohibiting some behavior or defining a general standard. For example, you will set up procedures with your students for collecting assignments, turning in late work, participating in class discussions, using the bathroom, and so on. Some procedures (such as use of equipment at a center) are so sufficiently complex or critical that you may want to post guidelines in addition to discussing them with the students. However, many procedures are not written because they are

"This class will stimulate your ideas and thoughts. And remember—no talking."
Reprinted by permission of James Warren.

very simple or because their specificity and frequency of use allow students to learn them rapidly.

Identifying School Rules and Procedures

In most schools, teachers are expected to enforce a set of school rules. It is to your advantage to do so. Rules applied consistently in all classes and areas of the building are easy for students to learn. The rules also acquire more legitimacy in the eyes of some students because the rules are everyone's rules. In addition to rules and procedures that regulate student behavior, all schools have certain administrative procedures that must be followed by every teacher (for example, keeping attendance records). You should know your school's rules and procedures before the year begins so that you can also incorporate them into your own classroom system. You can find out about school rules for students and administrative procedures for teachers at a school orientation meeting or from a teacher's handbook, a building administrator, or another teacher. Pay careful attention to the following:

1. Behaviors that are specifically forbidden (examples: running in the halls, bringing certain items to school) or required (being in possession of a hall permit when out of the classroom during class time, bringing a note for absence).

2. Consequences for rule violations. In particular, you need to note the responsibility you have for carrying out the consequence, such as reporting the student to the school office. If the school does not have a policy for dealing with certain rule violations, you will need to decide how to handle them yourself.

3. Administrative procedures that must be handled during class time. These procedures include beginning-of-year tasks such as assigning textbooks to students, collecting fees, and checking the class roster. Money collection (for school lunches, for example) will go on all year, so you will need some system of record keeping and a safe place to keep the money. Some administrative tasks will have to be conducted each day. These include taking and recording class attendance in your grade book, talking with previously absent students, and filing an attendance report with the office. You will also need a procedure for allowing students to leave the room to go to other parts of the building. Some teachers have an attendance chart where students designate when they are present each day. At one glance, you can tell who is absent without interrupting student activities.

Frequently, procedures in these areas will already be established and followed throughout the school. If uniform procedures have not been implemented in the school in some area, you may find it helpful to talk with experienced teachers about how they handle it.

Planning Your Classroom Rules

Once you have information about school rules and procedures, you will be ready to begin planning for your own classroom. Guidelines for rules will be presented separately from those for procedures.

Many different rules are possible, but a set of five to eight rules should be sufficient to cover most important areas of behavior. Five general rules that encompass many classroom behaviors are listed below. These or similar rules are often found in well-managed classrooms, although we do not intend that they be considered a definitive list. You may decide to use other rules (for example, a rule prohibiting a specific behavior) or different wording. Some teachers may find these rules too general, and they might prefer to have more rules with greater specificity. After each rule are examples of behaviors related to the rule. When presenting general rules, it is important to discuss your specific expectations with students. When discussing the rules and related behaviors, it is best to emphasize the positive parts of the rules rather than just their negative counterparts. When you do the former, you help students learn how to behave appropriately. You will need to be explicit about behaviors that are not acceptable when such behaviors might occur frequently (examples would be gum chewing, being out of seat, call-outs). These may be incorporated into your set of rules or discussed when presenting procedures associated with specific activities. Be sure your presentation includes concrete examples and that you explain any terms the children at your grade level might not understand.

CLASSROOM RULES:

NO ANYTHING!

"That's Ms. Clamhouse. She runs a tight ship."

Reprinted by permission of Tony Saltzman.

The set of rules you choose will be used later in several ways. First, you will discuss these rules with your students on the first day or two of class. You will also post the rules in the room or make certain that students have their own copies or both. A posted set of rules allows you to focus student attention on and create a strong expectation about behaviors that are important to you. Finally, you may refer to specific rules as needed to remind students of appropriate behavior during the year. It should be noted that your posted rules need not (and cannot) cover all aspects of behavior in detail. Procedures for specific activities and perhaps some ad hoc rules will be needed. For instance, you may wish to post separately your policies regarding student work. Examples of some commonly used rules follow.

RULE 1. BE POLITE AND HELPFUL.   This may be worded in various ways (e.g., be considerate of others, be courteous). For the rule to have meaning, the children must be given examples: Wait your turn; say "please" and "thank-you"; behave properly for a substitute. Some "don'ts" could include fighting, name calling, and bothering others.

RULE 2. RESPECT OTHER PEOPLE'S PROPERTY.   This rule may include guidelines such as (a) keep the room clean and neat; (b) pick up litter; (c) return borrowed property; (d) do not write on the desks; and (e) do not use another person's things without permission.

RULE 3. LISTEN QUIETLY WHILE OTHERS ARE SPEAKING.   Use of this rule will prevent call-outs and other interruptions of lessons. You can use the discussion of this rule to teach the students how to comment or ask a question (e.g., raise a hand and wait to be called on).

RULE 4. RESPECT AND BE POLITE TO ALL PEOPLE.   This rule is general; be sure to give sufficient examples and explanation so that both you and students clearly understand its meaning. You will need to define *polite*, and you may want to extend this definition to include not hitting, fighting, or name calling. You may also want to emphasize that "all people" includes you, the teacher.

RULE 5. OBEY ALL SCHOOL RULES.   Including this rule gives you an opportunity to discuss whatever school rules are pertinent to your supervision of students outside your classroom (such as on the playground or in the cafeteria). It reminds students that school rules apply in your classroom as well as out of it. It also suggests that you will monitor their behavior in the areas covered by the school rules.

Student Participation in Rule Setting

Some teachers involve students in rule setting to promote ownership of the rules and to encourage them to take more responsibility for their own behavior. Student involvement can take many forms, such as a discussion focused on reasons for having rules and on clarifying the rationale for and the meaning of particular rules. A discussion might begin with a consideration of why rules are necessary. After this initial discussion, rules can be presented one at a time. The teacher may first clarify the rule by describing (or asking students to describe) the area of behavior it covers. Students can usually supply concrete examples, although they will tend to give negative instances, such as "Respecting property means not marking on desks or not stealing." Consequently, you should be prepared to state positive examples. The discussion of individual rules may also include a rationale for those rules whose justification is not obvious.

Many teachers begin the process of developing classroom rules with a whole-class discussion. During this discussion, the students and teacher suggest possible rules for the classroom, and the teacher records each suggestion on an overhead projector, chalkboard, or large piece of chart paper. After all suggestions have been made, the teacher and students begin to arrange them into broad categories. They combine similar ideas and eliminate suggestions that are redundant or unnecessary. Once the suggestions are placed in these broad categories, the teacher and students develop a title for each category. If everyone agrees, this title becomes a classroom rule. In early elementary classrooms (K–3), this process may take several days to complete. In many classrooms, this activity is followed by role playing each of the rules. Role playing is crucial for student understanding of rules.

Another approach taken by some teachers is to permit student choice in particular activities or behaviors. For example, if gum chewing is not prohibited by a school rule and if you do not find it objectionable, then you could give your students a choice. It would be a rare class that decided to prohibit it! When students are given a choice, then you must also make them aware of their responsibility for making the chosen procedure or rule work and remind them they will lose the privilege if their behavior warrants it.

Another way to involve students in rule setting is to allow them to share in the decision-making process for specific rules. This is sometimes done at a school level (mainly in the intermediate grades) by having student representatives from each room or grade level participate in the identification of school rules. However, within individual classrooms, shared decision making is not common for several possible reasons. First, the domain in which student participation is acceptable is limited. Schoolwide rules must be accepted as they are. Second, policies essential to managing instruction cannot be left to student discretion. Third, elementary age students may require considerable prompting to produce a comprehensive list of general rules. Thus, most teachers prefer to develop and present their rules, including students in a discussion of examples and rationales.

It is important to note that many effective managers do not provide for student choice in rule setting. Instead, they clearly present their rules and procedures to students and provide explanations of the need for them. A teacher who establishes reasonable rules and procedures, who provides an understandable rationale for them, and who enforces them consistently will find that the majority of students is willing to abide by them.

PLANNING CLASSROOM PROCEDURES

If you have never analyzed the specific behaviors required of students in a typical elementary school classroom, you will be surprised by the complexity and detail in this section. Don't hurry through it, even though some of the items may appear trivial. These bits and pieces will combine to form the mosaic of your management system. Five categories are described: procedures for room areas, procedures for teacher-led instruction and seatwork activities, transitions into and out of the room, procedures for small-group work, and general procedures. A sixth area, keeping students accountable for work, is presented in Chapter 3.

As you read the items below, note ideas for procedures on Checklist 2.

Procedures for Room Use

Different areas of the room and furniture and equipment within the room need procedures to regulate their use.

TEACHER'S DESK AND STORAGE AREAS

The best procedure is that students may not remove anything from your desk or other storage areas without your permission.

STUDENT DESKS AND OTHER STUDENT STORAGE AREAS

Just as students may not tamper with your desk, students may not bother the desk or storage space of another student. You can also help students learn good work habits by setting aside a few minutes each week for students to clean out and organize their desks and materials. This is a good end-of-day activity on Friday.

STORAGE FOR COMMON MATERIALS

Some commonly used supplies (scissors, scrap paper, rulers, etc.) and resources (supplementary books, basals, encyclopedia, dictionaries, etc.) will be stored on shelves, in drawers, or in cabinets. Most teachers label these storage areas appropriately and tell students at what times these materials may be used and whether permission is needed for any of them.

DRINKING FOUNTAIN, SINK, PENCIL SHARPENER

A common procedure is to allow use of these by only one student at a time and only when the teacher is not conducting a lesson or talking to the whole class. Some teachers require students to request permission to use the fountain or sink except during specified break times.

BATHROOMS

When bathrooms are immediately accessible from or adjacent to the classroom, many teachers allow students to use these facilities, one at a time, without asking permission whenever the teacher is not conducting instruction. A system should be established to let a student know if the bathroom is occupied (examples: a reversible sign on the door with a green light and a red light; knocking and waiting). It is also a good idea to go over bathroom use procedures, such as flush toilet, wash hands, wipe off sink area, and dispose of paper towels.

CENTERS, STATIONS, AND EQUIPMENT AREAS

Procedures that need to be established include when the area may be used (perhaps during particular blocks of time only), whether special permission is needed, and how many may use the area at a time. Teachers often allow quiet talking in such areas as long as it does not disturb others. If talking will be allowed, then the area should be situated away from areas where students are expected to work quietly. Post rules or instructions for equipment use at each area.

Many teachers also post a number indicating how many students should be at a center at once. You will need procedures for assigning students to centers, or, if centers will be self-selected, for guiding student movement among centers. Posted instructions for cleaning up centers are also helpful.

Procedures during Individual Work and Teacher-Led Activities

Major concerns include keeping student attention, allowing for participation, and providing assistance when needed. Good procedures will prevent or reduce interruptions or distractions that can slow down content development activities or interfere with student learning.

STUDENT ATTENTION DURING PRESENTATIONS

It is important to consider how students should behave when you or another student are presenting information to the class or while you are conducting a discussion or recitation. Typically, students are expected to face the presenter and listen attentively. In fact, teachers often translate this expectation into a general classroom rule such as "Listen carefully when the teacher or another student is talking." Teachers also expect students to remain seated at all times during presentations, to remain quiet, and to have only the books or other materials needed for the lesson on their desks.

STUDENT PARTICIPATION

You will need to identify a procedure to enable students to ask a question, contribute to a discussion, or receive help. During presentations and discussions, the simplest procedure is to require that students raise their hands, wait to be called on, and remain in their seats. Some teachers teach students to call on the next speaker to avoid having all interactions channeled through the teacher. In most circumstances, it is not a good idea to allow students to call out answers or comments without raising their hands. Undesirable consequences of allowing call-outs include domination of participation by a few students, frequent inappropriate comments, and interruptions of discussions and presentations. Requiring that students raise their hands gives all students an opportunity to participate and allows you to call on students who do not have their hands up, if you choose. Two exceptions to the "no call-out" procedure are sometimes permitted. The first occurs when teachers want students to provide a chorus response; that is, when they want a whole class response to a question. This can be handled by telling students at the beginning of the activity that they do not need to raise their hands to respond. Also, children can be taught a signal for a chorus response; cupping one hand behind an ear or giving a verbal signal, such as prefacing the question with "everyone," can be used. A second exception may occur during activities in which hand raising might slow down or interfere with a discussion. Again, students can be told that it is not necessary to raise hands during that particular activity. It is worth noting that the variations from the standard procedure of requiring raised hands usually should not be used early in the school year. Instead, follow a simple routine for several weeks until you are certain that students understand it. Then, if you choose to depart from the procedure, clearly communicate the difference to the students at the beginning of the activity.

TALK AMONG STUDENTS

In many activities, quiet talk is an important part of problem solving. However, students must know when and how loudly they may talk. You will have to decide what your policy will be and communicate it to the students. The "no talking" rule is an easy rule to break. You must decide whether students may quietly ask a neighbor if they have questions. Then, try allowing students to help each other on a trial basis. If you decide to allow students to talk to one another and to work together during individual work activities, you will need to establish specific limitations. For example, you might tell students that during certain activities quiet talking is allowed, but if it gets too loud, the privilege will be lost. It would be best to demonstrate what "quiet talking" means and have students practice it to show you they know what is meant. If students are encouraged to help each other, you will need to establish procedures for how and when. For instance, some teachers establish the "3B4Me" procedure, which tells students to ask three other students for help before they ask the teacher.

OBTAINING HELP

When students are working at their seats and need help, have them raise their hands. It is not a good idea to allow them to call out or to come up to you whenever they wish. Once they have raised their hands, you may then go to them or have them come to you one at a time. Another procedure is to allow students to come up only if you are seated at your desk (or some other designated place) and not already helping another student. These procedures will eliminate long lines of chatty students around your desk. They will also allow you to control where you give individual assistance. If you choose to help students at a location other than their desks, choose one that allows you good visibility of the rest of the class. Some teachers help students think about their questions by having students ask themselves, "Can another student answer this?" If the answer is "yes," then the student asks another for help.

If students will work at centers and in groups, you will need to define with them how much noise is acceptable. Many teachers also find it helpful to have a "zero noise" signal for times when they need to get the whole group's attention. A "zero noise" signal could be your raising your hand or turning off the lights momentarily.

WHEN INDIVIDUAL WORK HAS BEEN COMPLETED

If students are assigned work at their desks, sometimes one or several students will finish before the next scheduled activity. This situation is frequently handled either by having students complete an additional enrichment assignment or by allowing these students to use the remaining time for free reading or work at a center or to help with classroom maintenance chores. You may also wish to have students who finish early serve as peer tutors for others. If you have enrichment activities that involve additional materials not in the students' possession, you will need to specify when these materials may be used, where they will be kept, and what the procedures are for returning the materials to the proper place. Note that if many students frequently complete their work early, it is evidence that assignments are insufficient or too much time is being allocated for seatwork activities.

Transitions into and out of the Room

BEGINNING THE SCHOOL DAY

You should establish a routine to open each class day. At the beginning of the year, this routine should be supervised and led by you so that it is done efficiently and helps students "settle in" to the classroom. During the course of the year, students may begin to lead this routine without the teacher's guidance. The routine need not be elaborate or time consuming. Many teachers begin with social items such as a riddle for the day, a discussion of the day's lunch menu, the pledge of allegiance, date and birthdays, discussion of school events, or other items of interest. Some begin each day with a class meeting or a planning session where students set their goals for the day. Such activities can be important community-building times.

You may also wish to collect money, permission slips, or other items brought from home at this time. If much time will be required for morning management tasks, have students begin work on a content-related activity to establish an academic focus to ensure students are not in dead time.

LEAVING THE ROOM

Your students will leave the room en masse at several times during the day: at recess and for lunch, physical education, music, or perhaps some other instruction. A common technique used is to have the children line up after appropriate materials have been put away, with the quietest table or row lining up first. Decide what behaviors are appropriate in line. Some teachers, particularly of younger children, find it necessary to specify where hands and feet should be while students are lined up. Some teachers have students clasp their hands behind their backs; others have students keep their hands at their sides. Line leaders can be helpful, and students enjoy the privilege. Because noise disturbs other classes, talking is usually forbidden while the line is passing through the halls. You will also need procedures for helping students know when and how to leave the room if they are working with a speech teacher, special education teacher, or peer mentor in another classroom.

RETURNING TO THE ROOM

It is important that procedures be established for this transition, particularly after lunchtime. If students know what activity they are to do on returning, they can get started instead of waiting for you to direct them. Common procedures are entering the room quietly and taking their seats; using the bathroom, sink, pencil sharpener, or drinking fountain one at a time in each area. Note that these procedures get students ready for afternoon activities.

When students return from an out-of-room activity that has left them noisy or unusually "chatty," or if they are very excited when returning from recess or lunch, your transition activity should give them time to wind down before you start academic work. For example, you might permit quiet social talk as they settle in and get ready for the next lesson. Some research has found that student attention is better after such transitions than when the teacher tries to enforce total silence and an immediate return to academic tasks. However, do not prolong the chatter unnecessarily and be sure to gain student attention when you begin the next activity. Monitor students so that "wind down" time doesn't become "wind up" time.

ENDING THE DAY

A routine is needed at the end of the day to ensure that the students' desks and work areas are cleared off, materials to go home are ready, and students leave on time. Planning ahead for the end of the day guards against hurried closings, lost papers, and a feeling of confusion and chaos. Possible routines include feeding room pets, straightening bookshelves, tidying up desks, and stacking chairs on the desks. Other important end-of-day tasks include briefly reviewing important things learned that day, foreshadowing coming events, and checking materials that will be taken home. If you have children who leave early to ride a bus, you may wish to do only the essentials with them and complete the rest of the routine after they leave.

Procedures during Group Activities

One complication with using small-group instruction is that the teacher is often working with one group while the rest of the class is engaged in individual work. The dual focus complicates monitoring, providing assistance, and dealing with problems that might occur. Well-planned procedures are a must if small-group instruction is to be carried out smoothly.

GETTING THE CLASS READY FOR THE ACTIVITY

Students must know what work they are going to do during the time they are not in the group. Therefore, you must post the assignments by group and discuss work requirements beforehand with the whole class. You should also note any materials that will be needed when the students come to the teacher-led group.

STUDENT MOVEMENT INTO AND OUT OF THE GROUP

These transitions need to be brief, quiet, and free from disruptions. Describe expected behavior to students: Walk, no talking, bring needed materials. You will need a signal to tell students when to come to the group area. They should not automatically come when they see other students leave, because you may want to check on student progress before working with the next group. Some teachers use a bell or a kitchen timer; others use a verbal signal.

EXPECTED BEHAVIOR OF STUDENTS IN THE GROUP

The rules for attention and hand raising used in the whole class can also be used in the small group. However, with smaller numbers of students, some procedures must change, and these must be taught. For example, some teachers have each student who responds select the next student to participate. Sometimes, the exchange between students can be more loosely structured.

EXPECTED BEHAVIOR OF STUDENTS OUTSIDE THE SMALL GROUP

You will have given instructions to students not in the group and posted their seat-work assignments. However, students may need help as they work. It is not a good idea to allow students to come up to you while you are in the group; therefore, some procedure must be established to enable students to get help. One such procedure is to allow students to help each other. Another procedure used by some teachers is to assign certain students the job of monitors. Students can then raise their hands and the monitor can assist them. Permission to interrupt the teacher is given only to the monitors and only when assistance is absolutely necessary. Often, students are told they should skip the part of the assignment they are unable to do and that the teacher will help them later. You should check on student progress even while you are working with the group. Look up frequently to scan the class for signs of difficulty. When you change groups, circulate around the room to help students before you call the next group. Students can raise their hands between groups to indicate a need for help, or they may write their names on the chalkboard to signal a need for assistance when you are available.

Procedures during Cooperative Group Activities

Some teachers use groups extensively for a variety of tasks, such as short- or long-term projects, peer coaching and other assistance, and review of content learned in other formats. Other examples include laboratory assignments in science, the preparation of group reports or projects in social studies and reading, or study groups organized to accomplish specific learning objectives. However groups are used, it is important to develop efficient routines that support the learning objectives.

Routines are typically introduced to the students whenever groups are first used and practiced thereafter until the groups are working well. It is important that students learn appropriate group behavior, especially if you intend to use groups extensively. Although you can monitor group work, the fact that six or seven groups may be working simultaneously at varying paces using a variety of resources precludes your being able to direct all the groups' activities. The procedures implemented for group work must be carefully chosen to encourage students to work more or less independently toward instructional goals, to promote desirable interaction among students in the group, and to support efficient use of time.

Teachers who use groups extensively often introduce the procedures early in the school year, giving careful attention to instructing students in what constitutes appropriate group behavior. This can be done by deciding ahead what group behaviors are desirable and communicating these expectations to the students. Common types of desirable group behaviors include staying on-task, participating frequently, listening carefully to others, and sharing and helping.

In addition to communicating positive expectations for these behaviors, you can give students feedback about their group behavior. Feedback can be given to individuals, to a specific group, or to the entire class. A commonly used strategy is to engage the whole class in a discussion about how well the groups are working and what can be done to improve them. It is helpful to stress each student's responsibility toward the common good. Teachers can ask students to take different roles to encourage particular behavior. Roles should be rotated to give each student an opportunity to practice different behaviors.

A number of procedures to help small group activities proceed smoothly are described next and in Chapter 5.

USE OF MATERIALS AND SUPPLIES

Small-group activities, particularly those that are run as part of a laboratory, frequently require the use of a variety of materials and equipment. To avoid traffic jams, you must plan distribution stations carefully and use more than one if necessary. When possible, save time by placing some or all materials on students' desks or worktables before class starts. Be sure to check equipment for proper functioning and have replacements on hand for use when needed. Student helpers may be assigned to distribute supplies and materials, to monitor supply stations, and to clean up work areas. This can often be one of the roles assigned to a member of each cooperative group. If students need to bring special materials for group or project work, they should be told far enough in advance so they can obtain them, and you may have to locate safe places for materials to be stored while work is in progress. If any of the equipment poses a potential hazard to students or can be easily damaged by careless use, you will need to identify safety routines and plan appropriate demonstrations.

ASSIGNMENT OF STUDENTS TO GROUPS

This topic is important for several reasons. Students who do not work well together should probably not be placed in the same work group. Also, a group composed mainly of poorly motivated students is not likely to accomplish much. A commonly used strategy is to assign students so that groups are reasonably balanced with respect to ability, ethnicity, and gender. If each person's grade is then based partly on the individual's accomplishments and partly on the group's accomplishments, everyone in the group has a stake in what everyone else does, and the chances for a successful experience are increased. To obtain groups that are well balanced, to discourage nonproductive talk during the assignment, and to save time in forming groups and getting started on the task, assignment of individual students to groups should be determined ahead of time by the teacher.

STUDENT GOALS AND PARTICIPATION

Students should be told the purpose of their group work and given direction about how they are to proceed, consistent with the task they are to accomplish. Cohen (1994) makes an important distinction about the nature of group tasks. She summarizes research indicating that the nature of teacher directions depends on the degree to which the group's task is structured. For outcomes that are well-defined and for which there is a limited range of suitable strategies (e.g., completing a worksheet, performing a specific laboratory procedure, answering comprehension questions, reviewing material presented in a text or by the teacher), teachers can give explicit instructions about steps to follow and can monitor the groups for satisfactory progress. On such tasks, the teacher might prepare a list of steps that should be followed and then display it on a chalkboard, on an overhead projector, or on a handout. A student can be assigned to monitor, noting when a step has been completed, or the whole group can be asked to keep track of progress.

However, when the task is less structured, and the nature of the product and steps to achieve it are not as evident, nor is there an easily identifiable strategy, teachers need to be less directive about how the group proceeds. The teacher might delegate some responsibility to the group to decide on its procedures and to select appropriate resources. Typically, the goal of such group tasks will include higher order thinking and problem solving. Too explicit a set of directions about how to proceed may stifle the types of thinking such a task is intended to promote.

For example, suppose a teacher's goal in assigning the development of a group report is to promote critical thinking and problem solving about the topic. If the teacher is highly directive about how the group is to function and what resources it can use, the students may simply try to develop a report that satisfies *pro forma* the assignment requirements. If, however, the teacher's directions offer the students latitude, and if responsibility is delegated, there is a better chance that students will draw on their own creativity and be more engaged in the group process.

If being overly directive has its disadvantages in terms of students engaging in higher order thinking, what is appropriate for teachers to do? First, guidelines should usually be given about the general direction the group should take. Thus, the task can be broken into a few parts and deadlines set for their completion. A range of possible resources can be identified. Students can be assigned different roles to contribute to the group. Second, general rules and specific procedures can be established to govern talk and movement behaviors as well as to facilitate appropriate student interaction in groups. Some areas of behavior, such as out-of-seat movement, contacting the teacher, and so on, can be managed using the same procedures as have been identified for seatwork activities. Obviously, quiet talk should be encouraged to facilitate group participation. Because the noise level may become a problem, the teacher should discuss what types of talk are permitted and when. Many teachers develop a signal to use to warn the class when the noise level becomes too high.

If you are planning to use groups, give careful attention to this activity before you introduce it. You may find it beneficial to start with group tasks that are well-defined and can be accomplished within the instructional time block. Such tasks may allow you to teach many important group procedures and to gauge student readiness for more complex tasks.

General Procedures

DISTRIBUTING MATERIALS

At the beginning of the year, books and supplies must be distributed to students. You will need procedures for recording book numbers, noting damage, and handling other details. These will be covered in Chapter 4 along with other procedures for beginning the school year. In addition to the beginning-of-year materials distribution, you will have supplies, papers, and books to pass out every day. Unless you establish efficient procedures, much time can be wasted. Many teachers have student helpers pass out materials such as manipulatives, calculators, or graded papers during opening activities. For the distribution of books or supplies, a student helper can be assigned to each group. If you collect papers from assignments by group or by row and preserve the order while you are checking them, you can then redistribute them to the class in the same way. This makes it easy to hand the materials to one student at each table or in each row.

INTERRUPTIONS OR DELAYS

If delays or interruptions occur while students are working, they should be taught to continue their work. Tell students they should be courteous and patient if you are interrupted in the middle of a lesson by a visitor or a phone call and that you will return to them as quickly as possible. If you will be detained very long, give the students something to do in case they finish their work before you return.

BATHROOMS

If bathrooms are located away from your classroom, a hall-pass system may be established to monitor the number of students out of the room and to let students know if they may leave. You might hang a bathroom hall pass next to the hall door to be placed by the student around his or her neck or carried en route to the bathroom. There may already be a schoolwide procedure, so be certain you know what it is.

LIBRARY, RESOURCE ROOM, SCHOOL OFFICE

When one or a small group of students must go to another area in the school, you will generally remain in the classroom with the rest of the students. For example, small groups doing research may go to the library. Schoolwide procedures are usually established to handle these situations. Find out whether a hall permit system or some other procedure is used to regulate movement of students in the halls. Also review any school rules that govern behavior in transit or at the locations. You will want to make sure your students understand these procedures.

CAFETERIA

Review the school policies for the cafeteria and be ready to explain them to your class before they go to lunch and after they return if needed. If you are planning to (or must) sit with the students, decide ahead of time who will get to sit by you and whether this will be at random, a privilege, or whether you will use assigned seats. If your students are too noisy or misbehave, you may wish to establish a reward system for good behavior or include lunchroom behavior as part of your in-class reward system.

PLAYGROUND

Safety rules are a must, and you should limit overly aggressive behavior and dangerous play. Also, if any of the equipment in the playground poses a potential hazard, you will need to talk about it with your students. Make clear to your students what part of the school grounds they may use for recess. You also should establish some signal for getting students' attention when it is time for them to line up and return to the classroom; this could be a whistle or a raised hand. If you plan to play a game on the playground, announce this before leaving the room, telling students where they should go once out on the playground.

FIRE AND DISASTER DRILLS

You need to know what school policies and routines have been established to protect the children and you. Although you may wish to wait a while before teaching these to your students, you should not wait until you know a drill is imminent. It is better to go over these procedures ahead of time and review them just before the first drill.

CLASSROOM HELPERS

Teachers often use students to help with such chores as erasing the chalkboard, passing out materials and supplies, carrying messages to the office, watering the plants, and feeding the animals. Students are often chosen to be line leaders. Some teachers use these activities as privileges or rewards for especially good or improved behavior, or they may use them to encourage some students to accept more responsibility. Some teachers have a chart or bulletin board with slots for the names of students currently serving as monitors or helpers. A card is then made for each child with his or her name, and this card is placed in the appropriate slot when that child has a particular room helper responsibility. Some teachers ask for volunteers for each job; others appoint students on a rotating basis or use jobs as rewards. Appointment is usually done at the beginning of the week, and the appointments last one or two weeks.

FURTHER READING

Castle, K., & Rogers, K. (1994). Rule-creating in a constructivist classroom community. *Childhood Education, 70*(2), 77–80.

> *Creating classroom rules together can be a meaningful experience for children and teachers and can help establish a positive sense of classroom community. Student participation in rule making encourages active involvement, reflection, meaningful connections, respect for rules, sense of community, problem solving through negotiation, cooperation, inductive thinking, and a sense of ownership.*

Cohen, E. G. (1994). Restructuring the classroom: Conditions for productive small groups. *Review of Educational Research, 64*, 1–36.

> *This article presents excellent ideas to consider for organizing group work. Particular attention is given to the nature of the work or task that students are expected to perform, factors that affect student interactions, and the teacher's role in promoting effective use of groups.*

Leinhardt, G., Weidman, C., & Hammond, K. M. (1987). Introduction and integration of classroom routines by expert teachers. *Curriculum Inquiry, 17*(2), 135–176.

> *Data from the classrooms of successful teachers show the importance of establishing and practicing routines from the beginning. Three types of routines are identified: management, instructional support, and teacher–student exchange. The authors point out that teachers build on simple routines to support more elaborate ones.*

Short, K. G. (1992). Creating a community of learners. In K. Short & K. M. Pierce (Eds.), *Talking about books: Creating literate communities* (pp. 33–52). Portsmouth, NH: Heinemann.

This chapter focuses on the ways in which the author and other teachers have established collaborative social contexts for learning. They believe that a community of learners is formed as learners (1) come to know each other; (2) value what each has to offer; (3) focus on problem solving and inquiry; (4) share responsibility and control; (5) learn through action, reflection, and demonstration; and (6) establish a learning atmosphere that is predictable and yet full of choices.

SUGGESTED ACTIVITIES

1. Identify the schoolwide rules and procedures you and your students are expected to observe. Be sure these are incorporated into your own classroom rules and procedures where appropriate.

2. Read Case Studies 2–1 and 2–2 on the following pages. They illustrate classroom procedures and rules for most major areas, and they will help you develop your own system of management.

3. Case Study 2–3 illustrates a more complex classroom organization that involves introducing multiple areas and centers for student activities. List some of the advance planning decisions Ms. Miller has made. What rules and procedures has she developed? How are these taught and monitored?

4. Use Checklist 2 at the end of this chapter to help organize your planning of classroom procedures. Be sure to think through your expectations for student behavior in each of the general areas and the instructional areas you will be using. Then develop a set of procedures that will communicate your expectations to your students.

5. If you have trouble developing procedures in some area or are not sure if the ones you have identified will work, ask other teachers for their opinions. They will usually be more than happy to share some of their "tricks of the trade."

6. Develop a list of five to eight general classroom rules. Be sure these emphasize areas of classroom behavior important to you and to the functioning of your classroom. Review these with an administrator or another teacher.

CASE STUDY 2-1

CLASSROOM PROCEDURES AND RULES IN A SECOND-GRADE CLASS

Mr. Abrams' students followed four rules: We use quiet voices in the classroom. We do our best work. We are polite and helpful. We follow all school rules. At the beginning of the year, Mr. Abrams and his students decided what "quiet voices" meant, and they practiced using quiet voices in different types of instructional activities. The students also role played situations in which students were and were not using quiet voices. When Mr. Abrams needed to get the attention of the class, he routinely used a bell as a signal. He practiced this signal with the students. He rang the bell once, and they stopped talking and looked at him. He explained to the class that using the bell was a shortcut to save time, that he would ring the bell only once and not several times, and that he expected students to respond immediately. He used the bell in a very consistent manner.

The rule "We do our best work" included listening carefully when the teacher was giving instructions, participating in class discussions, completing all assignments, turning in neat work, and using time wisely.

Student behaviors relating to the rule "We are polite and helpful" included listening quietly when the teacher or another student was giving a presentation, cooperating with other students during small group work, sharing materials and supplies, and respecting others' opinions. Mr. Abrams explained to his students that during some discussions, they could raise their hands and wait to be called on to allow everyone a chance to talk and be heard. His signal for this procedure was raising his right hand, and he practiced it with his students. At other times, students were allowed to contribute to a discussion without raising their hands. His signal for this procedure was placing his right hand by his ear. He also practiced this signal with the students several times. Other aspects of consideration and respect for fellow students, the teacher, and other adults in the school were also included under this rule. In addition, the school rules referred to in the fourth classroom rule governed student behavior in the halls, cafeteria, and other common areas of the school grounds.

Several other important classroom procedures provided guidelines for student behavior in Mr. Abrams' classroom. Students were expected to stay seated at their desks whenever he was presenting directions or instruction to the class as a whole. At other times, however, the students could leave their desks to get supplies, hand in papers, sharpen their pencils, and use the restroom that was adjacent to the classroom without asking permission, as long as they did not disturb other students. For example, students were allowed to sharpen a pencil without permission except when the teacher was talking to the class or when another student was addressing the class. No more than two students were allowed at the pencil sharpener at one time, one sharpening and one waiting. When the teacher was working with a small group or helping an individual, students were not to interrupt him. They stayed at their desks and raised their hands to request help. If students finished their work early, they could read books from the classroom library, go to one of the classroom centers, or play an instructional game. They could talk, using their quiet voices, but they could not disturb anyone still working on the assignment.

CASE STUDY 2-2

SMALL-GROUP PROCEDURES

It is the end of October, and Mrs. Bernard's fourth-grade classroom is a very busy place. She and her twenty-four students have begun an integrated study of the environment, and her writer's workshop is finally running smoothly. At the beginning of this unit, the students generated a list of questions about the environment they would like to answer. Mrs. Bernard and the students arranged the questions into three broad categories—recycling, natural resources, and pollution. Then, each student ranked the categories from 1 to 3, with 1 being the first choice for a research project, 2 being the second choice, and 3 being the last choice. After Mrs. Bernard collected these rankings from the students, she began to organize them into research groups. In this process, she assigned the students to their first or second choice, creating heterogeneous groups and paying attention to the group dynamics.

Today, Mrs. Bernard is going to work with each of the small groups during writer's workshop. Although students are accustomed to having individual conferences and peer conferences for editing and revising, this is the first time the teacher will be working with small research groups. As the students assemble on the carpet for their daily planning session, Mrs. Bernard decides to review the classroom procedures for writer's workshop to make the addition of the small research groups less noticeable. First, she reminds the students to make their plans for the day. The teacher has five headings written on the bottom, right corner of her dry erase board: brainstorming, writing, peer conferencing for editing and revising, typing/illustrating, and publishing. Before the workshop begins, the students write their names to show what they will be doing during this sixty-minute block of time. Because different areas of the room are set aside for each of the five writing stages, this procedure helps Mrs. Bernard know where the students should be. Second, Mrs. Bernard reviews the procedure that the students are to ask three other students for help in solving a problem before they ask her. She tells the class that as in her individual student conferences, she cannot be interrupted while she is meeting with the small research groups. Third, she reminds the students they are to use quiet voices when talking with others, especially during peer conferences. She asks a student to model a "quiet voice." Finally, Mrs. Bernard reminds the class that peer conferences are to be held in the back corner of the classroom, so they do not disturb the other students.

Mrs. Bernard also reviews general classroom procedures. She reminds the class that students could go to the bathroom one at a time, get a drink of water, and get necessary writing supplies when they were not working with her on their research projects. Before she gives directions for the small-group research projects, she asks if there are any questions. There are none, so she asks several students to repeat these procedures for their classmates to check their understanding.

Mrs. Bernard writes the research topic groups in the order she will meet with them—recycling, natural resources, and pollution. She also writes the names of the students in each group on the board. She tells the students that each group will meet for twenty minutes, and she will use the timer as a signal for the groups to change. When it is their time, the students are to put their writer's workshop materials at their desks and come to the small-group table in the front corner of the room. Mrs. Bernard asks the students to be quiet coming to and leaving the small-group table, so as not to disturb others.

At this point, writer's workshop begins. Mrs. Bernard circulates around the room briefly helping students get started as the eight members of the recycling group move to the small-group table. The teacher sits facing the class to monitor the students' behavior. As she meets with the group, Mrs. Bernard notices that two writer's workshop students raise their hands for help. She notices their hands, catches the students' eyes, and motions toward other students at the desks. This is a signal to these students to ask their peers for help while the teacher is working with the small group. A couple of other students write their names on the chalkboard as a request for the teacher's assistance when she is through with the small-group meeting.

When the timer rings, the students in the small group go to the writer's workshop areas they selected earlier, and the natural resources group moves to the table. During this brief transition, Mrs. Bernard quickly walks through the room to monitor students' progress and answer brief questions, beginning with the students who have written their names on the chalkboard. When the meeting starts with the natural resources group, she again keeps a watchful eye on the writer's workshop activities and redirects students as necessary.

When the timer rings again, this entire process is repeated with the pollution group. The completion of this third group signals the end of the sixty-minute writer's workshop. Mrs. Bernard and the students reassemble on the carpet for a debriefing of the workshop activities. Following their usual procedure, students carry their writing folders with them to the carpet. She compliments the students for following the writer's workshop procedures and tells them she looks forward to helping them with their research projects. She then dismisses them to put away their writing folders and to return to their seats in preparation for lunch.

CASE STUDY 2-3

USING CENTERS IN A MULTITASK CLASSROOM

Ms. Miller has designed her upper elementary classroom with centers for listening, reading, writing, and creating. Special interest centers on topics the class is studying in science, social studies, or math change every month or so. Although each child has a desk, students are seldom in their seats; instead, they work on a variety of projects individually, in pairs, and in groups. When they meet as a whole class, they often gather sitting on a carpet instead of in traditional rows of desks. On any given day in November, a visitor may see an active, busy, somewhat noisy place, but it takes only a few minutes to discern that there is a sense of order and purpose to the tasks in which the students are engaged.

This classroom didn't get this way all at once. Much of the first six weeks of school were spent preparing students to work independently and collaboratively. On the first day of school, Ms. Miller taught students cues for when to gather on the rug and when to return to seats. She explained that there would be times when they could talk to each other, but that during "rug time" they were to raise their hands so that only one person would be speaking at once. Ms. Miller prepared a poster with the day's schedule and "center time" clearly marked. She went over it with the students before posting it on a highly visible bulletin board. She made a habit of referring to the poster during the first weeks of school when giving students instructions for activities, or she asked students to tell her when certain activities were to start or stop.

Centers were introduced one at a time, over a period of several weeks. When each new center became available, Ms. Miller presented it to the whole class, demonstrating the material found there and pointing out times on the day's schedule when it would be available. She also pointed out two signs in each center. One sign lists the procedures for the center. For example, the sign in the reading center says, "Silent readers may leave the center to find a quiet place to read. Students reading aloud to each other should stay in the center." Every list of procedures ends with instructions for clean-up. The second sign lists the capacity of that center. For example, the listening center has only four sets of earphones, so its capacity is four. Ms. Miller explains to the students that they may sign up for centers each morning when they arrive at school. One period of the day is allotted to "free center time," when students may go to the centers they have chosen. During free center time, students cross their names off the sign-up sheets when they leave the center, so other students may enter. Another period is "assigned center time," when Ms. Miller decides who should be in each center. After each new center is introduced, Ms. Miller makes sure that every student visits it during assigned center time. She monitors the center's use carefully, making sure that all students understand the use of one center before another center is introduced. Even after all centers have been introduced, Ms. Miller continues to monitor their use and brings up any common problems she sees for discussion during rug time. She is careful to balance the available centers so that if activities at one center require her attention, the other centers have more familiar activities available on which students can work independently.

✔️ CHECKLIST 2

RULES AND PROCEDURES

Check When Complete	Subject	Procedures or Expectations
	Room use	
☐	A. Teacher's desk and storage areas	_____
☐	B. Student desks and storage areas	_____
☐	C. Storage for common materials	_____
☐	D. Drinking fountains, sink, pencil sharpener	_____
☐	E. Bathrooms	_____
☐	F. Centers, stations, or equipment areas	_____
☐	G. Chalkboard	_____

RULES AND PROCEDURES *Continued*

Check When Complete	Subject	Procedures or Expectations
	Individual Work and Teacher-Led Instruction	
☐	A. Student attention during presentations	_____
☐	B. Student participation	_____
☐	C. Talk among students	_____
☐	D. Obtaining help	_____
☐	E. When seatwork has been completed	_____
	Transitions into and out of the Room	
☐	A. Beginning the school day	_____
☐	B. Leaving the room	_____
☐	C. Returning to the room	_____
☐	D. Ending the day	_____
	Procedures during Group Activities	
☐	A. Getting the class ready	_____
☐	B. Student movement	_____
☐	C. Expected behavior in the group	_____
☐	D. Expected behavior of students out of group	_____
☐	E. Cooperative group activities	_____
☐	F. Materials and supplies	_____
☐	G. Assigning students to groups	_____
☐	H. Student goals and participation	_____
	General Procedures	
☐	A. Distributing materials	_____
☐	B. Classroom helpers	_____
☐	C. Interruptions or delays	_____
☐	D. Bathrooms	_____
☐	E. Library, resource room, school office	_____
☐	F. Cafeteria	_____
☐	G. Playground	_____
☐	H. Fire and disaster drills	_____

Managing Student Work

Wwhen we presented a set of procedures for establishing an orderly classroom setting in Chapter 2, we indicated that additional procedures would be needed to keep students accountable for their work. In this chapter, we describe the additional procedures, which are aimed at encouraging students to complete assignments and to engage in other learning activities.

Each day of the school year, you will give your students assignments they will be expected to complete in the classroom or at home. These assignments are important for learning and retention. Depending on the assignment, it may provide opportunities for exploration, for original thinking, for practice and application, or for repeated exposure to content. Such experiences are crucial for student learning.

Thus, the consistent and accurate completion of assignments is a critical goal for effective management. If students are not held accountable for their work, many problems in this area can occur. Consider the following hypothetical example:

> It is the second month of school, and Mr. Paul's third-grade class is nearing the completion of its fairy tale unit. As a culminating project, five cooperative groups are creating their own fairy tales. For this assignment, the group members must work together to write and illustrate a fairy tale, and on the last day of this unit, each group will present its fairy tale to the rest of the class.
>
> Mr. Paul is disturbed by the lack of cooperation in all of the groups. He has noticed that many cooperative groups have been off-task. Members have also been arguing about storylines, characters, and settings, and these arguments have led some students to work independently, not with their group members. Many of the students have also turned to Mr. Paul for answers, whereas he wants them to turn to their peers for help. Further, Mr. Paul has noticed that some of the groups did not follow the procedures he established for this activity. For instance, he asked the students to write and illustrate their books on only one side of their writing paper. Many have used both sides of the paper, and their markers and pens have bled through the paper, making the story and illustrations difficult to see.
>
> When groups present their fairy tales to the rest of the class, they are very disorganized. Many groups have not decided who will read and show the illustrations. Their presentation skills, such as talking loudly and displaying the fairy tales for everyone to see clearly, are also lacking.
>
> After the last group presents, Mr. Paul dismisses the students for recess and sits at his desk. He wonders what he can do to improve the cooperative groups.

It is apparent that many of Mr. Paul's students do not feel very accountable for their work. It is possible, of course, that the assignment is too difficult or was not explained adequately, but it is also likely that Mr. Paul's procedures are not helping the students develop good work habits or learn the importance of cooperation and effectively presenting information to others.

FOR REFLECTION

As you plan the academic activities in which your students will participate, think how you will help students be accountable for their work and create high quality products. Important areas of accountability are addressed in the questions below:

- ◆ Are the standards for quality and type of product clear to the students?
- ◆ How will you monitor student progress?
- ◆ What kinds of feedback do students receive about their progress as well as about their completed work? How soon do they get feedback?
- ◆ What are the consequences for incomplete or careless work?
- ◆ What are the incentives for careful, thorough, and timely completion of assignments? ■

This chapter will focus on aspects of classroom procedures that communicate the importance of assignments, that enable students to understand what is expected of them, and that help them make good progress. The critical areas include communicating assignments and work requirements, monitoring student progress, and providing feedback. Checklist 3 is provided to help organize your planning in these areas. In addition, three case studies of accountability systems of elementary teachers are provided at the end of the chapter.

CLEAR COMMUNICATION OF ASSIGNMENTS AND WORK REQUIREMENTS

Students need a clear idea of what their assignments are and what is expected of them. This means that you must be able to explain all requirements and features of the assignments. Verbal explanation alone will not be sufficient because not all students listen carefully, some students may be absent when the assignments and requirements are discussed, and the assignment itself may be complex. In addition, there is more to completing assignments than doing the work accurately. You must also consider standards for neatness, legibility, and form. While you do not want to encourage an overemphasis on form to the detriment of the learning objectives, standards in these areas must be set. The following three areas should be considered.

Instructions for Assignments

In addition to telling the students what the assignment is, routinely post the assignment and important instructions on a chalkboard, overhead projector, or flip chart. It is also a good idea to teach students to copy the assignment into their notebooks or on the first line of their papers so they will have a record of it if they need it to complete work at home. Go over instructions orally with the class, indicating where the instructions are displayed in the room. Whenever appropriate, use the overhead projector or the chalkboard to show students how their papers should look. After giving instructions, question the children and ask them to give examples so you can determine whether they understand what to do. One way to do this is to ask a student or students to restate the directions. Another is to have one group member share or restate directions for the group.

If you are giving directions for seatwork to several groups in preparation for reading group time, be sure the assignment for each group is clearly labeled. For primary grades especially, you might assign a color to each reading group. Use that color chalk or ink to put asterisks beside assignments or worksheets taped to the board to indicate the appropriate group, or write the whole set of assignments and instructions in that color. Use the same location for each group's assignment every day so they will know where to look without your reminder.

If you are giving directions for group work, move students into their groups first. Make sure you have everyone's attention again before thoroughly explaining your expectations. Check the understanding of at least one member of each group by asking questions such as, "What will your group need to do first?" For older students, it is helpful to provide a set of written instructions to each group, especially if the group task is a complex one.

Standards for Form, Neatness, and Due Dates

Develop a standard set of instructions for work requirements. Students will then learn what is generally expected, and you will have to explain only exceptions or changes to them as they occur. Students will need to know such things as what paper to write on, what heading to use, whether to write on the back of the paper, whether to color any part of it, how to number, whether to use pen or pencil, and whether to erase errors or to draw lines through them.

Decide on a standard heading for students to use on their papers. Post a sample heading and go over it with students the first time they are to use it. Remind them of it several times during the early weeks of school until they use it properly. Make the heading as brief and simple as possible.

Finally, due dates should be reasonable and clear; exceptions should not be made without good cause. Be sure to tell students your policy for turning in work on time and follow it consistently. Don't keep extending time limits; if you do, students may not learn to use time wisely. In general, insist that work not done on time be completed at home or after school. This assumes, of course, that students possess the necessary knowledge or skills to do the work on their own.

Procedures for Absent Students

A number of problems arise when students are absent. They miss instruction, directions for assignments, and assistance they may need in getting assignments under way. Establishing some routines for handling makeup work is helpful and avoids interruption of class. Perhaps you will not require that students complete each assignment they missed while they were absent, but a student who misses critical assignments may need to make these up. The following items should be considered:

1. Arrange to meet briefly with students who have been absent to point out what makeup assignments are required. If you post weekly assignment lists for each subject on a bulletin board or keep a folder with lists of assignments in an easily accessible place, you will be able to point out which of these are to be completed. For young children, you may need to have a packet of makeup work in a special "makeup folder." Be sure to let the students know how much time they have to complete it.

2. Establish a regular time, such as fifteen minutes before or after school, when you will be available to assist students with instruction they have missed. In addition, you can designate class helpers who will be available at particular times of the day (usually during independent activities) to help these students.

3. Designate a place where students can turn in makeup work and where they can pick it up after it has been checked (for example, baskets or trays labeled "Absent In" and "Absent Out").

4. Determine how students who have missed group work will make it up. Assist groups in planning for the inclusion of absent members and in catching up those members when they return.

MONITORING PROGRESS ON AND COMPLETION OF ASSIGNMENTS

Monitoring Work in Progress

Monitoring student progress helps you detect students who are having difficulty and also enables you to encourage other students to keep working. Once you have made an assignment, you should give careful attention to student work. Don't immediately begin work at your desk or go to help an individual student without first checking to see if all students are starting and are able to do the assignment. If you don't check, some students may not even start the assignment, and others may begin it incorrectly. Two simple strategies can help to avoid this situation. First, if everyone in the class is doing the same assignment, you can assure a smooth transition into independent work by beginning it as a whole-class activity; that is, have everyone get out paper or other materials and then answer the first question or two, or work the first few problems together as a group just as you would conduct a recitation. For example, ask the first question, solicit an answer, discuss it, and have students record it on their papers. Not only will this procedure help ensure that all students begin, but any immediate problems with the assignment can be solved. A second way to monitor student involvement in the assignment is to circulate around the room and check each student's progress periodically. This allows corrective feedback to be given when needed and helps keep students responsible for appropriate progress. Note the progress of all students, not just those who raise their hands for help. Check frequently with students who become easily confused or distracted. Also, be sure to check in with small groups as they begin working to make sure each group is on an appropriate track. Another way to monitor work in progress is to have students bring their work to you one at a time at some designated point in the activity. However, be careful to avoid lines of waiting students.

If you are working with reading groups while some students are doing independent work, don't wait until the end of reading time to check student progress. Go around to the students between meetings with groups to be sure the students are doing the work correctly.

Sometimes, assignments are given that are not due for several days or even a week or longer. Examples include notebooks, reports, and science or social studies projects. When this is the case, you will need to be especially careful to monitor

student progress. Define substages in the project or assignment and then set deadlines and goals for each of these parts or have students or groups develop work plans on which they report daily. Collect and check assignments at each of these stages and give students feedback. This will help students learn to organize their work and make it easier for you to monitor and evaluate their progress.

Monitoring the Completion of Assignments

Monitoring completion of assignments has several components. First, you will need to establish regular procedures for students to turn in completed work and for you to note whose papers have been turned in. Many different systems are possible. For example, you might have students put completed work in individual "mailboxes"; you can determine at a glance whose boxes are filled and whose are lacking assigned papers. Or you might have students put completed papers on a certain corner of their desks so they will be easy to spot and check as you move around the room. This procedure is especially appropriate when you do not intend to collect the papers. A third procedure is to have students turn in their work to different baskets for each subject. You must find time to check each basket frequently and record each completed assignment in your grade book. As an additional help, you may also provide students with individual checklists to help them keep track of their own assignments.

Give attention to how you will collect work. When all students will be turning in materials at the same time, the most efficient procedure is to have papers passed in a given direction until you have all papers in your hands. Materials such as notebooks or journals that are inconvenient or bulky might be collected by designated helpers and stacked in a particular spot. Papers or assignments turned in by students at varying times can be placed in appropriately labeled baskets, trays, or plastic containers. Avoid locating these drop-off spots in congested areas or where they might be distracting to nearby students. Be sure that students know the procedure you expect them to use. Following it consistently saves time and prevents confusion.

Maintaining Records of Student Work

An important part of your monitoring system is your record of student work completion. Generally, these records will be a part of your grade book. You should organize the grade book so that you have a place for recording the students who are absent each day; for example, by putting an *a* in the corner of the appropriate space. When setting up your grade book, you should devote several lines per student and record grades and scores for each subject on a separate line, or you can use a different page for each major subject. If you record grades for different subjects on the same line, you will need a code such as different colored pen or pencil to distinguish them. Or you can write in subject headings at the top of the page and separate them by heavy red vertical lines. If you have students from another teacher's class for instruction in a subject, be sure to leave space for those additional students on a page for that subject in your grade book. It will be your responsibility to supply the other teacher with report card evaluations, and it will be helpful to have all of the information in one place. Check with experienced teachers at your grade level for suggestions on organizing your grade book.

Record grades or other evaluations (E, S+, S, U) for major assignments and test results in your grade book. Whether to record an evaluation of other classwork such as worksheets or workbook pages is discretionary. This is not as common in the primary grades as in the intermediate grades, where more emphasis is placed on grading, and a more complete record of daily work in major subjects is useful.

MANAGING THE PAPERWORK

Keeping up with all the papers can be overwhelming. One way to avoid mountains of "back papers" is to look over, grade, record and return assignments quickly. Not only is this excellent feedback for your students, it also helps you to spot students who are "fading" or to diagnose areas needing whole-class remediation. Another approach is to have students assist with checking assignments. Although this must be supervised closely, the task should be well within students' capabilities. Also, be realistic about your grading capabilities. If you are behind in grading six sets of papers and are planning to assign essays due in two days, change your plans. Allow yourself enough grading time to do the job well—on the last paper as well as the first; try making a grading schedule to distribute a huge task into manageable segments rather than plowing through until you are exhausted. Instead of collecting, checking, grading, and returning each assignment, try another routine: Go around the room and check each student's work yourself and give oral feedback. You can record a grade if you wish, at the same time. This type of checking is especially effective for written assignments that require holistic assessment. It is also fast, personal, and efficient.

Upper elementary or middle school teachers often find themselves departmentalized and expected to teach 100 to 150 students each day. To manage the paperwork involved in distributing, collecting, keeping up with, and returning papers, you must have an organized system. A separate color code for each class can simplify the process. For example, if first period is coded red, place a red plastic tab on that roll page in your grade-book, place papers to be distributed or returned to first period in a folder having a red label, clip papers collected with a red spring clip, and place a red dot in the corner of report cards of all first-period students.

Distributing papers is made easier if they are counted out in class sets beforehand. This prevents your coming up one or two papers short and having to try to duplicate materials and teach class at the same time. It also enables you to place names of absent students on leftover papers, drop them in a coded file folder, and have them ready for those students when they return.

To collect papers, some teachers use a separate basket labeled for each period and have students place papers in the appropriate basket at a designated time. Others have students pass papers up in a designated pattern, clip papers together with a color-coded clip, and place the papers in an "in" basket. If you plan to have students pass papers up, you can prevent "straggler" papers by describing, modeling, and practicing how it is to be done.

Returning papers is simplified if they are already filed together, labeled by period, and even possibly organized by rows or groups. Papers may be distributed by students; consider using weekly "assistant teachers."

FEEDBACK TO STUDENTS

Good monitoring procedures provide the basis for feedback to students. Frequent and regular feedback is more desirable than sporadic appraisal because it reduces the amount of time students spend making errors if their performance is incorrect. Appropriate times for feedback will occur as you monitor work in progress and after it is completed. Try to give students immediate and specific feedback: Tell them what they need to do to correct errors, then check their corrections.

Feedback about completed work cannot occur until after an assignment has been checked. Checking should be done within a day of work completion so that students can benefit from the feedback, and you can keep track of their progress. If you find yourself bogged down with work to check, have your students help you. At most grade levels, students can exchange papers or check their own work occasionally. Use student checkers only for assignments they are capable of checking accurately, such as arithmetic worksheets or spelling quizzes that have specified right answers. Teach them a consistent system for marking right or wrong answers. Displaying correct answers with the overhead projector can make checking work in class proceed smoothly and accurately.

In the primary grades particularly, assignments are often short and easy to check quickly. Rather than collecting the work and checking it later, you can check each child's work as it is completed. If you have students bring their work to you, be careful to avoid the formation of long lines that distract others and waste time.

Another method is to check work as you monitor each student's progress. If students have finished, have them place the completed work at a corner of their desks so it is easy to see. This practice gives prompt feedback, cuts down on the amount of paper you must collect, and allows you to have students correct their errors much more quickly. Furthermore, you can offer suggestions even as students are completing an assignment. This feedback allows for altering and correcting work in progress.

Pay careful attention at the beginning of the year to the completion of assignments. The first time a student fails to turn in an assignment without an apparent reason, talk with him or her about it. If the student needs help, provide it, but require the student to do the work. If the student neglects two assignments consecutively or begins a pattern of skipping occasional assignments, call the parent(s) or send a note home. Be friendly, be encouraging, but insist that the work be done. Don't wait until the grading period is over to note problems with assignment completion or assume that the report card grade will communicate this information effectively. The parent or parents can be the teacher's strongest ally in assuring that the child takes school work seriously. And you should not hesitate to contact parents. Most parents will appreciate your concern and provide you with support from home.

Another procedure for communicating with parents is to have students take checked assignments home regularly. Be sure this includes good work and not just poor work. You can occasionally have parents sign and return the papers as a way of rewarding and motivating students to "keep up the good work." Use a large envelope or a folder with two ends taped to convey the materials home rather than leaving them loose. This envelope or folder also is a convenient holder for other important documents the child must transport home for signing or for the parents' information. Be sure the child's name is on the folder or envelope. Taping a signature sheet on the front that has a place for the date and the number of papers included can ensure that parents see all the student's work.

Another means of giving the children feedback is to display good work. Note that you should not make standards for "good" so stringent that some children can never meet them. Effort may be a more appropriate criterion in some cases.

Reprinted by permission of King Features Syndicate.

Finally, teach students how to keep a record of their own progress. Older children can keep a sheet with test scores or assignment grades. Steps on a ladder, circles on a caterpillar to color in for each completed assignment, or some other similar visual device can be a good motivator for younger students.

FURTHER READING

Anderson, L. M. (1985). What are students doing when they do all that seatwork? In C. W. Fisher & D. C. Berliner (Eds.), *Perspectives on instructional time* (pp. 189–202), NY: Longman.

This article provides a close look at how first graders spend time in seatwork and how they understand their seatwork assignments. This study found that students often cannot identify the goal of seatwork activities or, in some cases, perceive that the purpose of the activity is to finish it. The analysis provides insights into what is operating in seatwork settings that diverts student learning away from the instructor's goals.

Burns, M. (1995). The 8 most important lessons I've learned about organizing my teaching year. *Instructor, 105* (2), 86–88.

Many of the ideas in this article focus on planning for instruction. Their implementation would be a big step toward managing student academic work and are well worth considering by new or experienced teachers.

Crook, T. J. (1988). The impact of classroom evaluation practices on students. *Review of Educational Research, 58,* 438–481.

Students are greatly affected by the ways in which teachers evaluate their work. Some of the factors considered in this review of research include standard setting, the types of learning sought by the teacher, frequency and nature of evaluation, and its impact on motivation.

Doyle, W. (1983). Academic work. *Review of Educational Research, 53,* 159–199.

Key concepts considered in this article include the role of accountability in communicating the importance of specific academic content, problems in teaching toward higher cognitive level objectives, and special problems encountered by less prepared and immature learners. The teacher's role in creating the classroom environment for academic work is analyzed carefully.

SUGGESTED ACTIVITIES

1. Case Studies 3–1 to 3–3 illustrate accountability procedures that encourage student responsibility. Decide which ones you can incorporate into your classroom.

2. Case Study 3–4 illustrates problems that can occur if certain accountability procedures are not in place. Use the information in this and in previous chapters to diagnose Mr. Ambrose's problems. Compare your ideas with the keys in the Appendix.

3. Use Checklist 3 at the end of the chapter to organize your planning as you develop an accountability system. Can you think of any additional accountability procedures you will need?

CASE STUDY 3-1

MANAGING STUDENT WORK

To help students check their homework and to encourage them to help each other, Ms. Alvarez' fourth-grade students work in teams of four and go over the homework problems together. Ms. Alvarez has taught her students how to take turns reading the problems, answering the questions, and encouraging and helping one another. Each team member takes turns reading the problem aloud and then gives his or her answer to the problem. Team members rotate leading the discussion of the questions until all questions have been answered. From time to time, Ms. Alvarez plans activities and conversations that reinforce the collaborative environment she strives for in her classroom as well as reviewing procedures for her "group check."

The students use the "group check" process when checking their homework. When a team member reads the answer, the other members give a "thumbs up" if they had the same answer. If someone's answer differs, he or she says quietly, "I disagree." Each team member talks through the problem and reworks it so see where the error might be. This process continues until each team member comes to consensus about the homework problem.

On one question involving area, Jake did not draw his circle the same size as his team members did. When Anita gave her solution, Jake said, "I disagree. I think!" Jake and his team members discussed the different-sized circles and what they would need to do to draw to scale. The used their compasses and redrew the circle, being careful to note the radius given in the problem. As it turned out, Jake's answer was correct; he had drawn his circle to the correct scale. Jake and his team members marked the problems that were difficult for them on their papers. When Ms. Alvarez brought the class back together, she led a discussion about problems that were difficult for the team to agree on and what questions they still had.

Ms. Alvarez used this as a cue for the problems that were difficult for the majority of the class. She planned additional whole-class instruction to clarify these problems. Having the team members first check their work together freed Ms. Alvarez to move around the room and help teams that needed assistance. With her "group check" system, she knew that she did not have to stand at the front of the room and call out answers.

At the end of the morning activity, one person from each team takes the team's homework folders and files them in each team member's portfolios, stored on a nearby shelf. When Ms. Alvarez has a conference once a week with her students, their portfolios are within reach. Ms. Alvarez also returns the portfolios at a later time and checks the comments the students recorded on the assignment to be sure the students understand the concepts. If she notes that students need additional support, she works with then individually or in small groups.

CASE STUDY 3-2

KEEPING STUDENTS INVOLVED DURING CENTER ACTIVITIES

Ms. Avery designates a section of the chalkboard for listing the daily schedule for centers. Today's schedule consists of the following activities and times:

	Reading Group	**Research**	**Math**	**Science**
9:00–9:20	Spotted Owl	Gorilla	Panda	Panther
9:25–9:45	Panther	Spotted Owl	Gorilla	Panda
9:50–10:10	Panda	Panther	Spotted Owl	Gorilla
10:15–10:35	Gorilla	Panda	Panther	Spotted Owl

Center time typically consists of four stations, one of which is teacher-directed. At the beginning of center time, Ms. Avery presents directions and shows the students the necessary materials for each station.

The reading groups in Ms. Avery's class are flexible. Sometimes they are created around students' interests; sometimes they are formed to practice certain skills such as main ideas, cause and effect, and inferring. Presently, the class is studying endangered animals. The students have selected four animals for in-depth study (spotted owl, panther, panda, gorilla), and the reading groups were formed to study each animal. In addition to their reading groups, the small groups of students are developing research projects on their chosen animals.

During today's center activities, the students will meet with Ms. Avery for their reading groups. They will also continue with their research projects, using resources the teacher and students have collected. At the math center, they will complete a worksheet on long division. Manipulatives and other aids are provided for the students at this station. For science, the students will observe the animals in the class terrarium and record their observations in their science logs.

When Ms. Avery meets with each reading group, she sits so she can see the entire class. She scans the class frequently and signals children when necessary to keep them on task. She does so by making eye contact or sometimes calling individuals' names softly to prevent or stop inappropriate behavior. Because Ms. Avery does not want students coming to her for help while she is in the reading circle, she has assigned one helper for each group. To prevent excessive use of the helpers, Ms. Avery has taught the children to request assistance only for situations that prevent them from doing any work at all. If they can skip the problem or question and proceed with the work, they are to do so and wait for help from her.

When the timer rings, she dismisses the reading group, and the other groups clean up their stations, place their worksheets and journals in appropriate baskets, and move to their next stations. Ms. Avery circulates around the room checking on student progress, answering questions, and helping students. Between groups, checks usually take no longer than five minutes, after which she is ready to call the next group. Ms. Avery has made sure that circulation time is built into her schedule.

CASE STUDY 3-3

MATH ACCOUNTABILITY PROCEDURES IN AN INTERMEDIATE GRADE

In Mr. Wilson's fifth-grade class, math always follows the morning break. At the end of the break, Mr. Wilson displays four or five math review problems on the overhead projector screen and then rings a bell to signal the end of the break. At this point, students work the warm-up problems at their seats. The students are seated in groups of four and are encouraged to discuss the review problems with each other. Mr. Wilson sets a timer for ten minutes and spends the time helping the students with the problems, returning graded papers to students, and taking care of administrative matters. When math instruction begins, the warm-up problems are checked along with the regular assignment.

Mr. Wilson stresses the importance of being organized, and he has students keep a math folder with sections. The first section includes an assignment sheet on which students copy daily assignments. The second page in that section includes several reminders for math, such as, "Always use a pencil. Copy the whole problem unless told otherwise. If you are unsure of your answer, compare your work with other students at your table." Other sections of the notebook include warm-ups, class and homework assignments, and tests.

When checking work in class, Mr. Wilson usually reads the problem and asks for students to show their work on the overhead projector and explain how they solved the problem. Discussion is encouraged, especially when students have used different strategies to solve the problems. If several students seem confused about a particular method, Mr. Wilson makes a mental note to address this area during whole-class instruction. After checking the warm-up problems, the students write the number of correct answers at the top of the page, and Mr. Wilson collects the papers.

Mr. Wilson takes special care during the math lesson to present new material slowly and clearly, to check students' understanding of the strategies involved, and to allow ample time for classroom practice and questions. When students begin working on the class assignment, he walks around the room, systematically listening to group discussions, looking at students' papers, and asking probing questions. If he notices that several students need help, he will ask the students to pause, and he will hold a brief mini-lesson on this concept.

The grading system is easily understood by students. The warm-ups for one grading period total 100 problems, and the number of correct answers counts as one test grade. Classwork and homework grades make up 50 percent of the total math average and tests contribute the remaining 50 percent. In addition, Mr. Wilson provides bonus questions on tests, interesting problems, and math puzzles that students can complete for extra credit.

CASE STUDY 3-4

POOR WORK AND STUDY HABITS IN A FOURTH-GRADE CLASS

Mr. Ambrose's fourth-grade class has been fairly well behaved and exhibits little disruptive behavior. Most students follow his procedures for procedural tasks, such as staying in their seats during whole-class presentations, raising hands during discussions, and appropriately using the pencil sharpener, restroom, and other areas of the room. Some social talk occurs during seatwork activities, but it does not escalate into chaos, and students usually settle down when requested. However, students have been less task oriented lately, and many students have been tardy turning in assignments. They complain that they don't know when assignments are due, and some don't turn in their work at all. To make assignments very explicit, Mr. Ambrose has begun to record the daily assignments on the side chalkboard. Because some assignments are not due until the following day, he leaves the previous day's assignments on that chalkboard also, so students will know when each subject's assignment is due for both days.

Today, during a one-hour period of individual and group work, several students asked what they were supposed to do, despite the fact that Mr. Ambrose had listed the morning assignments on the chalkboard and repeatedly pointed out where they could be found. After several students turned in papers before they were called for, Mr. Ambrose explained, "Remember that class assignments not finished during class time are supposed to be kept until the next day, even if you get them done later in the day, unless I call for them. If you finish the homework during independent work time, it can be placed in the turn-in box then." Students continued to act confused, not only about when assignments were due but also about how to do the work.

Mr. Ambrose frequently works at his desk during seatwork time, but he allows students to come up one at a time if they need assistance. They follow this procedure well, although some of the lowest-achieving students seldom come up. Quite a bit of quiet socializing and other off-task activities go on among students whose seats are located away from the teacher.

Mr. Ambrose has ample activities for students. For example, during a recent one-hour segment, he gave students an assignment and then had them take a quiz (students were told to hold their papers until after the quiz was completed). Also an extra credit assignment was listed on the board for students who finished this regular work early. As he handed out the quiz and gave instructions, some students continued to work on the assignment. Later they had to go to Mr. Ambrose to find the instructions for the test, and several did not have enough time to complete the test. Mr. Ambrose has told students that they must work harder and do their best or their grades will suffer, but this seems to have had impact on only the most motivated students in the class.

What steps could Mr. Ambrose take to improve the situation in his class?

✔ CHECKLIST 3

ACCOUNTABILITY PROCEDURES

Check When Complete	Area	Notes
	Communicating Assignments and Work Requirements	
☐	A. Where and how will you post assignments?	_____
☐	B. What will be your standards for form and neatness? —Pencil, color of pen —Type of paper —Heading —Due dates —Erasures	_____
☐	C. How will absent students know what assignments to make up?	_____
☐	D. What will be the consequences of late or incomplete work?	_____
	Monitoring Progress on and Completion of Assignments	
☐	A. What procedures will you use to monitor work in progress?	_____
☐	B. When and how will you monitor projects or longer assignments?	_____
☐	C. How will you determine whether students are completing assignments?	_____
☐	D. How will you collect completed assignments?	_____
☐	E. What records of student work will you retain?	_____
	Feedback	
☐	A. What are your school's grading policies and procedures?	_____

continued

ACCOUNTABILITY PROCEDURES *Continued*

Check When Complete	Area	Notes
☐	B. What kinds of feedback will you provide, and when?	_____
☐	C. What will you do when a student stops doing assignments?	_____
☐	D. What procedure will you follow to send materials home to parents?	_____
☐	E. Where will you display student work?	_____
☐	F. What records, if any, of their own work will the students maintain?	_____
☐	G. How will you handle grading disputes?	_____

C H A P T E R $\quad$ **4**

Getting Off to a Good Start

The beginning of school is an important time for classroom management because your students will learn behavior, attitudes, and work habits that will affect the rest of the year. Of course, it is better if they start the year behaving appropriately.

Your major goal for the beginning of the year is to obtain student cooperation in two key areas: following your rules and procedures and successfully engaging in all learning experiences. Attaining this goal will make it possible for you to create a good environment for learning during the rest of the year.

A concern for establishing appropriate behavior does not imply a lack of concern for student feelings and attitudes. Instead, the intent is to create a classroom climate that helps children feel secure and that prevents problems from occurring. Therefore, some of the suggestions in this chapter will focus directly on cognitive goals, whereas others will incorporate student concerns and other affective considerations.

The major topics in this chapter are teaching your rules and procedures to the students, deciding on the classroom activities you will use during the first week of school, arranging these activities into workable lesson plans, and identifying needed materials. Special problems are discussed. A checklist is available to help organize your planning, and two case studies of the beginning of the year will give you many ideas about how to begin.

FOR REFLECTION

Can you remember what it was like to start school when you were attending elementary school? When adults are asked to recall school beginnings, they can rarely remember much detail about what teachers did, but they often remember their own personal experiences, problems, or concerns. How typical were your beginning-of-school experiences? How should teachers attempt to take their students' concerns into account at the beginning of the year? Because teacher personal concerns and anxieties also may be heightened during those critical days, how can teachers deal with their own feelings and accommodate student concerns at the same time? ■

TEACHING RULES AND PROCEDURES

One of the surest ways to communicate your expectations for student behavior is through a planned system of classroom rules and procedures. How best to teach this system to your students is an important consideration. The term *teach* is used purposely; you will not communicate your expectations adequately if you only tell students about rules and procedures.

Three aspects of the teaching process are important:

1. **Describing and demonstrating the desired behavior.** Use words and actions to convey what behavior is acceptable or desirable. Be as specific as possible. For example, do not simply tell the children you expect them to be good while you are out of the room; tell them what "be good" means—stay in seats, no talking, keep working. You should demonstrate desired behavior whenever possible. For example, if you allow "quiet talking" or "classroom voices" during center time, you should provide demonstrations of what this means. If the procedure is complex, present it in a step-by-step manner. For example, lining up requires that students know when to line up (e.g., the

teacher gives permission by tables or rows), where and how to go (e.g., push chairs under tables and then walk without talking), expected behavior in line (e.g., hands off others, no talking in halls, walk—don't run). You do not need to do all the demonstrating; many students enjoy the privilege of showing the class the correct procedure.

2. **Rehearsal.** This means practicing the behaviors. Rehearsal serves two purposes: It helps children learn the appropriate behavior, and it provides you with an opportunity to determine whether the children understand and can correctly follow a procedure. Complex procedures may have to be rehearsed several times. Practice is especially helpful for primary-grade children; however, the older elementary school child can benefit from rehearsal whenever the procedures are complex or have not previously been encountered.

3. **Feedback.** After you have asked students to follow a procedure for the first time, be sure to tell them if they did it properly and then praise them. If improvement is needed, be sure to tell them that, too. Be discriminating in your feedback—for example, "I liked how quickly you put your materials away, but I did not like the talking by the students at Table Two." If many students do not follow a procedure correctly, then you should repeat one or more of the above steps. If only a few students are off track, you might ask them to describe what they are supposed to do so that you can determine whether they understand your directions. Finally, the fact that students follow the procedure correctly once does not mean they will do so consistently. You should watch them carefully and be prepared to give reminders and feedback as appropriate.

Two examples that illustrate how to teach procedures are presented below. The first example shows the teacher instructing students on the use of the correct heading on their papers. This procedure was taught to students on the first day of school in a fourth-grade class as part of an assignment to write a brief account of their worst fear of fourth grade or "What would happen if. . . ."

> Mr. Samuels has written a sample heading for students' papers on the front chalkboard. He points to it, explaining to students that he wants this heading to be on every assignment they do. He points to the upper right-hand corner of the sample page and explains that students should write the heading there. Mr. Samuels tells students they should write both their first and last names on the first line. He points to the line below where he has written "Writing" and explains that this line is for the subject of the assignment and will change when students do an assignment in another subject. Students are instructed to put the date with the month spelled out under the subject name. The teacher points out the room calendar and suggests that students refer to it when they need to know the date. Mr. Samuels asks the class if there are any questions about the heading. When no questions are forthcoming, Mr. Samuels tells the students to take out a sheet of

paper and pencil and put the correct heading for a writing lesson on their paper. He circulates around the room, checking to make sure that every student is using the proper heading.

Note that Mr. Samuels demonstrated the correct form by having an example on the chalkboard; he described each aspect carefully and gave students an immediate opportunity to practice the heading and to receive corrective feedback.

The next example shows how a complex transition procedure was taught to a second-grade class. The teacher in this example teaches students to respond to a signal, put away their materials, and move to a rug area.

Ms. Stevens explains to her students that she expects them to move quickly and quietly from one activity to another so they will have time to do all the things planned. She shows them the kitchen timer and makes it ring. She tells the students that this will be a very important signal. When they hear this bell, the students should put away the materials they are using and move to the next activity as quickly as possible. "After reading, I will ring the bell, and you are to put your reading materials in your desk as quickly as possible. You should then get up from your desk and walk quietly to the rug so we can begin our Spanish lesson. Are there any questions?" A student asks if she will always ring the bell for Spanish, and Ms. Stevens says she will.

Ms. Stevens then tells the class that she would like them to practice. "You have paper and pencil on your desk that you have been using to write a story. I will give you time to finish the story later in the day. Right now, when I ring the bell, put your materials in your desk and come quickly and quietly to the rug." At this point, Ms. Stevens rings the bell. Students immediately begin putting away their materials and moving toward the rug. However, several students line up to get drinks of water and one goes to the bathroom. When everyone is on the rug in a circle around Ms. Stevens, she refers to the clock on the wall and says, "It took us three minutes to put the materials away and get to the rug. You are second graders now, and I think you can move faster than that. I think you should be seated on the rug in a circle in one minute. Also, it was not time to get a drink of water or to use the bathroom unless it was an emergency. Do you all understand?" The students all nod solemnly.

Ms. Stevens tells students to return to their desks, get out their paper and pencils, and get set to practice again. The students go quickly back to their desks and take out their materials. Ms. Stevens rings the bell again, and students go through the routine, this time more quickly. After all the students are settled, Ms. Stevens smiles and thanks the students. "You've done a super job. It only took you one minute to get to the rug. I'm really proud of you."

In the example, Ms. Stevens demonstrated the signal, described the desired behavior, and gave a rationale for it. The students were allowed to practice the process twice, and feedback was given to them each time.

PLANNING FOR A GOOD BEGINNING

You have already done a major portion of the planning for the beginning of the year if you have followed the guidelines in the first three chapters. Your room should be arranged, and you will have decided on your rules, procedures, and an accountability system. You now need to plan activities for the first several days of school.

Important Considerations

For the first days of school, plan activities that will allow all your students to be successful. Such activities will make students feel more secure and confident and encourage their continued good effort. Initial assignments should be easy and require only simple directions. In this way, the children will quickly learn lesson routines and encounter little difficulty in completing assignments.

Plan activities with a whole-class focus. For the first few days, you should limit the lessons to those that can be presented and explained to all the students at the same time. Do not try to group students for instruction for at least several days, and if you can, avoid individual testing or any activities or seatwork assignments that require you to work with individual students for long periods of time. Don't overload yourself or your students with unnecessarily complicated activities. Your students will already be learning many new procedures during the first few days of school. In addition, you will need to be free to watch students very carefully to detect problems and take appropriate action. If you are involved with a small group or with an individual, you may not see important behaviors and events.

Plan your activities to take into account the children's perspectives, concerns, and needs for information about the new and unfamiliar situation your classroom presents. A variety of activities, including some with physical movement, music, and provision for occasional short breaks will provide the changes of pace that help maintain interest and alertness throughout the day. In addition, you should stimulate the children's interest in the curriculum and associated activities. If you are excited about the wonderful things they will be learning this year, your students are more likely to feel the enthusiasm themselves. Foreshadow interesting units in science and social studies or tell them about skills they will develop in your class.

Some Typical Activities

Activities you will use in the first school day and for several days thereafter are described below. They are not necessarily presented in the sequence you will use, nor will you use each one every day, so you should carefully examine the two case studies at the end of the chapter to see how different teachers put the pieces together.

GREETING THE STUDENTS

Prepare student name tags ahead of time. Have extra materials on hand for unexpected students. Decide how name tags will be fastened. If you use straight pins, you may be inviting little dueling matches and surprise pricks and pokes. If you intend to use safety pins, be sure your students can fasten them or plan to do it for them. Other options are tape, commercial stick-on tags, or a length of yarn to allow the name tags to be worn like a necklace. In addition to name tags, you might also tape a card onto the top of the student's desk and write the student's name on it.

When students enter the room, greet them warmly, help them get their name tags on, and get them seated. If you have taped their names to a desk, the matter of seating is settled. In some cases, however, the roster of students is not definite, and you may not want to bother setting up a seating chart before the students arrive. In this case, let the students choose their desks. (Make a seating chart or label the desks with name tags as soon as practicable, making any necessary adjustments later.) Don't allow the students to wander around the room or become noisy. If students straggle in, and you cannot start class right away, provide a simple puzzle, a geography mind-bender, or a piece of paper with open-ended questions such as, "I am thinking about. . . ." "I have a question about. . . ." or "I wonder what _____ is like in school." This will give students something to do at their desks. As soon as most students are present, begin with the introduction. Remember later in the day to let students talk about how they solved the puzzles or what they wrote on their papers.

INTRODUCTIONS

You will want to tell the students something about yourself; however, an extended autobiography is not necessary. A few personal notes and something about your interests would be appropriate. Have students introduce themselves—nothing more than a name is necessary, but some teachers like to use a little more introduction, having the children tell something about themselves. The introduction activity should not take too long, however, as there will be plenty of opportunity later to get acquainted, and you do not want students to become restless.

ROOM DESCRIPTION

You will need to point out major areas of the room, particularly any areas that students will be using on the first day. As you do so, any procedures associated with room use that will be needed that day should be described to students. For example, show students where they may put their coats, lunches, or other items they bring from home; be sure they know where the pencil sharpener is and when they may use it, where frequently used supplies are stored, where the calendar, wastebasket, and clock are, and so on.

GET-ACQUAINTED ACTIVITIES

Teachers frequently include a get-acquainted activity as part of their first day plan. Such activities can help children feel that the teacher and other children know them better and care about them as individuals. Teachers often describe the goal of such an activity as helping students feel more comfortable with their classmates and more secure. The activities are also used to foster a greater sense of class cohesiveness. One of the get-acquainted activities described below can be used early in the first day's plan of activities. It will provide a change of pace after the room description or after the initial discussion of rules and major procedures.

◆ Ask students to introduce themselves and to name a favorite activity or hobby or tell about something they did during the summer. Keep this activity moving briskly because student attention will wane during long introductions. A variation of this activity is to use reciprocal introductions. Have pairs of students learn each other's name and something about the other person (hobbies, interests). Then have each person introduce his or her partner.

◆ Use a name game to help students remember names and to add interest to introductions. For example, have students make up an adjective to go with their own name (e.g., Happy Holly, Curious Carl) or have students think of a game they like (Nintendo Nick). As students introduce themselves, have them name the other students who came before them (or perhaps the last five students) along with their adjectives.

◆ Make ditto copies of a line drawing of the school's mascot. Have each child sign his or her copy and write personal facts (names of brothers or sisters; pets; likes and dislikes; favorite activities, foods, and so forth) on the drawing. Post these on a bulletin board so students can read about each other.

◆ Have students complete a brief questionnaire identifying their interests, favorite subjects, hobbies, etc. Upper elementary students can complete a series of open-ended statements that reflect their interests or preferences (e.g., "Today I feel. . . ." or "The thing I do best is. . . .").

The activities described below can be used the first day or later in the week, after students are more acquainted with one another or after you have time to prepare for the activity.

◆ Make a puzzle with student names. For example, leave out a few letters in each name for students to fill in. Or list first and last names in separate columns in scrambled order and let students match names, or students can identify names arranged in a "seek and find" puzzle.

◆ Set aside a few minutes before the children leave in order to review the day's activities and to discuss with the students what they learned, found difficult, liked best, and so forth. Say a few words about upcoming events and activities that the children will look forward to. Comment on good work and behavior to reinforce your expectations and to keep the tone positive.

◆ Have students from last year's class—you'll need to plan this well ahead— write letters to students in this year's class, telling them what to expect, what was fun about the year, suggestions for study, and what they learned during the year. Share these letters with your students.

◆ Have students bring a paper bag with three to five objects, such as books, pictures, or toys, that tell something about themselves. Let students use these props to introduce themselves on the second or third day of school. Split the activity into two segments if necessary to maintain attention and interest.

◆ Make up a questionnaire in the form of a scavenger hunt; for example, "Name a student who has three brothers and who plays kickball." Let students work in groups to see how many of their classmates they can identify.

◆ Have students bring in one item that represents them for a bulletin board. Each student will explain the meaning of his or her item to the class and put it on the bulletin board, forming a collage of student interests and experiences.

PRESENTATION AND DISCUSSION OF RULES, PROCEDURES, AND CONSEQUENCES

Soon after the introductions, usually after the initial room description, present the major rules and procedures. School rules should be covered along with your classroom rules. Major consequences associated with the rules should be described at the same time. Plan to review the rules later, perhaps on the second and third days, to confirm their importance and help students remember them. Posting the rules will serve as a reminder to students. You may have copies made of the rules and procedures and send these home for parent signatures. Important procedures should also be taught. Teach these procedures as they are needed, rather than all at once. For example, during this initial discussion, you will probably want to teach procedures for using bathrooms and pencil sharpener, moving about the room, obtaining help, asking questions, and talking. Later in the day, as they are needed, teach other important procedures such as those for major transitions (ending the day, leaving and entering the room at lunch time, etc.) as well as procedures associated with recess, cafeteria, or other out-of-room areas. Your opening routine (see Chapter 2) will probably be used on the second day of school, so you may wish to wait until then to describe it to the students. Procedures for special equipment can wait until you're ready to use a particular piece of equipment, and small-group procedures should not be introduced until those activities are to begin. The idea is to provide students with the information they need to complete successfully the activities required of them in the first days of school and to help them feel confident in their new classroom environment.

On the second day of school, review the rules and major procedures students need to know. This reinforces your expectations for appropriate behavior and reminds students of rules and procedures they may have forgotten. When correcting students' behavior at the beginning of school, it is important to remind students

"The hardest part about goin' back to school is learning how to whisper again."

Reprinted with special permission of King Features Syndicate.

of what rule was broken. In the primary grades particularly, you will need to observe students carefully for several weeks to be sure they are following procedures correctly and to give reminders, cues, and prompts to help them learn class routines.

When you present your class rules and procedures to students, set a positive tone by emphasizing the benefits to everyone: "These rules are intended to help us have an enjoyable class in which everyone can learn. We all know that our classroom will work better when everyone respects each other's rights," or "When we allow someone to speak without interrupting, we are showing that we are good listeners." If some procedure or rule is difficult to follow, you might acknowledge this as you discuss it: "I know it isn't easy to remember to raise your hands before speaking when we are having an interesting discussion, but doing so will give everyone a chance to participate," or "It will be hard not to start using the equipment right away, but we need to wait for directions so no one is injured." Explanations such as these help students understand and accept what might ordinarily be seen as arbitrary rules.

CONTENT ACTIVITIES

Be sure to select activities that are uncomplicated and that can be presented to the whole class. Seatwork assignments should allow for differences in speed of completion; be sure to have backup activities for students who complete work early. Consult your teachers' manuals and curriculum guides and talk with experienced teachers to get ideas about appropriate beginning content activities for different subjects at your grade level.

TIME FILLERS

Periodically, you will need to fill in time between activities or before and after major transitions. For example, students may complete a seatwork assignment earlier than you anticipated, but there may not be enough time to begin another activity before the next scheduled event. Or there may be times when the students need a short break after an intensive lesson. Filling these times with constructive activity is better than trying to stretch out an already completed task or just letting students amuse themselves. Ideas include having a good book to read to the children or some simple games that can be played in the classroom (Seven Up, Name Bingo, Hangman, Baseball Math, Spelling Bee). Keep on hand dittos or other handouts with puzzles, riddles, or story starters for creative writing. You can also lead the children in group exercises, sing songs, listen to a good children's tape, or have a bulletin board of creative writing ideas. You could also have a "share and tell" time in which students focus on telling what they know about a particular topic (e.g., pets, hobbies). Ask other teachers for ideas and accumulate a file so you will be ready with a filler whenever one is needed.

ADMINISTRATIVE ACTIVITIES

If you will use textbooks, you will need to distribute them to students. You may wish to issue one or two textbooks on the first day; some teachers wait a day or two before distributing textbooks and use handouts and dittos for assignments, especially if class enrollment is likely to change. When you do give out books, you need to record book numbers for each student, perhaps using a standard form. You should also determine school policies in this area. For example, some schools require that books issued to students be kept covered at all times. If so, you will need a supply of covers on hand, and you will need to be prepared to teach the children how to cover the books. In lower grades, it might be better to do the job yourself or enlist the help of parents or an aide. Even in higher grades, some students will have forgotten how to cover books. Plan to show the whole class and schedule plenty of time for this event.

Determine whether there are any materials that students must take home with them on the first day or later in the week (this might include information about the breakfast and lunch program, school policy on attendance, time of arrival and departure for children, etc.).

Communicating with Parents

It is a good idea to prepare a letter to send home to parents explaining any essential information not already conveyed via school handouts. Sometimes, teachers at one grade level get together and collaborate on the letter. If not, write one of your own and get it ready to go home with the children at the end of the first day. Its purpose is to establish a link with parents and to communicate important information to them. The letter should include information on:

◆ Materials or supplies their child will need

- ◆ Your conference times and how parents may contact you
- ◆ Information about curriculum units you will teach or special field trips coming up during the year
- ◆ Special events for parents (e.g., back-to-school night, open house)
- ◆ Information on breakfast and lunch programs if not already provided by the school

A cheerful, friendly letter that is neat, legible, grammatically correct, and free of misspellings will create a good impression and communicate a professional image to the parents. It is easy to get extremely rushed at the beginning of the year and to let this letter be slipshod. Have a friend proofread the letter before you duplicate it to be sure it is clear, correct, and easy to read. A handout describing class rules and major procedures (especially those relating to student assignments) might be sent as an enclosure with the letter. Having parents sign and return this handout will provide you with assurance that parents received your letter and enclosures.

Special Problems

It is not possible to predict every problem that could occur in the first few days of school, but it is possible to identify several that occur commonly, occasionally, or rarely. If you are prepared for the commonly occurring problems and at least not surprised by the occasional or rare event, you will be able to cope.

"And then, of course, there's the possibility of being just the slightest bit too organized."
Reprinted by permission of Glen Dines/KAPPAN.

INTERRUPTIONS BY OFFICE STAFF, PARENTS, CUSTODIANS, AND OTHERS (COMMON)

If you can manage the interruption without leaving the room, do so. Ask the interrupter into your room and face your children as you talk with the person. If the interruption is likely to last more than a few seconds, or if you must leave the room, give the children something to do before continuing the conference. Let the interrupter wait, not your class. Ask your students to continue working if they are already involved in an activity. If not, tell them they can use the time to read a book they have at their desks or to rest their heads on their desks. It is a good idea to have materials for one or two planned activities ready for an unforeseen or lengthy interruption.

LATE ARRIVALS ON THE FIRST DAY (COMMON)

Greet late arrivals as warmly as you did the other students. Tell them you will talk to them about what they missed as soon as you can but that for now, they must wait in their seats. Show them where to sit. When you have the total class involved in some activity, meet with these children to explain anything they may have missed.

ONE OR MORE CHILDREN ARE ASSIGNED TO YOUR CLASS AFTER THE FIRST DAY (COMMON)

Try to arrange to meet with these students before school so that you can explain rules and procedures to them and handle necessary paperwork. If you have already distributed books to the class, make sure these students also get texts. If you can't meet these students ahead of time, use the first available opportunity while the rest of your class is occupied. Appoint one or more responsible students to be "buddies" with the new students to help familiarize them with the classroom and school procedures and rules. The amount of assistance you can expect from these buddies will depend on their grade level. Be sure to monitor new students carefully to help them adjust to your class and to learn appropriate behavior.

A CHILD FORGETS LUNCH MONEY OR SUPPLIES (COMMON)

Be familiar with your school's policies. The principal or school nurse may have an emergency fund for students without lunch money. Some schools allow students to charge a lunch in an emergency. It's a good idea to keep a couple of lunches' worth of small change on hand. Also, have one day's worth of supplies available for students who forget theirs. If a student continues to forget supplies, you may need to check with parents to see that they are aware that the materials are needed. If you suspect that the problem is that the family cannot afford the supplies, see if your school or parent–teacher organization has funds for helping such students.

LARGE AMOUNTS OF PAPERWORK DURING THE FIRST WEEK OF SCHOOL (COMMON)

Do as little of this during class time as possible. Plan to spend extra time before and after school and arrange your personal schedule to accommodate it. This will pay off in reduced tension over the long run. If you must do clerical work during class time, do it quickly while the children are engaged in activities. Monitor the class while you work and avoid losing eye contact with your students for long periods.

A CHILD FORGETS HIS BUS NUMBER OR MISSES HER BUS (OCCASIONAL)

Help to avoid these problems by rehearsing bus procedures with students (especially younger students). Have bus numbers and parents' and emergency phone numbers on hand for when these situations do arise. Make certain the child is not left alone while waiting for a ride and reassure the child that you will not leave him or her.

INSUFFICIENT NUMBERS OF TEXTBOOKS ARE AVAILABLE, OR VITAL EQUIPMENT AND MATERIALS ARE MISSING (OCCASIONAL)

Before school begins, check on the availability of textbooks and your equipment and find out your school's procedures for getting the needed materials into your room. When you discover shortages, report them to the proper person from the school office. If you must begin the year without enough texts, you may be able to have students share books, or you might arrange to share a class set with another teacher. If you have no texts at all in some subject, you can probably find earlier editions of the text in the book storage room to tide you over. Depending on the subject, dittos or other teacher-prepared materials may be sufficient.

ONE OF YOUR STUDENTS HAS A HANDICAP THAT SERIOUSLY INTERFERES WITH HIS OR HER ABILITY TO UNDERSTAND OR TO FOLLOW DIRECTIONS (OCCASIONAL)

Seat the child close to you and engage him or her in simple activities. Work individually with this student only after the rest of the class is busy. As soon as possible, talk to the child's resource teacher to determine what the child is capable of doing, then plan the child's educational program. If possible, talk to the child's teacher from the preceding year for suggestions. You will also find it helpful to set up a conference with the child's parents soon after the year has begun. For further suggestions, see Chapter 9.

CRYING (OCCASIONAL)

Younger children especially may tend to cry for no apparent reason early in the school year. The crying will usually stop fairly quickly if you can distract the child and engage him or her in some activity. Sometimes, it helps to assign a friend to accompany the child to get a drink of water, wash his or her face, and then come back to join the class. Be understanding but do not reinforce crying by giving the child excessive attention or sympathy. If the crying is not disruptive, the child can remain in his or her seat until the episode is over. If the crying is disruptive, take the child out of the room or have someone from the office come to get him or her.

WETTING (OCCASIONAL)

Although accidental wetting is more common with younger children, it sometimes occurs even in the upper grades, especially during the first few days of school. This kind of accident is extremely embarrassing to the child, and the teacher should make every effort not to add to the child's discomfort. Have paper towels on hand to facilitate the cleanup and handle the matter as privately as possible. Arrange to call home or have an office worker phone to bring a change of clothes to school. Later, talk privately with the child to determine why he or she did not go to the restroom in time. With some younger children, you may need to contact the parents and keep a change of clothes at school as a precaution. In general with younger children, the teacher needs to schedule regular bathroom breaks and even remind some children to use the bathroom regularly.

A CHILD BECOMES VERY SICK OR IS INJURED (RARE)

If the child has a known medical condition (such as epilepsy), and you have been previously informed of what to do, follow directions and stay calm. In other cases, phone the office or send a messenger requesting someone to come to get the child. Do not leave the child unattended.

FURTHER READING

Edwards, C., & Stout, J. (1990). Cooperative learning: The first year. *Educational Leadership, 47* (4), 38–43.

In this article, two teachers offer suggestions about critical elements in the process of implementing cooperative learning activities. These ideas will be helpful to anyone considering introducing this type of instructional program, whether at the beginning of the year or later.

Emmer, E. T., Evertson, C. M., & Anderson, L. M. (1980). Effective classroom management at the beginning of the school year. *The Elementary School Journal, 80* (5), 219–231.

This article traces the means by which routines are established in the beginning of the school year and their relationship to classroom management throughout the year. Observations of elementary school teachers starting the school year distinguished between teachers who maintained higher levels of task engagement and cooperation in classroom tasks and low levels of inappropriate and disruptive behavior and those who did not in the ways they established and reinforced classroom norms, monitored, paced lessons, and prevented misbehavior from occurring.

Evertson, C. M. (1989). Improving elementary classroom management: A school-based training program for beginning the year. *Journal of Educational Research, 83* (2), 82–90.

> *This article describes the results of a classroom management training program for inservice elementary teachers. Findings showed that teachers who participated in the program had smoother instructional routines at the beginning of the year and less off-task and inappropriate student behavior.*

Randolph, C. H., & Evertson, C. M. (1995). Managing for learning: Rules, roles, and meanings in a writing class. *Journal of Classroom Interaction, 30* (2), 17–25.

> *The authors argue that management and content are interwoven. As teachers and students negotiate ways of interacting with academic content and with each other, and as they define the roles that each plays, they establish meanings that influence what academic content can be learned and how it is learned.*

Wiske, M. S. (1994). How teaching for understanding changes the rules in the classroom. *Educational Leadership, 51* (5), 19–21.

> *This article discusses how attempting to share authority and responsibility with students violates traditional classroom and school norms. The author implies that teachers must remain open to and accepting of the uneasiness this change causes both in themselves and in their students.*

SUGGESTED ACTIVITIES

1. Read Case Studies 4–1 and 4–2. They describe teachers beginning the year in diverse settings. As you read them, consider the following questions:
   a. To what extent are the principles described in this and previous chapters in evidence in each case?
   b. In spite of subject matter and grade level differences, there are similarities between the teachers. Identify as many of these as you can.
   c. What differences are apparent between the teachers in their beginning-of-year activities? Which one(s) would you use? Why?
   d. In Case 4–1, the teacher uses a literature-based approach to frame activities for students. In Case 4–2, the teacher makes extensive use of groups for Cooperative Learning. How do these approaches affect how each teacher begins the year?

2. What do you think your students' goals and concerns will be at the beginning of the year? How can your classroom management plan accommodate them?

3. Use Checklist 4 at the end of the chapter to organize your planning activities for the beginning of school.

4. Talk with teachers who have had several years of experience at the grade level you will be teaching. Ask them what activities they use during the first few days and how they sequence them. Teachers are often willing to share handouts and ideas. You might also ask someone to look over your lesson plan for the first day and give you suggestions.

CASE STUDY 4-1

BEGINNING THE YEAR IN A LITERATURE-BASED PRIMARY CLASSROOM

First Day Activities

Time/Activity	Description
8:00–8:35 Greeting students	Ms. Gonzalez greets the children as they enter, helps them put on their nametags, and checks the pronunciation of their names. She gives the students laminated strips with their names on them and tells each one to choose a desk and place the strip on it. She also tells students to put their lunch boxes in the basket, hang their bookbags on their labeled coat hook, and place their supplies on the round table at the side of the room. As the first students settle at their desks, Ms. Gonzalez has them select a piece of construction paper, write their names on it, and decorate it. Once they have finished, they are to choose a cubby, which will hold their personal belongings, and tape the construction paper to the back wall of the cubby. She has conveniently placed a tape dispenser at each end of the cubbies for the students to use. Ms. Gonzalez also asks these students to help their classmates. As the rest of the students arrive, Ms. Gonzalez busily helps them settle into the classroom, checks supplies, talks with parents, and monitors students' progress.
8:35–8:40 Teacher introduction	After all of the busses have arrived and she feels that her students are settled, Ms. Gonzalez moves to the next activity. She does not have to call roll because she can tell who is absent by the remaining laminated strips. She fills in her attendance card and places it outside her door. Ms. Gonzalez, who has taught at this school for many years and already knows many of her students, briefly introduces herself and tells the children that she is looking forward to an exciting year with them. She notices that many of the children are curiously looking around the room, so she starts by describing the classroom and a few of her procedures to them.
8:40–9:00 Description of the room	She begins by pointing out the classroom library, and she tells students they may get books from the library after they have finished assignments. The students may use the bean bags and comfortable pillows while they are in the library, or they make take the books to their desks. She also shows the listening center next to the library. This center can accommodate only two children at a time, and she

shows how to operate the tape recorder. Four computers are next to the listening center. Ms. Gonzalez says they won't be using the computers until next week, but she does tell the students what kinds of activities they will learn to do with the computers. She also highlights materials in the science discovery center, gives procedures for this area, and tells the students that four children may work at this center.

Ms. Gonzalez also shows the students other interesting areas of the classroom. Next to the dry erase board is a large space entitled "Message Board" where she and the students can display messages to the class. She also points out the student bulletin board, which is divided into twenty-four large rectangles. The students can use their rectangles to highlight their interests and achievements. Last, she shows the students their mailboxes.

9:00–9:25
Drawing
self-portraits

Ms. Gonzalez shows the class her self-portrait, which she drew the previous day, and they discuss what self-portraits are. Ms. Gonzalez then distributes construction paper to the students and asks them to draw their own self-portraits. She also asks them to write two things about themselves on the back of the pictures.

As the children begin, Ms. Gonzalez circulates, offers assistance, and monitors their progress. When some children become concerned about their spelling, she tells them to try their best, listen to the sounds in the words, and write what they hear. A few children finish early, so Ms. Gonzalez tells them to select a book from the class library or go to the listening center.

9:25–9:30
Procedures

At 9:25, the timer rings. Ms. Gonzalez tells the children that she uses the timer to signal the end of an activity. When they hear the timer ring, they should look at her for further directions. Ms. Gonzalez sets the timer again, and the students practice this procedure. She tells the children that it is time to go to the playground, so they need to practice lining up to leave the classroom. She says she will dismiss them by tables, and they should push the chairs under their desks. She demonstrates pushing in chairs and asks a student to show how it can be done quietly. She then asks students to get in line quietly without crowding the person in front. She dismisses each table and compliments students for following directions.

9:30–10:00
Playground

While students are on the playground with another teacher, Ms. Gonzalez writes a message to the students and posts it on the message board.

10:00–10:30
Sharing

When the students return from the playground, several students notice the message. Ms. Gonzalez reads the message to the class and invites students to post notes on the board.

After all of the students are at their desks, Ms. Gonzalez sets the timer and reviews the procedures. When all of the students are looking at her, she asks them to bring their self-portraits and quietly form a circle on the floor. Everyone, including Ms. Gonzalez, shares the self-portraits and two interesting things about themselves.

10:30–11:00
Story and song

Ms. Gonzalez follows this activity by reading a story about self-esteem. She then teaches the students a song called "I Like Me." She has written the words and has drawn several picture cues on a large sheet of chart paper. They practice reading the words several times, then Ms. Gonzalez sings the song for her students. She repeats the song, and the students join in the singing.

As she dismisses the students from the circle, they give her their self-portraits. Ms. Gonzalez chooses this time to review lunch procedures. Students practice getting their lunchbags and quietly lining up for lunch. Before they leave, Ms. Gonzalez reviews the lunchroom rules.

11:00–11:30

Lunch

11:30–11:50

Recess

11:50–12:00

As the students reenter the room, Ms. Gonzalez goes over the bathroom procedures. She lets one or two students practice with the bathroom passes. She also lets them practice knocking to be sure no one is in the bathroom before they open the door. Students then leave their seats to use the bathroom and to wash their hands.

12:00–12:20
Read aloud

Ms. Gonzalez sits in a rocking chair, and the students gather around her on the rug. She reads a story aloud and explains that the twenty minutes after lunch and recess will always be set aside for read aloud time. The students will select the books that are read.

12:20–12:30
Discussing school rules

The class remains seated around the rocking chair, and Ms. Gonzalez explains the school rules. There are two: (1) Remain quiet in the hallways; and (2) Every student must have a hall pass. After they discuss the rules, Ms. Gonzalez asks two children to repeat them to the rest of the class and explain what they mean.

12:30–1:00
Developing classroom rules

The discussion of school rules leads directly into the development of the classroom rules. The students remain seated on the rug but shift their attention to the dry erase board. Ms. Gonzalez moves the over head projector next to the students and projects it on the board. She asks a student to turn off half of the classroom lights so the class can see the screen.

She tells the students they will need to raise their hands and wait to be called on during the discussion because everyone will need to hear all of the suggestions. She asks the students to suggest rules they feel are necessary for their classroom. The students raise their hands, Ms. Gonzalez calls on them and writes their responses on the overhead. At this point, she is careful not to make evaluative comments on the students' ideas. She wants them to brainstorm suggestions. The students discuss their ideas and often expand, connect, or modify them.

Ms. Gonzalez ends this activity when she notices the students' attention beginning to fade. She tells them this is a good start to their classroom rules, and they will continue with them tomorrow. At the end of this activity, the students return to their desks.

1:00–1:35 Graphing activity	Ms. Gonzalez focuses the students' attention on the dry erase board where she has hung a large graph. The graph is drawn on brightly colored butcher paper and is titled "How I got to school today." The graph is divided into four columns. A picture of a car, a bus, a bicycle, or a pair of shoes is at the bottom of each column. She asks the students how they got to school this morning. Did they come in a car? Did they ride the bus? Did they ride their bikes? Did they walk? As the students raise their hands, Ms. Gonzalez gives them a picture of a car, bus, bike, or shoes. The students write their names on their pictures, color them, and tape them in the appropriate columns on the graph. After all of the pictures are placed on the graph, Ms. Gonzalez asks them to count the number of pictures in each row and determine which row has the most and the least. She draws a bar graph that corresponds with the number of pictures in each row. She explains that the class will be learning a lot of new things this year. They will be doing science projects, math, writing, etc. She asks them to think about things they would like to know about.
1:35–2:15 "What do I want to study this year?"	Ms. Gonzalez hangs another large piece of butcher paper next to the pictures. In the middle of the paper is the question, "What do I want to study this year?" Again, she asks students to raise their hands and wait to be called on, because everyone should listen to the topics. Ms. Gonzalez creates a semantic map with all of the suggestions. She knows that many of the topics will be covered because they correspond with her curriculum guide. Other topics will be pursued through individual and small-group projects.
2:15–2:30 Getting ready to go home	Ms. Gonzalez reviews the day's activities by asking, "If your mom or dad asks you what you did today, what would you tell them?" She also asks questions about the procedures and school rules. She reminds the students to check their personal belongings and check their mailboxes for notes that need to go home. She asks them to leave their nametags on their desks, so they can use them tomorrow, and she shows them how to put their chairs on the desks so they won't fall. She checks to see if everyone has the things they need to take home.

She rehearses with them the proper procedure for being dismissed. They are to leave their desks table by table and line up by the door. She asks two students to demonstrate lining up. When the bell rings, she leads the students out the classroom door, down the hall to the proper outside door for dismissal.

Second Day Activities

Time/Activity	Description
8:00–8:20 Greeting students	The teacher greets the students at the door and asks them to put on their nametags and get their journal notebooks from their cubbies. On the board, she has written the journal topic "What I liked best about my first day of school." She tells the students they may either write or draw a picture. She takes attendance, fills in the lunch count, and assists the students as they write. The timer rings to signal the end of this activity, and the teacher asks everyone to close the journals. She lets them go by tables to put their journals in their cubbies and gather on the floor. She reminds them of the procedures for leaving their desks and gathering on the floor (quickly and quietly).
8:20–8:50 Introducing morning activities	Ms. Gonzalez shows the students the helper chart. Every student has a job, and the jobs rotate daily. She asks the pledge leader to come to the front of the room and lead the class. She helps the pledge leader point to the words as the students repeat the pledge. She then asks the calendar person to add today's date to the calendar and name the month, day, and year. The weather person tells today's forecast and uses the weather section from the newspaper to record today's expected high and low temperature. Ms. Gonzalez guides the weather person through the forecast. The song leader leads the students through the "I Like Me" song they learned the previous day. Again, Ms. Gonzalez helps the student point to the words while the class sings. Then, Ms. Gonzalez asks who wants to share what they wrote in their journal. Three students volunteer. While those students get their journals, Ms. Gonzalez tells the class that journal writing will usually be the first activity every morning. The students share, and Ms. Gonzalez tells each student one thing she liked about his or her writing.
8:50–9:25 Developing classroom rules	Ms. Gonzalez then asks the class to look at the dry erase board. She turns on the overhead projector and reviews the ideas they brainstormed yesterday for classroom rules. She asks the students if any of the rules are alike. As the students begin to group the similar ideas,

Ms. Gonzalez reminds them to raise their hands. She writes their ideas on another overhead transparency. After they develop six broad categories, she asks the students to think about a title for each category. When titles are proposed for each category, she asks the students if these would be appropriate classroom rules. After some minor rewordings, the children and Ms. Gonzalez are satisfied with the rules.

9:25–9:30
Procedures

The teacher dismisses the students to line up at the door. Several students use this time to get a drink of water or go to their cubbies. Ms. Gonzalez asks everyone to come back to the rug, and she asks a student to repeat the procedures for lining up. Ms. Gonzalez dismisses the students again and compliments them for remembering the procedure.

9:30–10:00
P.E.

While the students are in physical education, Ms. Gonzalez writes the classroom rules on a piece of chart paper.

10:00–10:30
Role playing
classroom rules

When the students reenter the room from PE, they go to their seats and the teacher points out the rules and asks each student to sign. She lets each table go to the chart paper in turn. She asks the students where the rules should be posted, and it is decided to hang them on the wall by the dry erase board.

Small groups of students volunteer to role play an example of each rule. The small groups practice for ten minutes and present their demonstration. The other members of the class guess what rule the group is presenting.

10:30–11:00
Math activity

The teacher asks the students to return to their seats and when they are seated, she asks for their attention. She is standing at the front of the room and holding geometric figures (circles, triangles, squares) made from different colored construction paper. Magnets are attached to the figures so they will stick on the board.

She tells the students they are going to play a guessing game. She is going to make a pattern on the board with these figures, and the students will have to determine which figure goes next in the pattern. After they complete several of these examples, Ms. Gonzalez tells the students they are going to continue this game with a partner.

Because this is the first time the students will be working cooperatively, she has them begin with partners as opposed to groups of three or four. As she passes out the materials, she asks them what classroom rules should apply to this activity. Several respond that they should listen to their partners and not interrupt them. Others say they should help each other. The teacher tells the students they can remain at their seats or move to a spot on the floor. She allows them one minute to move. As the students make patterns for their partners, she circulates throughout the room and offers assistance. She sets the timer to signal the end of the activity.

When the timer rings, the majority of the partners stop their patterning activity and turn to the teacher. A few continue to work, so she asks a student to repeat this procedure. Then she sets the timer again. When it rings, everyone turns to her. She asks the partners to put the geometric figures in a storage bag. When she dismisses the students, they give her their bags of figures and quietly line up for lunch.

11:00–11:30	Lunch
11:30–11:50	Recess
11:50–12:00	Bathroom break

12:00–12:20
Read aloud

Ms. Gonzalez sits in the rocking chair, and the students gather around her as she reads a story they have selected.

12:20–1:00
Writing sample

Ms. Gonzalez likes to collect a writing sample from each of her students early in the year. This sample is placed in the student's portfolio and will serve as a baseline for the student's writing progress. Because the class has been sharing about themselves, this writing sample will take the form of a book called, *All About Me*. Ms. Gonzalez has prepared a small book with lines at the bottom of the pages for writing and spaces for illustrations. She brainstorms ideas for the book with the students and reminds them to use invented spellings if necessary.

When the students return to their seats, Ms. Gonzalez monitors their progress and pays close attention to students who are frustrated. Several children are concerned about their writing, so she tells them to draw the pictures first and then write about the pictures. A few students finish before the timer rings, and they go to various centers in the room.

1:00–1:15
Sharing

When the timer rings, Ms. Gonzalez asks if anyone wants to share his or her book. She collects the books from the students who do not want to share, and everyone gathers on the rug. Four students share, and the class listens attentively. Students comment on the books and applaud the volunteers.

1:15–1:55
"Getting to
know you"

Ms. Gonzalez had asked each student to bring something to school today to share with classmates. She had suggested that they bring a favorite book, picture, or stuffed animal. As on the previous day, the class formed a circle and everyone, including the teacher, shared.

1:55–2:15
Sustained
silent reading

While they are still in the circle, Ms. Gonzalez explains the procedures for sustained silent reading. She says this will be the last activity every day. The students will select one or two books or magazines and find a quiet place to read. Once they choose a place, they will remain there until the timer rings. Ms. Gonzalez says she will also be reading during this time.

She dismisses the students two at a time from the circle. They put away their objects from sharing time, select books, and quietly choose a place to read. After they are reading, Ms. Gonzalez reminds a few students to be quiet. She also reads but keeps a close eye on the students.

Even though twenty minutes are set aside for today's sustained silent reading, Ms. Gonzalez knows that after the procedures are taught, the students will read for only seven or eight minutes. This amount of reading time will steadily increase throughout the school year.

| 2:15–2:30 Getting ready to go home | When the timer rings again, Ms. Gonzalez dismisses the students two at a time to return their books and collect their belongings to go home. After the students are ready to go, Ms. Gonzalez leads a brief review of today's activities and the classroom rules. |
| 2:30 Dismissal | Ms. Gonzalez reminds the students how to line up and calls the bus children to line up first. She compliments the students on another good day and leads them out of the room. |

CASE STUDY 4-2

BEGINNING THE YEAR IN A SIXTH GRADE MATH CLASS USING COOPERATIVE LEARNING

Ms. James teaches math in a departmentalized sixth grade. She repeats the same lesson with three groups of sixth graders each day. The following narrative describes the first day of class for the second group of students.

First Day Activities

Activity	Description
Before the bell	Desks are arranged in seven groups of four or five students each. The teacher collects a folder from the previous class for each group of desks and replaces it with another folder of a different color, marked with the period and group number. As students enter, Ms. James tells them they may sit wherever they choose today but that seats will be assigned later in the week.

Initial greeting (4 minutes)	The teacher smiles and states her name. She introduces herself, telling students about her family and some out-of-school interests. She tells students she is a hard worker, and she also expects them to work hard. She says she will be in her room starting an hour before school, and she will stay in her room until 4:30 each day, so students can come in for help if they need more explanation or assistance. "The most important thing in this class is trying. We will all make mistakes and get stuck, but by working together we will be able to solve the problems and learn a lot of new things."
Introduction (10 minutes)	Ms. James notes that students have all studied math for the past five years, but she is curious whether they know how important and useful it is. She leads a discussion in which she elicits student ideas about how math might be useful. She asks students to raise their hands and wait to be called on before speaking during this activity. During the discussion, she calls attention to a bulletin board that has several colorful posters highlighting math applications. During the discussion, Ms. James thanks students on several occasions for raising their hands and for listening well. When a couple of students call out, she reminds them to raise hands before she calls on them. Ms. James comments on the grouping of desks. She explains that in her classes, students work in groups much of the time and that this activity can be very helpful in learning. She says they won't always work in groups; they will also keep an individual notebook and take tests by themselves. For many assignments, however, they will be expected to work together and assist each other in understanding the content and solving problems. She comments that students often find this to be not only a good way to learn but an enjoyable one as well. A student asks if she can choose her group. Ms. James responds that she must reserve the right to arrange the groups. Because group membership will change at different times, however, students will have an opportunity to work with a variety of other students. Ms. James also emphasizes that working in groups with others is a good way to get to know other students. "It's important that you're able to work with anyone in school, just as you'll have to outside of school," she comments.
Initial presentation of procedures (6 minutes)	Ms. James thanks the students for raising hands before speaking. She says she has a few other procedures that will be needed for the class to run smoothly. She will go over some of these now and save the others for later, when they start group work. She says that during class, when she is talking or when a student is presenting something to the whole class, they are to remain in their seats. If they wish to comment or ask a question, they should raise a hand and wait for their turn. At other times, when they are working in groups or on individual assignments, they may talk if it is to someone in their group

and it is about the assignment. If they need to sharpen a pencil or get materials during work times, they may do so without permission, as long as they do not disturb other students.

Initial group task (8 minutes)	The teacher designates students in each group as Chair #1, Chair #2, Chair #3, etc. She tells them that when they work in different groups Chairs will have different roles, and that these will be rotated so that each student gets a chance to do different things. "Chair #1, please open the group folder on the desk and look in the right-hand pocket. Take out a yellow card and a class card for each student." She asks Chair #1 to distribute these items in each group. Ms. James then has students make name cards for their desks and fill out name cards for her. While students work on this task, she returns to her desk for a couple of minutes to attend to some administrative matters. She then asks Chair #1 to collect the cards.
Description of procedures (10 minutes)	She asks Chair #2 to look in the left-hand pocket and get out the blue sheet listing classroom policies and procedures and to give one to each group member. She tells students that everyone will need a three-ring binder for this class, and that this page should be the first one in it. She then reviews the classroom and school policies regarding absence and tardiness, leaving the room, make-up work, tests, and detention for violating rules. She explains that if she gives a warning to a student and it's ignored, then she will assign a lunch detention and the student will need to bring lunch to the room at noon and eat it there. She says, "If I have to come find you, it will be doubled."
End of period	Ms. James notes that time is almost up. She says that she'll explain her grading policies and class activities tomorrow. "Chair #3, if there is a new student in class assigned to your group tomorrow, would you please be responsible for helping him or her get a copy of the class policies, name card, and class card?" She asks the students to return their cards to the folder. She asks students to remain in their seats until she dismisses each group, which she does when materials have been returned to the folder and each group is seated and quiet.

Second Day Activities

Activity	Description
Before the bell	Ms. James collects folders from each group from the preceding period, replacing them with the next period's folders. She greets students as

they enter, asking them to take seats with the same group as yesterday. She directs a few new students to join groups.

Opening the period (3 minutes)	The teacher greets the students warmly as soon as the bell rings. She reminds them they are in groups and have a designated number that will be the same as yesterday's. She reminds Chairs #3 of their responsibility to help new members of the group.
Diagnostic test (15 minutes)	"Before we get started on today's lesson, I'd like you to answer some questions. This will not be for a grade, but I would like you to do your best. Your answers will help me understand what topics need review and also help me make group assignments." Ms. James distributes the diagnostic test and tells students to show their work. She monitors as students complete the test.
Description of procedures and grading policies (8 minutes)	The teacher reviews talk and movement procedures in groups. "Use group voices, please. Talk loudly enough to be heard by others but not so loudly that groups near you will hear. Like this . . . (she demonstrates)." She gives students a one-page handout describing grading policies. She explains these in detail and asks students to place this handout in their notebooks.
Preparation for group activity (4 minutes)	Ms. James announces a first activity. She tells students this is an activity to learn about working in groups as well as to learn math concepts. She asks students to volunteer ideas about what it takes to be a good group member. Stressing positive examples, Ms. James supports especially the ideas of sharing, helping, listening, encouraging, and working hard.
Math Lesson (20 minutes)	The teacher begins by reading an article from *USA Today,* which states that the average sixth grader in the United States watches 1000 minutes of television a week. She asks the students if they are surprised by this fact and then asks them to estimate about how many hours of television that would be each day. She stresses that they are estimating and that exact computations are inappropriate. Next, she asks students to share what they think the article means by "the average sixth grader." She then explains that the students will be calculating how many days of television the average sixth grader watches in one year. She asks Chair #4 at each table to open the folders and distribute the materials. She says she will ask someone in each group to report on the group's solution. After the groups have worked for about five or six minutes, Ms. James calls on one person from each group to report on their results; she prompts students as needed as they describe the solution process their group used.
Wrap-up (5 minutes)	Ms. James asks students to comment on their roles in their groups. She also asks for suggestions about what works best for different roles.

She praises the students for their creativity in developing different solution methods and for their effort. She dismisses the class as the next group begins to gather at her door.

Third Day Activities

Activity	Description
Organization (5 minutes)	Ms. James tells students to check the name list at each group of desks to find their group. She tells students they will stay in their groups for several weeks. She assigns Chair numbers to the group members.
Textbook check-out (12 minutes)	Ms. James asks Chair #4 from each group to get texts from several stacks at the back of the room. While students cover their books, the teacher circulates from group to group and records book numbers.
Content activity and a new teaching strategy (15 minutes)	The teacher reviews concepts from yesterday's lesson. She asks Chair #2 to distribute materials from a box in each group. Students use the materials to work along with the teacher as she demonstrates different ways problems can be solved. She tells students they will now work in pairs, and she writes "Pair Share" on the chalkboard. Students will work in pairs to solve a problem, and then they are expected to take turns explaining the solution or demonstrating the steps to each other. "It is not enough just to work out a solution. Each of you must be able to explain to your partner how you arrived at it." Afterward, Ms. James has volunteers come forward to demonstrate and explain their solutions.
Group work (17 minutes)	Students are now given problems to solve as a group. These are somewhat more difficult and require several steps. Ms. James asks each group to work together to develop a way to solve each problem. She asks Chair #4 to be recorder of the solutions and Chair #5 to be moderator to make certain that everyone contributes. The teacher reviews briefly, based on yesterday's discussion, what these roles entail. As the groups work on the problem, the teacher checks on progress. She has several groups report to the class. Afterward, students are given an assignment, due the next day, which they work on for the remainder of the class. Students may work together on problems, but they are expected to show their own work on the assignment.
Wrap up (5 minutes)	With about five minutes remaining in the period, the teacher asks students to put away their work. She says that unfinished problems should be completed as homework. Then she initiates a short discussion

about appropriate helping by asking students what it feels like not to understand something. She also asks about ways they might react if they were in that situation. "Everyone will experience those feelings and do some of those things, especially if they're made to feel unintelligent. In this class, though, we will learn from our mistakes, and no one should be embarrassed by not understanding something. Also, helping other students is a great way to gain in understanding. I certainly understand math much better after I have taught it than I did when I was a student." Ms. James explains that everyone will have opportunities to explain problems and answer questions in this class. But if there is something they don't understand, they need to ask for another explanation. She and the class then discuss how to explain in ways that are most helpful. The class is dismissed.

CHECKLIST 4

PREPARATION FOR THE BEGINNING OF SCHOOL

Check When Complete	Item	Notes
☐	1. Are your room and materials ready (see Chapter 1)?	_____
☐	2. Have you decided on your class procedures, rules, and associated consequences (see Chapters 2, 3, and 6)?	_____
☐	3. Are you familiar with the parts of the school that you and your students may use (cafeteria, office and office phone, halls, bathroom facilities, resource room, etc.) and any procedures for their use?	_____
☐	4. Do you have a complete class roster?	_____
☐	5. Do you have file information on your students, including information on reading and math achievement levels from previous teachers, test results, and any other information?	_____

PREPARATION FOR THE BEGINNING OF SCHOOL *Continued*

Check When Complete	Item	Notes
☐	6. Do you know if you have any students with disabilities who should be accommodated in your room arrangement or in your instruction?	_____
☐	7. Do you have adequate numbers of textbooks, desks, and class materials?	_____
☐	8. Do you have the teacher's editions of your textbooks?	_____
☐	9. Do you know the procedure for the arrival and departure of students on the first day? For every day after that?	_____
☐	10. Are the children's name tags ready? Do you have blank ones for unexpected children?	_____
☐	11. Do you have your first day's plan of activities ready?	_____
☐	12. Does your daily schedule accommodate special classes (e.g., physical education, music) or "pull-out" programs (e.g., Chapter 1 reading, resource room students, programs for the gifted)?	_____
☐	13. Do you have time-filler activities prepared?	_____
☐	14. Do you have a letter ready to send home to parents with information about needed school materials?	_____
☐	15. Do you know when and how you can obtain assistance from school staff members (e.g., the resource teacher, school nurse, librarian, office personnel, counselor)?	_____

C H A P T E R **5**

Planning and Conducting Instruction

Let's assume that the steps you have taken so far to ensure that your classroom will run smoothly have worked. Your classroom is organized, you've developed and taught your rules and procedures, and you have systems in place to manage student learning. Now that your students are attentive and ready to participate, what do you do? Remember, your purpose is not only to have a smoothly running classroom; your purpose is to help students learn. It is at this point that management and instruction meet. Well-planned lessons with a variety of developmentally appropriate activities support the positive learning environment that your careful management decisions have begun to create. Dry lessons with limited opportunities for student participation are boring and lose students; this is when management problems begin. Interesting, well-planned lessons are the key to holding students' attention.

This chapter describes how to plan and conduct instruction in ways that support the kinds of learning you want for your students regardless of content area. Combining this information with information from your content area courses will help you teach each subject more effectively. The chapter is divided into three sections. The first part discusses the planning decisions you must make before you step into the classroom. The second section discusses how to implement those plans as you conduct instruction. The final section discusses common problem areas such as transitions between activities and clarity of instruction.

FOR REFLECTION

Brainstorm a list of the types of activities you would like to orchestrate in your classroom and the content with which they will be used (e.g., pair discussions of student writing). As you continue reading this chapter, modify your list. ■

PLANNING INSTRUCTIONAL ACTIVITIES

When teachers choose instructional activities for their classes, they consider several things. Primarily, they think about whether an activity will lead to student learning and what kind of learning they want to encourage. Activities that lead to better memorization are different from those teachers will choose to enhance reflective thinking or problem solving. Next, teachers also must consider whether the activity will maintain student involvement. The sequence of activities in and the amounts of time spent on the various subjects in the curriculum must also be weighed. Such considerations lead many elementary teachers to plan reading and at least some language arts activities (or a combined literacy block) for the first two hours or so of the morning. These activities usually require sustained effort and often involve a combination of small-group, whole-group, and individual work formats. Student involvement in these activities would be more difficult to maintain later in the day when students are less alert and more fatigued.

It is wise to establish a daily schedule with specific times allocated to different subjects. Doing so will help you remain conscious of time so that you do not shortchange subjects taught later in the day. Furthermore, students will be better able to pace their own work if they know what schedule will be followed. When you plan your schedule, try to arrange change-of-pace activities to follow periods of sustained effort or intense concentration. For example, you might schedule recess, art, physical education, or music following the reading/language arts activities. If you cannot schedule such activities conveniently, at least give students a brief break and lead them in exercises, a song or two, or give them a little time to stand and stretch if they have not had the opportunity to move around.

When you begin to plan your daily schedule, you may find that your school district has established guidelines for the amounts of time to be allotted to different subjects. Also, special teachers may be assigned to teach a particular subject for certain days and times of the week. Thus, you may find that your class will be taught physical education on Tuesday and Thursday from 1:30 to 2:00 and will have music on Monday and Wednesday from 10:30 to 11:00. Obviously, your schedule will need to be set accordingly.

At the beginning of the school year, good planning requires extra effort. Overplanning—preparing more activities than can be accomplished in a particular time—and underplanning—preparing too little for the amount of time available— can occur, particularly with inexperienced teachers. It is better to overplan, then be flexible in implementing the plan. Activities not completed one day can serve as starters for second and third days.

Types of Planning

You will engage in several levels of planning, both long range (i.e., by the year and by the term) and short range (i.e., by the unit, the week, or the day). Each of these levels of planning should be coordinated. Accomplishing the longer plan requires dividing the work into terms, the terms into units, and the units into weeks and days.

The lesson outcomes you envision will determine your planning goals and objectives, and your plans should reflect these intended outcomes. Thus, your plans provide road maps that help transform the available curriculum into activities, assignments, and learning experiences for students. In developing your plans you should keep two important considerations in mind: first, what skills and concepts students must learn; and second, through which activities they can best learn them. The next section describes some possible instructional activities.

Types of Instructional Activities

For each subject you teach, you will choose a series of activities to help students acquire skills or new learning, practice the skills, consolidate and extend their knowledge, and receive feedback about their learning. In this section, the major types of instructional activities used to reach these goals are described. Several concepts are discussed that are essential for the management of activities: sequencing, clarity, and activity flow.

CONTENT DEVELOPMENT

Although teachers sometimes present content to students individually or in small groups, whole-class presentation is often the major vehicle for introducing and teaching content activities. In our discussion, we will assume that content development activity is taking place in a whole-class format. During content development, the teacher presents new information, elaborates on or extends a concept or principle, conducts a demonstration, shows how to perform a skill, or describes how to solve a problem. Whole-group content development activities are appropriate for learning goals such as exposure and familiarity and for the efficient presentation of new material.

During content development, the teacher takes an active role focused on making students think about the new content, relate it to what they know, and apply it. One chief management concern is making sure that students are active, not passive. Student involvement in the development of the lesson should be encouraged. Teacher questions are also used for this purpose, allowing the teacher to check student understanding, to encourage students to contribute to steps in problem solving, to apply concepts or principles, or to analyze ideas being presented.

In addition to teacher presentations and questions, content development should include student activities such as sample problems or other demonstrations of understanding of the new content. These short activities not only help students learn the new content but also provide the teacher with information about how well the class is understanding the lesson. Activities and teacher questions should be thoughtfully designed to expose students' thinking and understanding. For example, when a student gives a correct answer, the teacher can probe with further questions: "What led you to that answer?" "What do you mean by . . . ?" "What would come next?" "How else could you do that?"

Another way to develop content is for students to engage in research and problem solving, individually and in groups. Review Case Study 2–2 and see further information in the chapter about considerations when planning group work.

STUDENT WORK IN GROUPS

This activity should not be confused with small-group instruction, which is described next. During student work in groups, two or more students work together on a task that requires their cooperation. This activity might be used for discussion of problem solving, preparing for a group report, building a display or other art project, reviewing for a test, working on a science or social studies activity, or practicing new vocabulary or spelling words. Small groups work best when goals are clear and the steps to achieving them are understood by the students.

When assigning and managing group work, do not assume that your students possess the necessary skills for working together effectively. Instead, plan to teach them how to listen to others, take turns, summarize, reach consensus, etc. Such skills should be explained or demonstrated before beginning group activities and reviewed when necessary.

If you plan to use groups extensively, as is the case with cooperative learning methods, pay extra attention to issues of management. The following suggestions are derived from several sources on group learning (Kagan, 1992; Slavin, 1995; Bennett & Dunne, 1991) as well as from our own observations of classes making frequent uses of these approaches.

Promoting group cohesiveness. Working together to achieve a common goal, product, or outcome usually improves group unity and positive interpersonal relationships. Occasionally, however, students have difficulty cooperating or just don't get along with other students. To encourage cooperative behavior, teachers often stress the value of learning to work with many different types of individuals, not just one's best friends. Also note how teamwork, such as team sports, band and other musical groups, drama, medicine, manufacturing, or science, is important in areas both in and out of school. Another feature that can promote cohesiveness is receiving recognition or a reward for the group's accomplishments. If intragroup relations are a problem that can't be resolved, change group membership as needed.

Monitoring noise levels. Students must talk if they are to work in groups, but the volume of that talk can become a problem. Expectations for talk during group work should be discussed ahead of time so students can understand why monitoring the noise level is important. Teachers often provide guidelines such as, "Talk only loud enough to be heard within your group; other groups shouldn't be able to hear your conversations," or "Use twelve-inch voices in groups." If you are planning to involve young children in group work, it is helpful to practice with them how to lower their voices.

Another useful guideline is to have specific procedures for when students may and may not talk between groups. One procedure might be to raise hands to obtain permission to talk with another group. It is also important to have a procedure for obtaining silence if noise levels are too high. Common ones include turning out the lights, moving to the overhead projector or to another specified area of the room, or using a hand signal accompanied by the direction "eyes to the front."

Ensuring participation. Student engagement in group activities is usually as good or better than in most other classroom activities. If, however, a group is frequently off-task, discussing the situation with them, correcting any condition that might be affecting their focus, and obtaining a commitment to change their behavior can be first steps toward improvement. Also, reexamine the task the students are given and make sure it is appropriate to their age and ability levels. It is a good idea to define for students what you mean by good participation. This definition can include sharing information and explanations with other group members, being a good listener, and respecting other students' ideas and feelings.

A good way to ensure participation is to assign roles to group members. For example, each student in a group can be assigned a number (e.g., 1, 2, 3, 4). The teacher then assigns roles by number. For example, #1 can be asked to be responsible for reviewing the group's assignment and explaining what must be done; #2 could be asked to obtain and organize materials; #3's task could be to lead the group discussion and see that each group member has a chance to participate; #4 can be responsible for recording the group's progress or results. Other roles, such as pacer, turn-maker, encourager, summarizer, or reporter can be incorporated. Case Study 4–2 describes one teacher's way of orchestrating group work using these guidelines. In addition to final reports, at an appropriate time during the activity, the teacher can call for progress reports from one or more groups by asking all #1's (for example) to summarize their work. In sharing expectations for appropriate group behavior, desirable attributes of group members should be emphasized, so students know what is expected.

SMALL-GROUP INSTRUCTION

In this activity, the teacher works with small groups of students, one group at a time, while the rest of the class works independently. This mode of instruction is most commonly used for reading and frequently used for mathematics. Its purpose, of course, is to accommodate a wide range of achievement levels in basic skill subjects. Because small-group instruction is used so extensively for basic skills, we will describe its features in detail.

A critical aspect of small-group instruction is that at least two different activities occur simultaneously. A teacher leads a group while students outside the group participate in a variety of independent activities. Because the teacher is actively involved with the small group, it is more difficult for him or her to monitor the behavior of other students and give them assistance. And because students may work independently for a long period, very careful planning and extra effort are required to keep them involved in their work.

The first step in setting up effective small-group instruction is to set the stage for the out-of-group activities. Give directions to the whole class at once, including the following: instructions for each assignment; a description of materials that will be needed; and, to help students pace their work, a suggested time for completing each activity. This list of assignments should also be posted or written on the chalkboard. Check whether students understand the directions by asking students in each group to review them before beginning.

Before calling the first group, monitor the beginning of independent work for a short time. After you are certain that students have started, signal the first group. During your work with the small group, monitor out-of-group students by scanning the room frequently. If you observe inappropriate behavior that is interfering with work, try to stop it with eye contact or some nonverbal signal, by calling the student's name once, or by reminding the student of what he or she should be doing. A "time-out" desk near you can also be used for a student who persists in misbehavior: You can signal such a student to go to the desk for a while, without your having to leave the group.

Another issue to consider is how students needing help on an independent task can obtain it without interrupting the teacher. Some teachers tell students to skip work they cannot do and go on to another activity until the teacher is available to assist them. Others allow students to help each other, or they assign a few students (perhaps one for each table or group) the role of helper. This works best if students are seated in mixed-ability groups. Finally, students can sign up on the chalkboard or on a clipboard sheet to indicate the need for assistance when you are available. If you must leave the small group to help a student or to deal with a problem, be sure to give students in the group something to do. One student in the group may be able to lead the activity for a short time.

When work with one small group has been completed, the next group should not be called immediately. Instead, take the opportunity to check the progress of the students who will be continuing individual assignments and help them with any problems they have encountered. Briefly inspect all students' work and whether

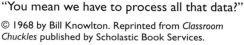

"You mean we have to process all that data?"

© 1968 by Bill Knowlton. Reprinted from *Classroom Chuckles* published by Scholastic Book Services.

they have requested assistance. Students who were off-task while you were teaching the small group can be given delayed feedback at this time. Be sure to encourage and give positive feedback to students who are participating appropriately. The students who have left the small group and are moving to other activities should also be monitored to be sure they begin their activity promptly. Then signal the next group to come for instruction.

DISCUSSION

Discussion is used to encourage students to evaluate events, topics, or results; to clarify the basis for their opinions; to help them become aware of other points of view; or to help them improve their oral expression skills. Sometimes, discussions are begun with a recitation activity, described next, in which the facts of the content to be discussed are reviewed. Compared to a recitation, however, discussion questions are more likely to elicit the students' judgments, impressions, ideas, and opinions; also, teachers are less likely to evaluate the student responses directly. Instead, students are encouraged to express themselves, to examine their opinions and beliefs, and to understand other perspectives. Students may respond to each other rather than only to the teacher. The teacher's role becomes one of encouraging, clarifying, and using student ideas rather than evaluating their correctness.

Management of a discussion calls for a number of skills, including warmth or friendliness (to promote security), conflict resolution, and encouraging expression of divergent points of view (to foster acceptance and openness). Although it is more common for some students than others to contribute to a discussion, the teacher should not allow a few students to monopolize the discourse; thus, less oral students need to be included skillfully. Inviting reticent members to speak from time to time by asking for their opinions or views of what has previously been discussed is a good way to do so. Giving students opportunities to paraphrase, clarify, and elaborate on their own or other students' remarks is useful to keep a discussion moving and on target, perhaps allowing the teacher to transfer some of the responsibility for maintaining the discussion to students. Getting students to listen to each other rather than treating the discussion as a dialogue with the teacher is sometimes difficult. Therefore, it is important to emphasize that students need to respond to each other and not only to the teacher's comments or questions.

If you choose to use a whole-group discussion format, you will need to plan questions. This can keep the discussion focused and productive. However, many teachers encourage students to formulate their own discussion questions, especially if these follow from group or individual research projects. Whether discussions are student-led or teacher-led, it is important that ground rules for participation are clear (for example, raise hands, listen carefully, respect others' rights to speak).

RECITATION

This activity is a question-and-answer sequence in which the teacher asks questions, usually of a factual nature, and accepts, guides, or corrects student responses. The sequence of question/answer/evaluation is repeated frequently, with many students being asked to respond until a body of content has been covered. In effect, a recitation is a form of checking that is done orally. It can be used as a skill drill or to review student understanding of a previous lesson or assigned reading. It can also be used to check spelling, knowledge of vocabulary words, or other factual recall.

When recitation is used to check student understanding, it is important to distribute questions to all students, not just to those who are eager to answer. Calling on only those who volunteer can give you an inaccurate impression of the class's understanding. Develop a way to check systematically who gets a turn to answer. This can be done by using a checklist or a shuffled stack of name cards. It is helpful to ask the question, allow time for students to think, and then call on individual students. Limit the time you call on only those students who volunteer. Sometimes, teachers use choral or whole-group responses as a way of keeping everyone alert and active. These kinds of responses are usually helpful only at the beginning of concept development as new material is being introduced and practiced. Sometimes teachers do not allow students enough time to respond, thus reducing opportunities for students who are slow to answer. Some experts recommend a "wait time" of several seconds—e.g., three seconds—before giving a prompt or calling on another student.

INDIVIDUAL WORK

In this activity, students engage in assignments that build on presented material. In the upper elementary grades, that portion of the assignment not completed in class often becomes a homework assignment unless the materials or resources needed to finish it are available only in the classroom. (Procedures for independent work have been discussed in Chapter 2.)

Good management of individual activities has several components. First, adequate content development must precede the independent student activity so that students can work productively on their own. Second, the teacher needs to communicate clearly the requirements and objectives of the students' work and arrange for student access to needed materials or resources. A good strategy to adopt is to begin the independent work assignment as a whole-class activity (for example, by working several of the exercises, problems, or questions together) before the independent work phase. This gets students started, gives them an opportunity to ask questions, and enables the teacher to observe and correct common problems in a whole-class format rather than having to deal with the same problem with multiple individuals. Third, the teacher should actively monitor the students' work so that problems are detected early and corrective feedback is provided.

Independent activities are best used for consolidating or extending prior learning rather than for acquiring new content. Therefore, we urge that you not overuse independent activities; a rule of thumb is to devote at least as much time to content development as to independent work. Moreover, student engagement is more difficult to maintain in lengthy individual work activities. If you do find yourself assigning long periods of time to individual assignments, try breaking the activity into smaller segments and having a discussion or review between segments. The change in lesson format will help refocus student attention, and it will give you an opportunity to check student comprehension and clear up problems before students continue.

CHECKING

In this activity, students check their own seatwork or homework. The activity is appropriate only when the judgment of correctness can easily be made. Checking provides quick feedback to students, and it allows the teacher to identify and discuss common errors on assignments. Careful monitoring during checking is important to be sure that students are doing it correctly. Students must be taught to check papers accurately, so it is important for you to explain the procedures as well as model them and allow students opportunities to practice. When student checking is used, you should collect the students' papers and examine them, even when you record grades in class, to keep abreast of student progress and problems.

Arranging Activities within a Lesson

In any given subject, lessons usually consist of a series of activities. A common activity sequence in basic skill areas is:

1. Checking or recitation

2. Content development

3. Classwork

4. Independent work, group work, or discussion

The first activity allows the previous day's assignment or homework to be corrected. If there was no homework, the teacher leads a review of prior content important for the day's lesson. During content development, new content or skills are taught.

Following this, a short classwork activity is used to review the new content and to preview the new assignment. Then, practice is provided through independent work, group work, or discussion.

The problem with this sequence is that it requires that the presentation of lesson content and the practice period each be handled in two, usually lengthy, segments. A variation of the sequence that accommodates more complex content and that does not demand as much sustained student attention is:

1. Checking or recitation

2. Content development

3. Classwork or independent work, usually brief, with checking

4. Content development

5. Classwork, usually brief

6. Independent work, group work, or discussion

This sequence allows the teacher to divide the lesson content into two parts, with practice and feedback following the first content development activity. Teaching new content in two parts with an intervening practice period will help students consolidate learning from the first part before they are asked to contend with the new learning required in the second part. The sequence also allows the teacher to check student understanding and to provide prompt feedback before moving on to more complex content. Furthermore, when individual activities are divided into shorter segments, student attention is usually easier to maintain. A problem with the sequence is that it produces more transition points and thus greater potential for student disengagement. Usually, these transitions can be managed without difficulty, however, because student movement, new materials, or drastically changed lesson focus will not be required in the content development–classwork–independent work cycle. Thus, the various activities will blend together, usually without conspicuous transitions.

Of course, not all lessons will fit either of the activity patterns described above. For instance, a science or social studies lesson may consist of a relatively long period of active student exploration or problem solving in small groups followed by a whole-class content development discussion. Ongoing projects may entail long segments of individual seatwork or small-group work interspersed with short segments of whole-class or small-group instruction. Nevertheless, the two common patterns described above provide useful frameworks for building most teacher-directed lessons.

Planning for Clear Instruction

Once you have an idea of the range and sequence of activities available to you, examine the content, concepts, and goals of the lessons and units that you will be teaching. One way to start is to review the unit and lesson in the teacher's edition of your textbook(s). Pay careful attention to suggestions for lesson development and activities. Study the exercises, questions, problems, and other activities in the textbook and decide which items would provide appropriate review of lesson objectives. Note examples, demonstrations, and key questions and activities to use in the development of the main concepts. Try to anticipate problems students may encounter in the lesson or assignments. Check for new terms and be ready to define them and present examples. Do some of the classwork or homework assignment yourself to uncover hurdles students will face. You can then build helpful hints into your lesson or give extra emphasis to these difficult areas. If some items in the assignment go beyond the lesson scope, do not assign them as classwork or homework until you can teach the necessary content. If the content is not essential and you do not plan to teach it later, assign such items only as enrichment or extra-credit activities.

Consider the interest the lesson is likely to have for students. Will you be enthusiastic about teaching this material to your class in this way? Your enthusiasm about the lesson is contagious and signals to students how you feel about its importance. If you find it interesting and exciting and you communicate this excitement to your class, students will probably respond with interest. However, if you find yourself unenthusiastic about a lesson or topic, chances are your students will share your feelings. Consider approaching the lesson in a different way. For example, rather than giving a lecture presentation of material, perhaps you can find ways for students to contribute through large-group or small-group discussions that address the same issues.

Finally, organize your lesson parts into a coherent sequence. If the lesson is complex, write down or outline the main components. Then, you will be well prepared for a clear lesson presentation.

PRESENTING NEW CONTENT

If students understand where a lesson is going, they are more likely to be there with you at the end. Tell students what the lesson objectives are, either at the

Reprinted by permission: Tribune Media Services.

beginning of the activity or during it. If the lesson is at all complex, give students an outline to help them follow its organization. An outline helps organize the content for the students and provides a road map to keep them on course.

If students are to understand content from silent reading or from viewing a film or filmstrip, provide a content outline with a few items filled in and spaces for students to supply the rest. This task focuses attention and provides motivation for careful reading or watching. Go over these items with the class after the film, especially if the students use the outline for further work or study. Alternatively, use the video as an opportunity to teach note-taking skills. Guide students in determining the questions they need answered by the film and then help them identify important information as the film progresses.

As you present a lesson, stay with the planned sequence unless an obvious change is needed. Avoid needless digressions, interruptions, or tangential information. Inserting irrelevant information into a lesson only confuses students about what they are expected to learn. Displaying key concepts, new terms, major points, and other critical information on the overhead transparency screen or the chalkboard will underscore their importance.

Presentations should be as focused and concrete as possible. Use examples, illustrations, demonstrations, physical props, charts, and any other means of providing substance and dimension to abstractions in the lesson. Avoid the vague expressions and verbal time fillers that, at best, communicate little information and make presentations difficult to follow. Allow students time and opportunity to process the information you're presenting.

CHECKING FOR UNDERSTANDING

Find out whether students understand a presentation during the lesson; do not wait until the next day. As content development activities unfold, ask students questions to verify their comprehension of main points. You can also ask students to provide a written response to key questions and then check some or all of the students' answers either orally or by examining the written work. Asking students to demonstrate comprehension at several points during a presentation not only allows you to verify their progress but also keeps students more involved in the lesson.

You can also check student understanding and emphasize main points by conducting an oral recitation after a presentation. Do this by asking a series of questions that recapitulate the lesson sequence and its major concepts. Be sure to involve many students in answering these questions so that you can identify the overall level of understanding in the class and reteach what has not been satisfactorily learned.

Other methods of checking for understanding include having students respond to your questions by the following:

◆ Displaying the correct one of two or more possible answers by holding up prepared color-coded cards.

- Using designated body movement (i.e., thumbs up or thumbs down, arms crossed or arms uncrossed).

- Folding a piece of notebook paper into fourths, using each of the eight sections to write responses, and holding them up for you to see.

- Writing in their own words explanations of the concept studied and turning these in for your inspection.

- Pairing with a designated neighbor and quietly explaining a concept or process to the other while you circulate and listen.

- Writing a question about the concept studied to ask a partner (any that cannot be answered are turned in for whole-class explanation).

- Keeping a journal or a learning log that includes entries on each lesson in a particular unit.

KOUNIN'S CONCEPTS FOR MANAGING WHOLE-GROUP INSTRUCTION

A central theme in managing teacher-led activities well is the idea of activity flow; this means the degree to which a lesson proceeds smoothly without digressions, diversions, or interruptions. Lessons with good flow keep student attention and are less likely to offer opportunities for deviation because most of the cues for student behavior during the lesson will be directed toward behaviors appropriate for the lesson. When lesson flow is jerky, with frequent interruptions and side trips, there is more competition for student attention from cues external to the focus of the lesson. Therefore, there will be a greater tendency for students to go off-task.

A series of classroom research studies by Kounin and his colleagues (Kounin, 1970; Kounin & Gump, 1974) identified several concepts that contribute to effective management of interactive group activities, leading to smooth activity flow.

According to Kounin, activity flow is maintained through three types of teacher behaviors: preventing misbehavior, managing movement, and maintaining group focus. Within each class of behavior there are two or three related concepts. Let us look at how each is defined and consider some examples. These concepts are summarized in Table 5–1.

Preventing Misbehavior

Classrooms are complex settings. Many events can occur at the same time. One cannot always predict with certainty what will occur when. New teachers run the risk of focusing too closely on single events or on select areas of the classroom and

TABLE 5-1   How Effective Managers Maintain Activity Flow (Kounin, 1970)

Issue	Skills	Definition	Example
Preventing misbehavior	✓ Withitness	Communicating general awareness of the classroom to students; identifying and correcting misbehavior promptly and correctly	The teacher makes eye contact with a student who is about to "shoot a basket" with a wad of paper. The student puts the paper away. A student behind him, who has seen the interaction, decides he's not likely to get away with shooting a basket either.
	✓ Overlapping	Attending to two or more simultaneous events	The teacher is leading a class discussion when a student comes in late. The teacher nods to him, continuing the discussion. Later, when students have begun a seatwork assignment, she checks in with him and signs his tardy slip.
Managing movement	Momentum	Keeping lessons moving briskly; planning carefully to avoid slowdowns	The teacher notices that explanation of a relatively minor concept is taking too long and distracting attention from the primary focus of the lesson. The teacher makes a mental note to go more in-depth on this concept in a separate lesson the next day, and moves on.
	Smoothness	Staying on-track with the lesson; avoiding digressions and divergences that can lead to confusion	While being responsive to student interests, the teacher avoids comments that tend to draw attention away from the key points of the lesson.

TABLE 5-1 *Continued*

Issue	Skills	Definition	Example
Maintaining group focus	Group alerting	Engaging the attention of the whole class while individuals are responding	Each student has a number that was drawn from a hat on the way into class. The teacher draws numbers and uses them to call on students during a fast-paced review.
	Encouraging accountability	Communicating to students that their participation will be observed and evaluated	At the end of the discussion and practice of a new skill, students are told to turn to a neighbor and explain the process to him or her.
	High participation formats	Using lessons that define behavior of students when they are not directly answering a teacher's question	While some students work problems at the board, students at their desks are instructed to check them by working the problems on paper.

missing the big picture. Understanding of two of Kounin's (1970) concepts, *withitness* and *overlapping*, helps to prevent this mistake.

Withitness is the degree to which the teacher corrects misbehavior before it intensifies or spreads to more students and also targets the correct student when doing so. A teacher who is not "with it" either will fail to stop the problem until it has escalated and may require a major intervention or else will fail to catch the perpetrator and instead target the wrong student. It is apparent that underlying aspects of withitness include good monitoring and prompt handling of inappropriate behavior, concepts that will be discussed in detail in Chapter 6.

Overlapping refers to how the teacher handles two or more simultaneous events: For example, a visitor comes to the door in the middle of a lesson; a child from out of the group comes up to the teacher during reading group time; several students get into a squabble while the teacher is busy helping other children across the room. A teacher who has good overlapping skills will handle both events in some way instead of dropping one event to handle the other or else ignoring the second event. To handle an interruption, for example, a teacher might tell the class or group to continue working, or to get out some work, and then deal with the interrupter. The squabble taking place away from the teacher might be handled by eye contact or a brief verbal desist while the teacher stays where he or she is.

Calvin and Hobbes   by Bill Watterson

Notice that a teacher who is with it and exhibits good overlapping skills is able to insulate lessons from the intrusions that student misbehavior or external interruptions might cause. Furthermore, by reacting promptly to problems (but not overreacting), the teacher will often be able to use simple measures (eye contact, redirection, a quiet desist) that will not interfere with ongoing activities or distract students very much. If a teacher is not with it or does not overlap when needed, lessons may be interrupted by student misbehavior and by the teacher's subsequently more visible and tardy reactions.

Managing Movement

Whereas withitness and overlapping are accomplished by handling external interruptions and student intrusions into the flow of the lesson, movement management is accomplished by avoiding teacher-caused intrusions or delays. Good movement management is achieved through momentum and smoothness.

Momentum refers to pacing and is indicated by lessons that move along briskly. Teachers can cause slowdowns in momentum by dwelling on individual parts of a lesson, direction, or skill and by unnecessarily breaking an activity into too many parts. For example, teachers should provide a standard heading for assignments that can be used routinely rather than altering its form and having to explain it over and over.

Smoothness, as opposed to jerkiness, is epitomized in lesson continuity. A smoothly flowing lesson keeps student attention, whereas one that jumps from hither to yon distracts. Kounin used graphic labels to depict ways a teacher might diverge from a smooth lesson. He described these divergences as "flip-flops," "dangles," "thrusts," and "stimulus-boundedness." These problems are compared in Table 5–2.

Maintaining Group Focus

Classroom instruction involves teaching children in groups, often a whole class at a time. Doing so means that a teacher needs to be conscious of the group influence

TABLE 5-2   **Common Problems in Maintaining Momentum and Smoothness (Kounin, 1970)**

Problem	Definition	Example
Dangle	Teacher leaves a topic or activity "dangling" to do something else or to insert some new material.	"All right, please take out your math books. Turn to page. . . . Oops, I forgot to send this form to the office. Raise your hand if you ride the bus. All right, where were we?"
Flip-Flop	Like a dangle, except that the topic inserted is left over from an earlier activity.	"OK, let's leave vocabulary now. We'll pick up the discussion tomorrow. Please move your chairs into your writing groups. Take your pencils and a blank piece of paper, and that's all." (Students move into their groups, and the teacher begins to give instructions for today's writing activity.) "All right now, does everyone understand what I want you to do? Oh, and did everyone remember to write down your vocabulary workbook assignment? I put it on the board, pages 235–242. OK, go ahead and start."
Thrust	Teacher inserts some information at a point where students are involved in another activity, and it seems irrelevant to them.	Students are working quietly on a standardized test. The teacher has been circulating and offering help; otherwise, there is scarcely a sound in the room. The teacher looks up and comments quietly, "When you're done, bring your test booklets to the front table and put your answer sheets in this box." Students continue to work quietly. When they begin completing their tests, the teacher must explain to each one individually where to put the test booklet and answer sheet.
Stimulus-bound	Teacher is distracted by some outside stimulus and draws the class's attention to it and away from the lesson.	Students are taking turns reading their writing aloud. Each student's reading is followed by comments from the rest of the class. During one such discussion, the teacher notices a student reading a paperback. "What are you reading, Alice?" she asks. "Have you read anything else by that writer?"

on the instruction. Like a conductor leading an orchestra, the teacher must elicit the performance of the individuals and still provide signals and direction to the whole class. Group focus can be maintained through several techniques.

Group alerting means taking action to engage the attention of the whole class while individuals are responding. It can take the form of creating suspense, telling students they might be called on next, calling on students randomly, asking students not reciting to listen carefully because they might be called on to add to the answer, or by using some new visual aid, display, or attention-getting strategy. In contrast, poor group alerting would be engaging in a dialogue with one student or calling on students before asking questions.

Accountability occurs when the teacher lets students know that their performance will be observed and evaluated in some manner. It does not require a letter grade or a score (although it might), just communicating some degree of awareness of how students are performing. For example, the teacher might ask everyone who knows an answer to raise a hand and then call on one or more of those students; or the teacher could have all students write answers and circulate to check them. The teacher might also have students keep notebooks and check them from time to time.

High participation formats are lessons that program the behavior of students when they are not directly involved in answering a teacher question. Such lessons have a higher built-in rate of participation than do lessons that merely assume that students will sit and watch when other students respond. Higher participation formats occur when students are expected to write answers, solve problems, read along, manipulate materials, or perform some other concurrent task.

Some activities lend themselves more to one type of group focus than another. When planning instruction, it will be helpful to consider which of the three aspects to use. For example, during a demonstration that involves expensive materials, it might be difficult to use a high participation format, but group alerting might be easy to incorporate.

Kounin's concepts for managing group instruction not only help identify key aspects of effective teaching, but they can also be used to diagnose instructional problems and identify possible solutions. For example, if lessons seem to drag, and student response is unenthusiastic, there may be a problem with group focus; a solution may be to work on alerting or accountability or to increase the degree of participation. Activities that take too long and that seem to get off-track constantly might have a problem with movement management. Perhaps the teacher should check for slowdowns and jerkiness.

TROUBLESHOOTING COMMON PROBLEMS IN CONDUCTING INSTRUCTION

Two areas give many teachers difficulty in conducting instruction: transitions and clarity. This section focuses on common problems in these areas and suggests possible solutions.

Transitions

The interval between any two activities is a transition. Several management problems can occur during transitions, including long delays before starting the next activity and high levels of inappropriate or disruptive behavior. Transition problems can be caused by a lack of readiness by the teacher or the students for the next activity, unclear student expectations about appropriate behavior during transitions, and faulty procedures for transitions. Following are examples of transition problems along with suggested ways of correcting them.

Transition Problem

Students talk loudly at the beginning of the day. The teacher is interrupted while checking attendance, and the start of content activities is delayed.

Students talk too much during transitions, especially after a seatwork assignment has been given but before they have begun working on it. Many students do not start their seatwork activity for several minutes.

Students who go for supplemental instruction stop work early and leave the room noisily while the rest of the class is working. When these students return to the room, they disturb others as they come in and take their seats. They interrupt others by asking for directions and assignments.

During the last afternoon activity, students quit working well before the end; they begin playing around and leave the room in a mess.

Suggested Solution

Establish a beginning-of-day routine and clearly state your expectations for student behavior at the beginning of the day.

Be sure students know what the assignment is. Post it where they can easily see it. Work as a whole class on the first several seatwork exercises so that all students begin the lesson successfully and at the same time. Watch what students do during the transition and urge them along when needed.

Have a designated signal that tells these students when they are to get ready to leave, such as a special time on the clock. Have them practice leaving and returning to the room quietly. Reward appropriate behavior. Leave special instructions, in a folder, on the chalkboard, or on a special sheet at their desks, for what they are to do when they return. Or for younger students, establish a special place and activity (e.g., the reading rug) for returning students to wait until you can give them personal attention.

Establish an end-of-day routine so that students continue their work until the teacher gives a signal to begin preparations to leave; then instruct students to help straighten the room.

Transition Problem	*Suggested Solution*
Whenever the teacher attempts to move the students from one activity into another, a number of students don't make the transition but continue working on the preceding activity. This delays the start of the next activity or results in confusion.	Give students a few minutes' notice before an activity is scheduled to end. At the end of the activity, students should put all the materials from it away and get out any needed materials for the next activity. Monitor the transition to make sure that all students complete it; do not start the next activity until students are ready.
As the teacher gives directions during a transition, many students continue to work and do not pay attention, put their materials away, or get out new materials.	Don't try to give instructions during a transition except to individual students. Instead, give the whole class instructions before the transition begins. Don't begin explaining the new activity or presenting content until everyone is ready and listening.
A few students always seem to be slowpokes during transitions, delaying the rest of the class.	Don't hold up the rest of the class for one or two students. Go ahead and start but be sure to monitor the dawdlers in later transitions to find out why they are having trouble. Then give them individual feedback and close supervision.
The teacher delays the beginning of activities to look for materials, finish attendance reporting, pass back or collect papers, or chat with individual students while the rest of the class waits.	Have materials organized ahead of time and once transitions begin, avoid doing anything that interferes with your ability to monitor and direct students.

The preceding items summarize the major problems that occur in classrooms at and around transition times. If you feel that your class is wasting time or if you are having difficulty keeping control during transitions, a look at the suggested solutions may prove helpful.

Clarity

Communicating information and directions in a clear, comprehensible manner is an important teaching skill. Clear instruction helps students learn faster and more successfully; it also helps students understand your directions and expectations for behavior more readily. Although clarity is important in all classroom activities, it is crucial during content development when nearly all new subject matter is introduced and taught. This section will focus on ways to improve clarity during this critical portion of your lessons.

Clear instruction results from several factors: the organization of information into a coherent sequence, use of an adequate number of illustrations or examples, precision and concreteness of expression, keeping in touch with student comprehension, and providing enough practice to ensure mastery. The following chart illustrates some of the many ways teachers can be both clear and unclear in their instruction.

Poor Clarity	*Being Clear*
Communicating Lesson Objectives	
Not describing the lesson's purpose or what students are expected to learn	Stating goals or major objectives Telling students what they will be accountable for knowing or doing
Pointing Out Important Information	
Not calling students' attention to main points, ideas, or concepts	Emphasizing major ideas Reviewing key points or objectives at the end of the lesson
Presenting Information Systematically	
Presenting information out of sequence, skipping important points, or backtracking	Outlining the lesson sequence and sticking to it
Inserting extraneous information, comments, or trivia into the lesson	Sticking to the topic, holding back on complexities until the main idea is developed
Moving from one topic to another without warning	Summarizing previous points, clearly delineating major transitions between ideas or topics
Presenting too much complex information at once or giving directions too quickly	Breaking complex content into manageable portions, giving step-by-step directions, and checking for understanding before proceeding
Giving group instructions orally without written backup	Providing instructions on chart paper or a handout; going over these and checking for understanding
Being Specific	
Presenting concepts without concrete examples	Providing a variety of illustrations
Using overly complex vocabulary	Using words students understand; defining new vocabulary terms
Overusing negative phrases (e.g., not all insects, not many people, not very happy)	Being specific and direct (e.g., the beetles, one-third of the people, discouraged)

Poor Clarity	*Being Clear*
Being ambiguous or indefinite: maybe, perhaps, sort of correct, more or less right, you know	Referring to the concrete object precisely, stating what is and is not correct and why.

Checking for Understanding

Assuming that everyone understands, or simply asking, "Does everyone understand?"	Asking specific questions or obtaining work samples to be sure students are ready to move on
Moving to the next topic because time is short or no students ask questions	Asking students to summarize main points to verify comprehension; reteaching unclear points
Not calling on slower students, relying only on feedback from a few volunteers	Checking everyone's understanding
Assigning tasks to work groups without accountability	Asking groups to report about findings or work-in-progress orally or in writing; having specific questions for students to answer to assess their progress
Not explaining students' roles in work groups and how they are performed	Describing and modeling different group roles such as notetaker, time monitor, etc.; assigning responsibilities to individual group members

Providing for Practice and Feedback

Not assigning classwork or homework	Being sure students have adequate practice so that critical objectives are mastered
Giving assignments that cover only a portion of the content	Reviewing assignments to be sure all of the lesson's skills are reinforced
Not checking, reviewing, or discussing students' assigned work	Checking work regularly, re-explaining needed concepts, reteaching when appropriate

FURTHER READING

Alvermann, D. E., O'Brien, D. G., & Dillon, D. R. (1990). What teachers do when they say they're having discussions of content area reading assignments: A qualitative analysis. *Reading Research Quarterly, 25,* 296–322.

Although teachers often say they utilize discussion activities, this study found that the nature of discussion varies greatly from class to class. Maintaining control was very important to many of the teachers, and the more this dominated their perspective, the more their discussions resembled recitation rather than open forum for expressing views.

Brophy, J. E., & Alleman, J. (1991). Activities as instructional tools: A framework for analysis and evaluation. *Educational Researcher, 20* (4), 9–23.

> *The authors provide a detailed analysis of the design, selection, and evaluation of activities, with a central concern being how activities contribute to student learning. Several major principles underlying activity design are proposed in this comprehensive analysis.*

Casey, M. B., & Tucker, E. C. (1994). Problem-centered classrooms: Creating lifelong learners. *Phi Delta Kappan, Oct.,* 139–143.

> *The authors give guidelines for establishing a problem-centered instructional program. They address the teacher's role in posing open-ended questions, teaching the steps in thinking, and connecting lessons to children's interests. Their summary of strategies at the end of the article is especially useful.*

Cooperative learning [Special issue]. (1989/90). *Educational Leadership, 47* (4).

> *This thematic issue focuses on group learning approaches. Articles by researchers and teachers describe different forms of cooperative learning, applications to different content fields, and teaching strategies and tips.*

Stigler, J. W., & Stevenson, H. W. (1991). How Asian teachers polish each lesson to perfection. *American Educator, 15* (1), 12–20, 43–47.

> *If you have a stereotype of Chinese or Japanese lessons as led by an authoritarian lecturer endlessly drilling students in rote tasks, your view will change after reading this article. Teachers in these two Asian cultures emphasize well-constructed, coherent lessons that focus on meaningful learning and active student participation.*

SUGGESTED ACTIVITIES

1. Use Checklist 5 at the end of the chapter to plan one or more lessons.

2. Read Problems 5–1 through 5–3, which describe problems three teachers are experiencing with the management of instruction. After reading each paragraph, review this chapter and decide what strategies they might use to help overcome their problems (other chapters may also provide useful suggestions). You might use each problem as a basis for a group discussion and generate a list of many possible solutions or strategies. Then compare your list with the keys in the Appendix.

3. See how many examples of Kounin's concepts you can find in Problem 5–4. Compare your list with the keys in the Appendix.

4. Case Study 5–1 illustrates problems that can arise in conducting instruction. Use the concepts in this and in previous chapters to diagnose Ms. Lake's problems. Compare your list with the keys in the Appendix.

PROBLEM 5-1

Ms. Kendall is beginning her first year of teaching fourth graders. She is writing out her plans for the first few days of class. She has familiarized herself with the scope and sequence of the fourth-grade curriculum. One of the first decisions she will make is about her class schedule. She must decide how best to organize her students' day.

What should she consider as she develops her daily schedule?

What long-term plans should she make to ensure that students learn to manage their own academic work and develop good work skills?

PROBLEM 5-2

During reading instruction, Mr. Hart generally works with a small group of students while the remaining students do assigned work. Lately, Mr. Hart has noticed that some students are not following seatwork directions and never finish their work, although he feels he allows appropriate amounts of time for work to be completed and gives thorough instructions before the reading groups start. A few students finish early, turn in their papers, and then wander around, interrupting other students and socializing excessively. Mr. Hart has to stop his work with the group to quiet the students. What can Mr. Hart do to get students to work more productively during seatwork?

PROBLEM 5-3

Ms. Jackson is trying to include more science lessons in her curriculum. She wants to try a discovery approach with her third graders. For a lesson on how sound is made, Ms. Jackson passes out paper cups in two sizes to students. Her plan is to have them hum into the cups and feel the different vibrations. However, as soon as students receive their cups, they begin to plop them noisily on the desks. Some students poke holes in the bottoms with pencils. Other students place them over their ears and show their neighbors, while another group is trying to figure out how to make the cups stay on their heads as hats. Ms. Jackson cannot get their attention back to the lesson. How could advance planning have helped her to avoid these problems? Use Checklist 5 to help you analyze this lesson.

PROBLEM 5-4

As he is about to begin class after lunch, Mr. Case makes eye contact with two students who are exchanging notes; the students quickly get out their class materials. "Let's begin by working some of the exercises at the end of the chapter; you will need a piece of paper with a heading." As students begin to get out their materials, Mr. Case calls out, "Oops! I forgot to tell you to bring money for tomorrow for the field trip. How many of you will be going?" After a brief discussion, students finish getting out their materials. Mr. Case says, "We'll go through these exercises orally, but I also want you to write the answers on your papers as part of today's classwork. I'll come around later and check your answers. Now, who can answer the first question? Hands please. Tyrone?"

Mr. Case conducts the lesson by calling on various students, some with hands up, others seemingly at random from the nonvolunteers. About halfway through the exercises, a student enters the room and says that he is new to the school and has been assigned to the class. Mr. Case goes to his desk, sits down, and says, "Okay, come here. I'll check out some of your books to you. I wish the school office wouldn't send children in the middle of the day. Where are you from, anyway? That's a nice shirt you are wearing."

After finishing with the student and sending him to a seat, Mr. Case leaves his desk and says to the class, "Now where were we? Oh, yes, question 7. Say, where did Kim and Lee go? I didn't give them permission to leave."

After several more minutes, Mr. Case calls a halt to the activity and says, "Now, I'd like us to discuss the test coming up this Thursday. Let's make sure that you are all clear on what will be on the exam and what you will need to get ready for it." After a pause, he adds, "I almost forgot. Get your questions from before and look at the next to the last one. We need to add an important point that was left out. . . ." After finishing the item, Mr. Case turns the topic back to the upcoming test: "Now, where were we? Oh, yes. I need to show you some items that will be similar to those on the test. Here's one." He writes it on the chalkboard, then pauses: "Well, I don't want to give away the test, do I?"

Without discussing the test further, he turns to another topic: "Just wait until you hear about the video tape we will be viewing tomorrow. I borrowed it from another teacher, and she said that her students thought it was one of the most interesting, exciting stories they had ever seen!"

CASE STUDY 5-1

A SCIENCE LESSON IN A SIXTH-GRADE CLASS

Ms. Lake has been having great difficulty obtaining acceptable or even completed work from many of her sixth-grade students. They never seem to be able to follow instructions or directions, even for assignments in the textbook. Only the most able four or five pupils are actually doing good-quality work. Ms. Lake likes to challenge the students with new ideas to stimulate their curiosity and promote independent thinking. Although much of the class appears to enjoy her presentations, the students don't seem to be able to transfer their enthusiasm to their assignments. For example, in a recent science assignment, students were supposed to draw pictures illustrating stages in the evolution of birds from reptiles; most students did not perform satisfactorily. The lesson preceding this assignment included the following components: a five-item test covered questions on birds, reptiles, and vertebrates, reviewing some content covered during the preceding week. Students checked their own answers to this test in class and then passed them in. Although it was not a difficult test, most students got three or fewer items correct. After the checking activity, the teacher began a twenty-minute presentation on the possible evolution of birds from reptiles. The following topics were discussed:

◆ The meaning of adaptation, with an example supplied by students.

◆ An example of environmental action in the local community. This topic was introduced by a student, and other students added comments.

◆ The possibility of life on other planets, including a discussion of the number of solar systems in our galaxy.

◆ A consideration of the question of why birds might evolve from reptiles, with a student's answer, "To get away from enemies, they would take to the air," as the only reason given.

◆ The classification system of living organisms: kingdom, phylum, class, order, family, genus, and species.

At this point in the presentation, students were instructed to copy the classification system from the board. Ms. Lake also provided an example of classification, using the lion in the animal kingdom, vertebrate phylum, mammal class, etc. Two similar examples were also presented and listed on the board. The teacher asked if students understood and if they had any questions. No questions were forthcoming, so the teacher gave the assignment of illustrating the stages in the evolution of a reptile to a bird. Students were given twenty-five minutes and told, "Use some color in your picture, make it neat, and use three stages." As was the case with many of the assignments Ms. Lake gave, only a few students completed their work satisfactorily, although most seemed to make an effort to do some drawing, and many students checked frequently with Ms. Lake to see if their pictures were acceptable.

What problems are evident and what changes might Ms. Lake make to achieve more success in helping students complete assignments satisfactorily?

✔ CHECKLIST 5

PLANNING FOR INSTRUCTION

Check When Complete	Before the Lesson Ask Yourself	Notes
☐	1. What are the most important concepts or skills to be learned?	_____
☐	2. What kind of learning is your goal (memorization, application)?	_____

PLANNING FOR INSTRUCTION *Continued*

Check When Complete	Before the Lesson Ask Yourself	Notes
☐	3. Are there difficult words or concepts that need extra explanation?	
☐	4. How will you help students make connections to previous learning?	
☐	5. What activities will you plan to create interest in the lesson?	
☐	6. What materials will be needed? Will students need to learn how to use them?	
☐	7. What procedures will students need to know to complete the activities?	
☐	8. How much time will you allocate for the lesson? For different parts of the lesson?	
☐	9. If activities require students to work together, how will groups be formed? How will you encourage productive work in groups?	
☐	10. What examples and questioning strategies will you use? Prepare a list of examples for explanations and list higher order questions.	
☐	11. How will you know during and after the lesson what students understand?	
☐	12. What presentation alternatives are there if students have trouble with concepts? Peer explanation, media, etc.?	
☐	13. Are there extra- or special-help students?	
☐	14. How will you make sure that all students participate?	
☐	15. How will you adjust the lesson if time is too short or long?	
☐	16. What kind of product, if any, will you expect from students at the end of the lesson?	
☐	17. What will students do when they finish?	
☐	18. How will you evaluate students' work and give them feedback?	
☐	19. How will the concepts you present be used by students in future lessons?	

CHAPTER 6

Maintaining Appropriate Student Behavior

As you have seen in the first five chapters, good classroom management depends on very careful planning of the classroom's organization, rules, procedures, initial activities, and instruction. All of this planning and preparation will pay large dividends once the students arrive. However, being ready is not sufficient to sustain good behavior throughout the year. You will need to be actively involved in maintaining student cooperation and compliance with necessary classroom rules and procedures. You cannot assume that students will behave appropriately just because you carefully taught them what was expected of them. In primary grades, children are in the early stages of learning "going to school" skills, so constant attention to prompting good behavior will be needed. Even in the intermediate grades, children need teachers who encourage good behavior by using their rules, procedures, and consequences consistently.

In particular, you should not be lulled into complacency by the good behavior of your students at the beginning of the year. Most elementary classes are quiet and subdued on the first day or two of school. Without careful teacher attention to maintaining good behavior, even a class that seems to begin very well may ultimately become disruptive and difficult to control. The following brief example illustrates such a class and also suggests some of the reasons why management problems might develop.

> Ms. White carefully discussed her classroom rules and procedures with her fifth-grade class at various times on the first several class days, and students were generally well behaved. However, at the start of the third week, problems are beginning to occur. While leading whole-class discussions, Ms. White stands at the front chalkboard to jot down important points. When she turns away from students to write on the board, students at the back of the room begin talking quietly among themselves. Some pass notes, throw paper wads, and wander around the room during quiet work time. If Ms. White reprimands students for talking, they say they do not understand what to do and that they are seeking help from each other. If she allows students to help each other, before long everyone is talking, few are working, and the noise level becomes high.
>
> At first, students raised their hands for permission to speak. Later, some students called out comments, and rather than ignore the contributions, Ms. White began to accept them when they were substantive. Now, more and more students have become loud and distracting. Because discussion activities do not seem to work well, Ms. White has begun to reduce the amount of time spent on these activities and to assign more individual work.
>
> During reading instruction, Ms. White meets with students in small groups while the rest of the class works on individual assignments. While working with the small group, Ms. White is interrupted more and more frequently by students who are having problems with the individual assignments. At other times, she has to interrupt small-group instruction to deal with misbehavior outside the group. At the end of the small-group instruction period for reading, Ms. White frequently is dismayed to see what little progress students have made on their independent work.

Problems such as those occurring in Ms. White's class often have a gradual onset, developing over several weeks or even months. It is usually possible to avoid these problems, but to do so you must first understand why the problems occur and what you can do to prevent them. Because they develop gradually, the causes are not always apparent to the teacher or even to an observer unfamiliar with the history of the classroom. However, the capsule account of events in Ms. White's class suggests several reasons why things are beginning to go awry. One source of problems is that Ms. White is not monitoring student behavior carefully enough.

Talking, inattention, and misbehavior are going undetected until the noise or commotion level is high. In addition, Ms. White is not checking student progress on assignments frequently enough. This reduces student accountability and prevents the teacher from providing the assistance that students may need to achieve the learning objectives.

A second problem is that Ms. White is being inconsistent in her use of procedures and in her reaction to students when they do not follow the procedures. By accepting some call-outs and by allowing noisy talk during independent work, she invites students to continue to test the limits until the procedures finally break down.

A third problem, related to the first two, is that too many inappropriate behaviors are being ignored. As a result, students are unsure of behavior standards, and minor events are escalating into major disruptions involving substantial numbers of students. A fourth problem is the teacher's attention becoming more and more directed at inappropriate behavior; no attention or incentives for appropriate behavior are evident.

These problems can be prevented or handled by the following four important guidelines:

◆ Build a positive climate with an emphasis on reinforcing appropriate behavior.

◆ Monitor student behavior and academic progress carefully.

◆ Be consistent in the use of procedures, rules, and consequences.

◆ Deal with inappropriate behavior promptly.

The remainder of the chapter considers how these guidelines can be implemented.

FOR REFLECTION

Think back to your elementary school years and recall a teacher or a year when you were in a class with a positive climate. List characteristics of that class and what the teacher appeared to do to promote it. Compare notes with a friend. To what extent do you recognize concepts from this chapter in those recollections? How can you put these into practice in your own classroom? ■

MONITORING STUDENT BEHAVIOR

To monitor classroom behavior effectively, first you must know what to look for. Two categories of student behavior are especially important to monitor:

1. Student involvement in learning activities.

2. Student compliance with classroom rules and procedures.

Reprinted by permission of Tribune Media Services.

Student involvement is indicated by many behaviors, including attention during presentations and discussions and satisfactory progress in individual work and other assignments. Students' compliance with classroom rules and procedures will be easy to monitor if you have a clear set of expectations for student behavior and have communicated these to the class.

Monitoring student behavior during whole-class presentations requires that you stand or sit so you can see all the faces of the students and so you scan the room frequently. Some teachers are not effective monitors of student behavior during whole-class activities because they focus their attention on a limited number of students (usually those seated in the middle rows or tables and at the front desks); other teachers "talk to the chalkboard." In either case, the teacher does not have a very clear perception of overall student response to the presentation, nor is he or she fully aware of what may be occurring at the periphery of the classroom. During your presentations, therefore, try to move around and develop "active eyes." If you notice a commotion involving several students and you have no idea what is going on, this is a sign you have not been monitoring closely enough.

When instructing a small group of students while the remainder of the class is engaged in individual seatwork, sit where you have an unobstructed view of all the students. Don't become so absorbed in working with the small group that you lose track of the other students. Look up frequently and be alert for problems. After finishing with one group, circulate around the room and provide needed assistance before calling the next small group.

When students are working on individual assignments and you are not instructing a group, monitor the class by moving around the classroom and checking each student's progress periodically. You will of course help students who request assistance; however, you should not just "chase hands," or you will not be aware of the progress of other students. One way to prevent having to chase hands is to establish a procedure by which students can ask questions of members of their group or their neighbors. This can free you to work with other students.

It is difficult to monitor student progress on assignments from your desk or from any other fixed location, so spend as little time in one place as possible. If you must work at your desk for a time, get up periodically and circulate around the room, looking at each student's work. If you must spend a long time (more than a minute or two) helping an individual student, avoid doing it at the student's desk unless you can monitor the rest of the class from that position. If the student's seat is in the middle of the room, for instance, half of the class will be behind you. In such a case, call the student to a small-group work table, to your desk, or to some other location from which you can easily see all the students. Finally, when you work at your desk or at any other location, don't let students congregate around the area. They will obstruct your view of the class, and they will probably distract students seated nearby. Instead, call students to you one at a time.

Monitoring cooperative groups can present special challenges. To be sure each group understands your expectations, move fairly quickly from group to group as students begin to work. Then stop and spend more time with each group, listening and occasionally contributing as a group member. In this way, you can gather information about the group's progress, provide a model for how to participate in a group, and help guide discussions to higher levels when needed.

A critical monitoring task is checking assignments. Collect them regularly and look them over, even when students check their own work in class. Keep your grade book current so you will be able to detect students who skip assignments. If you give a long-term assignment, be sure to check progress regularly. You may even give a grade or assign points toward a grade at these points. In upper elementary grades, you may also have students keep a checklist of assignments and due dates.

Keep in mind that an important part of monitoring is checking student progress and understanding. Build into your assignments ways to monitor these areas. For example, ask small groups to report on their progress; have individuals make and update daily or weekly work plans; follow up individual work time with brief discussions of concepts with oral checks for understanding. See Chapter 5 for ways of checking for understanding.

CONSISTENCY

The dictum "be consistent" has been repeated more frequently than the pledge of allegiance. It is still worth discussion, though, because its meaning is not always clear. In the classroom, consistency means retaining the same expectations for appropriate behavior in an activity at all times and for all students. For example, if students are expected to work silently during independent work on Monday, the same procedure is in effect on Tuesday, Wednesday, and the rest of the week. Penalties should also be applied consistently. For example, if the penalty for missing assignments is losing one's place on an honor list, the teacher must make sure that all students who skip assignments receive the penalty. This procedure should be followed even when it is inconvenient to administer it or in spite of the pleading of individual students that an exception be made. Obvious inconsistency in the use of procedures or in the application of penalties will cause confusion about what is acceptable behavior. Students will then frequently "test the limits" by not following the procedure or by repeating whatever behavior was to have evoked the penalty. These events can rapidly escalate and force the teacher either to abandon the procedure or to tolerate high levels of inappropriate behavior. Because neither outcome is desirable, it is best to avoid the problem by learning to be consistent from the start. Of course, it is not possible to be totally consistent; there will be occasions when the most reasonable course of action will be to make an exception to a rule or procedure. Thus, a deadline for an assignment may be extended when a student has a valid reason, or some procedures might be ignored during an emergency. Note that using certain procedures routinely for some activities but not for others is not inconsistent. For example, you may require that no students leave their seats without permission during discussions or presentations, but you may allow them to get materials, sharpen pencils, or turn in papers as needed without permission during seatwork. Differentiate between these activities when you explain the procedures to the students.

Undesirable inconsistency usually arises from three sources. First, the procedures or rules as presented are not reasonable, workable, or appropriate. Second, the teacher fails to monitor students closely and detects only a fraction of the inappropriate behavior. This creates the appearance of inconsistency. Third, the teacher may not feel strongly enough about the procedure or rule to enforce it or to use the associated penalty. If you find yourself caught in an inconsistency that is becoming a problem, your alternatives are:

1. Reteach the procedure. Take a few minutes to discuss the problem with the class and to reiterate your desire that they follow the procedure. Then enforce it.

2. Modify the procedure or consequence and then reintroduce and use it.

3. Abandon the procedure or consequence and possibly substitute another in its place.

Your choice of the alternatives depends on circumstances and the importance of the item to your classroom management system.

PROMPT MANAGEMENT OF INAPPROPRIATE BEHAVIOR

Inappropriate behavior must be handled promptly to keep it from continuing and spreading. Behaviors that you should be concerned about include lack of involvement in learning activities, prolonged inattention or work avoidance, and obvious violations of classroom rules and procedures. It is not a good idea to ignore such behavior: Prolonged inattention will make it difficult for the students to learn and to be able to complete assignments; violations of rules and failure to follow procedures create many problems we have already discussed. These behaviors should be dealt with directly but without overreaction. A calm, reasoned tone or approach will be more productive and less likely to lead to confrontation. The following alternatives are recommended.

Four Ways to Manage Inappropriate Behavior

1. Make eye contact with or move closer to the student. Use a signal, such as a finger to the lips or a head shake, to prompt the appropriate behavior. Monitor until the student complies.

2. If the student is not following a procedure correctly, simply reminding the student of the correct procedure may be effective. You can either state the correct procedure or ask the student if he or she remembers it.

3. When the student is off-task—that is, not working on an assignment—redirect his or her attention to the task: "Sammy, you should be writing now," or "Cynthia, the assignment is to complete all the problems on the page." Check the student's progress shortly thereafter to make sure he or she is continuing to work.

4. Ask or tell the student to stop the inappropriate behavior. Then monitor until it stops and the student begins constructive activity.

Sometimes, it is inconvenient or would interrupt an activity to use these procedures immediately. If the behavior is not disruptive or is not likely to spread to other students, make a mental note of the problem and continue the activity until a more appropriate time occurs. Then tell the student you saw what was happening and discuss what the appropriate behavior should have been.

The four procedures outlined above are easy to use, cause little interruption of class activities, and enable students to correct their behavior. However, if a student persists in an unacceptable behavior, other alternatives should be used. If the rest of the class is working appropriately and does not need your immediate attention, a brief talk with the student may be sufficient. If that doesn't settle the matter, or if an immediate conference is not desirable or feasible, stop the child's behavior and assess whatever penalty is appropriate. Some teachers use a "time-out" desk or chair as a holding area for erring students; others have students wait outside the classroom until time can be found for a conference. Before you do this, however, be sure school policy permits waiting in the hall. Note that the four procedures apply to relatively minor forms of misbehavior. Many additional measures to deal with problem behaviors are described in Chapters 7 and 8.

BUILDING A POSITIVE CLIMATE

This chapter emphasizes maintaining appropriate behavior by applying procedures and rules consistently, handling problems promptly, and using nonintrusive interventions when possible to maintain activity flow and student involvement in lessons. We now want to emphasize the importance of keeping a positive perspective and avoiding overdwelling on misbehavior or inadequacies. Sometimes, teachers get caught in the trap of seeing only faults and problems and overlooking the better features of students' behavior. Instead of rejoicing when twenty-nine students are involved in learning, we complain about the one student who is off-task.

> Mr. Acerbic's sixth-grade physical education class could do no right. Although most of the students initially participated willingly in the class activities, students never seemed to perform quickly or well enough for their teacher. "Come on, you horseflies, quit buzzing and listen up," he would yell when he heard talking. "Laps" around the gym were given for even slight infractions such as brief inattention; there always seemed to be three or four students making the rounds at any given time. Instead of feedback about good performance, criticism was usually given for inadequacies. Although students took the constant carping in stride, they displayed little zest for the class.

Although poor performance should not be ignored—students need specific, corrective feedback to know what they need to improve—it is important that the climate for learning be positive. This means that students should look forward to the class. They should expect to learn and to receive assistance when they encounter difficulty and should feel supported in their efforts. Such a climate can be fostered by communicating positive expectations to students, by praising good performance, and, at times, by using additional rewards.

Teacher expectations can be communicated in a variety of ways, some obvious and others subtle. (For a thorough description of this aspect of teacher behavior, see Good and Brophy, 1994.) Teachers can:

◆ Identify appropriate instructional goals and discuss them with students so they are clear about what is expected.

◆ Insist that students complete work satisfactorily.

◆ Refuse to accept excuses for poor work.

◆ Communicate acceptance of imperfect initial performance when students struggle to achieve new learning.

◆ Convey confidence in the student's ability to do well.

◆ Display an encouraging "can do" attitude that generates excitement and self-confidence.

◆ Avoid comparative evaluations, especially of lower-ability students, that might cause them to conclude they cannot accomplish the objectives.

By communicating positive expectations, teachers lay the foundation for students to attempt new tasks and reach new goals. When students know that their teacher believes them to be capable, they are more likely to try harder.

A positive climate for learning is also created by appropriate teacher praise. When used well, teacher praise can be uplifting and provide great encouragement to a student. The most powerful type of teacher praise provides the student with information about what aspect of student performance is praiseworthy and also demonstrates that the teacher is impressed with the quality of the student's work. In other words, effective praise provides both informative feedback and genuine teacher approval. It can also accompany suggestions for improvement (constructive criticism) without loss of effect.

For children from about the third grade and up, public praise that focuses on student accomplishment works better than praise for student effort. When teachers praise them for "working hard," many older elementary students are likely to assume that the teacher thinks they aren't very able. When you know that a student put forth considerable effort and you want to acknowledge it, be sure the praise also includes an emphasis on the student's achievement. "Gloria, all your hard work paid off because your project was beautifully done. The organization of ideas and the extra details in the descriptions were outstanding!" Likewise, praise should be deserved and it should not be too easily obtained. Public praise of a student for success on an easy task can communicate to the rest of the class (and the student who was praised) that the teacher believes he or she has little ability.

It is a good idea to look for private ways to provide praise. Written comments on papers, tests, and other assignments or a personal note offer excellent opportunities for quality praise. Private conversations, conferences with parents, notes home, and informal contacts also offer opportunities for praising students. Private praise avoids some of the complications of public praise and permits the teacher to include a greater variety of performances and behaviors as the focus of praise. Further discussion of the uses of teacher praise can be found in Emmer (1988) and Brophy (1981).

IMPROVING CLASS CLIMATE THROUGH INCENTIVES OR REWARDS

Extra incentives or rewards can help build a positive climate. The improvement in class climate occurs because the incentives add interest or excitement to the class routine while also directing attention toward appropriate behavior and away from inappropriate behavior. Moreover, students are more likely to respond positively to the teacher, contributing to a mutually supportive pattern of interaction.

Before using an added incentive, consider several factors that might affect its appropriateness and effects. Check your school or district policies, because sometimes certain incentives are prohibited, and you would not want to promise a field trip or party only to find out that it was not allowed. Your rewards should target the behaviors you would like to encourage. Rewards too easily earned or too difficult to achieve lose their motivational effect. Also, be concerned about whether the use of a reward takes too much class time for record keeping or other administrative tasks. Avoid using complex systems that distract you and your students from a focus on learning. Start with simple procedures and add to them if that seems reasonable.

Be careful not to set up incentives that only the most able students can achieve. Systems that encourage excessive competition for scarce rewards will discourage those students who don't have much chance. The examples in this section and in the activities at the end of the chapter include a variety of types. Combine these ideas with those of other teachers and your own experience to develop alternate rewards for use at various times of the year.

Many different types of rewards, including symbols, recognition, activities, and materials, can be used with elementary students. Each of these types is described later in this chapter, with examples.

Recognition

Recognition rewards involve some means of giving attention to the students. Examples are displaying student work; awarding a certificate for achievement, for improvement, or for good behavior; and verbally citing student accomplishments. Recognition rewards may be given on a weekly or monthly basis using a system such as "Super Stars of the Week," a class honor roll, or "Good Worker's Award." Be sure to explain the basis for awards—for example, good attendance, achievement, improvement, hard work, good conduct, or citizenship. The more specific you can be when describing the desired behavior, the more likely you will be to obtain it.

Some teachers encourage competition among student work teams or other groups. These competitions may be simple and short (for example, in a first-grade class, the teacher might say, "Let's see which table is ready first!"); at higher grade levels, competitions may run for a week, a month, or a grading term and may be based on behavior or a specific academic task. If competition among groups is encouraged, this fact should be kept in mind when the teacher forms the groups. Group composition should be balanced so that all groups have an equal chance to succeed. Competing for awards and prizes can be fun and will spur interest and effort. If you want to maximize the effect for all students, be liberal when giving awards—use second and third place and honorable mention awards so that everyone who participates appropriately receives recognition.

Activities

Permitting or arranging for students to do something special or enjoyable constitutes giving an activity reward. Sometimes, you can let students choose what this might be. If they have a voice in what the activities are, they are more likely to "buy in." Examples are privileges such as free-reading time, game time, visits to the school library, or appointment as a room monitor, game leader, or special helper. A more elaborate activity reward is the field trip or party. Because school policy may affect your use of the latter activities, clear any such activity with the appropriate administrator before announcing it to your class. Be certain to describe clearly what students need to do to receive such privileges.

When activity rewards are used as incentives for the whole class, students can participate in their identification and selection. Thus, ideas for activity incentives can be solicited from students during a discussion, or the teacher might start with a short list and ask students to suggest additions to it; either way, the class can vote for a favorite. Some whole-class activities that might be used as incentives include watching a videotape, fifteen minutes of free time, playing a game, listening to music, having a popcorn party, or no homework. A group activity reward should be made contingent on specific desirable behaviors; if the group cooperates, they receive the incentive. If not, they lose some or all of the time in the activity. Because the purpose of using an activity reward is, at least in part, to promote positive climate building, it is important not to let one or two students spoil the fun for the rest of the class. A chronically uncooperative student can be invited to participate but can be excluded from the reward if he or she persists in noncompliance. In most cases, however, positive peer pressure will encourage such a student to cooperate without the teacher having to resort to exclusion.

Symbols

Elementary teachers use a variety of symbols to communicate a positive evaluation of student work. Examples include letter grades and numerical scores, happy faces, checks and check pluses, and stars and stickers with an appealing design. At all elementary-grade levels, the teacher's positive evaluation and written comments are a source of satisfaction for students. For younger children, especially, this reward should be provided as soon as possible after they complete a task and on a daily basis. Assignments in the early grades can usually be checked quickly, so there is no

Reprinted by permission: Tribune Media Services.

reason to delay feedback. One effective procedure for checking assignments such as worksheets, writing, or math is to have the children place them on a corner of their desks when finished. As you circulate through the room, you can check completed assignments, write an E, put a star, check, or other symbol on the paper, and praise good effort, correctly done work, or neatness.

In the upper grades, where assignments are sometimes more complex or somewhat lengthy, you are more likely to collect assigned work to check it and record the grades in your grade book. Acquire a box of stars or other stickers, or buy hand stamps with a happy face or other symbols to supplement your numerical or letter grades. Be liberal in your use of these. Reward improvement and good effort so that all students have access to these incentives. Obviously, you should not reward poor performance, but do give feedback and encouragement so the student can improve.

In addition to their use for daily feedback, symbols are also used on report cards. Elementary-grade children, even first graders, place a positive value on high grades (or "lots of E's"), and it is not uncommon to hear young children comparing report card grades. However, most first or second graders are not likely to have a clear conception of a specific relationship between daily work and long-term grades. Consequently, report card grades are not particularly useful incentives for encouraging young children to complete daily work. In the upper elementary grades, however, students are better able to understand a connection between their effort on daily assignments and the grades they receive in particular subjects. Therefore, it is a good idea to explain your grading policies to these children so they will understand that the value you place on good effort and performance on daily work will translate into a report card grade. However, do not expect report card grades to be the major source of motivation for most students; plan to rely more on the daily use of symbols, positive feedback to students, and other rewards.

Material Incentives

Material incentives are objects of value to students. Examples include food, a pencil or eraser, discarded classroom materials, games, toys, or books. You will have to consider your own financial circumstances as well as school policy before deciding to use such rewards.

A procedure combining several types of rewards is the use of an honor roll system (an all-star list, super stars, gold record club) or competition among groups or teams in conjunction with other incentives. Badges, stickers with appealing designs, food treats, activity privileges, or a party can be used as rewards along with the recognition of being an award winner. It is best to spread the honors around and include a good portion of the class. Do not give awards only for outstanding achievement; have awards for improvement, excellent effort, good conduct, and so on.

When using a class party or field trip as an activity reward, you will need to be particularly careful. If only half the class can meet the criteria you establish for receiving this award, you will have to figure out what to do with a large number of unhappy students during the party or field trip. For such a reward, it would be better to establish criteria that all students could meet (such as good citizenship). In this way, you can encourage a class norm for good behavior that is attainable by everyone.

A major consideration in the use of rewards is their feasibility. Some rewards require a great deal of planning, record keeping, or other preparation. For example, a field trip, party, or major group activity needs careful planning. If some (presumably a very few) students will be denied the activity, arrangements must be made for their supervision. In addition, transportation may need to be arranged, other adults may be needed for supervision, and expense may be incurred. Other rewards require little preparation or effort. Examples are giving positive verbal feedback, placing a symbol or other positive comment on an assignment sheet, and awarding simple privileges such as leading the line to lunch, passing out materials, taking up papers, and being a room monitor.

Between the two extremes of much effort and little effort are a large number of rewards that require a modest amount of the teacher's time or effort. These include things such as awarding free time for reading, play, or games; sending home a positive note to parents; awarding prizes such as a pencil with the school name on it; allowing extra time in the library or for some other activity; and establishing an honor roll or "Super Star" list. Don't try too much too soon in the way of reward systems. Systems that require extensive record keeping or constant attention or complex arrangements will be a substantial drain on your time. Start with simple procedures and add to them if you can. The case studies at the end of the chapter illustrate a number of possibilities.

CAUTION IN THE USE OF REWARDS

Some researchers (e.g., Deci & Ryan, 1985; Lepper & Greene, 1978) have urged caution in the use of extrinsic rewards by pointing out that in some cases their use may erode students' intrinsic motivation to engage in the activity that is rewarded. Results from their studies and other research suggest that receiving a reward for engaging in an activity or performing an altruistic behavior reduces subsequent motivation if the extrinsic reward is later removed.

Explanations of this dampening effect on motivation usually focus on the implicit messages that are communicated when individuals are given rewards. For example, an implicit message might be, "This is an unpleasant or boring task, so a reward is needed to get anyone to do it." Consequently, the recipient tends to devalue the rewarded activity.

Before concluding that teachers should never use incentives, however, it should be noted that research in this area has several limitations. Much of it was conducted in laboratory settings where the task and its accompanying reward occurred on only one occasion. Also, the rewarded tasks in these studies were highly interesting ones, such as games or puzzles. Thus, the research setting and the tasks

Calvin and Hobbes   by Bill Watterson

Panel 1: I'VE GOT AN IDEA, DAD.

Panel 2: MAYBE I'D GET BETTER GRADES IF YOU OFFERED ME $1 FOR EVERY "D", $5 FOR EVERY "C", $10 FOR EVERY "B", AND $50 FOR EVERY "A"!

Panel 3: I'M NOT GOING TO *BRIBE* YOU, CALVIN. YOU SHOULD APPLY YOURSELF FOR YOUR OWN GOOD.

Panel 4: RATS. I THOUGHT I COULD MAKE AN EASY FOUR BUCKS.

CALVIN & HOBBES © 1989 Watterson. Dist. by UNIVERSAL PRESS SYNDICATE. Reprinted with permission. All rights reserved.

were not representative of real classrooms. Furthermore, some research has found that incentives can actually enhance interest rather than reduce it. Bandura (1986) argues that the conflicting findings mean that the effect of extrinsic rewards on intrinsic motivation is weak, and many other factors operate to influence the effects of the use of incentives.

The most reasonable application of the research results for classroom use of rewards is to be thoughtful about their use. No purpose will be served by rewarding activities that are already highly interesting to students. In fact, the evidence suggests that to do so will reduce motivation. However, many classroom tasks are not highly interesting, especially those in which extensive repetition is needed to produce skilled performance and learning. When student motivation flags, external incentives may be necessary to maintain engagement. Actually, the use of incentives is more desirable than lowering expectations and accepting poor performance or resorting to punishment or threats.

Finally, when rewards are used, the teacher can counteract the potentially negative effects on intrinsic motivation by pointing out to students the usefulness of the skill to be learned, by choosing materials and activities that have high potential for sustaining interest, and by modeling and demonstrating personal interest and enthusiasm for the task.

FURTHER READING

Maehr, M., & Midgley, C. (1991). Enhancing student motivation: A schoolwide approach. *Educational Psychologist, 26,* 399–427.

Student motivation contributes to classroom climate and to maintaining desirable behavior. This article provides an organizing framework for considering classroom goals and motivational strategies that can be applied by teachers throughout a school.

Marshall, H. H. (1987). Motivation strategies of three fifth-grade teachers. *The Elementary School Journal, 88* (2), 135–150.

> *Marshall identified three patterns of motivational strategies in the statements three fifth-grade teachers used to frame lessons, maintain lessons, and handle responsibility for learning. She describes the characteristics of these three patterns, which she calls "learning-oriented," "work-oriented," and "work-avoidance."*

Raffini, J. P. (1996). *150 ways to increase intrinsic motivation in the classroom.* Boston: Allyn & Bacon.

> *Many useful strategies are presented in this compendium of classroom activities designed to enhance student motivation. Teachers looking for alternative ways to build classroom climate will find Chapters 4 and 6 especially relevant.*

Strengthening student engagement [Special issue]. (1995). *Educational Leadership, 53* (1).

> *This issue of the journal* Educational Leadership *contains several articles that focus on maintaining student involvement in the classroom. Topics in the issue include the use of rewards, student views of schoolwork, strategies for engaging students in specific content areas, and cultural factors in improving classroom climate.*

SUGGESTED ACTIVITIES

1. Read Examples 6–1 through 6–4 and consider how you might adapt these descriptions of reward systems to your own classroom. Analyze each example using the following questions as starting points:
   a. What teacher and student roles are encouraged?
   b. Is the system primarily intrinsic or extrinsic?
   c. Is the system cooperative or competitive?
   d. What kind of classroom environment is the system likely to foster?

2. Find out about school policies that will affect your use of rewards. Also, note any schoolwide system that you will need to incorporate into your own classroom procedures.

3. Review Checklists 2 and 3 in Chapters 2 and 3 and identify the rewards you intend to use with your major conduct and accountability procedures. By planning ahead, you will be better able to explain these incentives and be consistent in their use.

4. In Problem 6–**1**, Ms. Greene is encountering problems maintaining her management system. Use the information in this and previous chapters to diagnose her problems and to suggest what she can do to improve student behavior. Refer to the key in the Appendix for other suggestions.

5. How can you help students see the intrinsic rewards in activities in your classroom?

   ◆ *Example 6–1: Shoot for the Moon* Mrs. Li used a reward system called "Shoot for the Moon" to give feedback to second-grade students for behavioral and academic performance. She decorated a large bulletin board with blue paper, a large round moon, a few clouds, and a title, "Shoot for the Moon." Each child's name was written on a small construction paper spaceship. The spaceships were lined up at the bottom of the bulletin board at the start. At the beginning of the year, Mrs. Li discussed with her class the kinds of behaviors that would result in the movement of each spaceship closer to the moon. Daily completion of assignments and good behavior in the classroom, at lunch, and on the playground would result in the spaceship moving two inches closer to the moon. For bad behavior (such as misbehavior in the lunchroom or during instruction, not working in class, or not turning in an assignment), a student's spaceship would be moved one inch away from the moon. When students reached the moon, they were rewarded by being able to keep their spaceships decorated with a star. The teacher then started another spaceship for them at the bottom of the board. Sometimes, students were required to reach the moon by a certain deadline to get a special reward such as a privilege or a popcorn party. Mrs. Li was consistent in rewarding appropriate behavior each day and in penalizing inappropriate behaviors, and she also occasionally rewarded individual students for being especially quiet or helpful or for improving their work or grades. This worked well with students who had particular behavior or academic problems.

◆ *Example 6–2: Regular Feedback*   Ms. Harmony's first-grade class functioned smoothly and productively without many obvious rewards and penalties. Although she only occasionally rewarded individuals or groups with public compliments, Ms. Harmony maintained a high level of student involvement through interesting, well-paced lessons and assignments with a high level of student success and by promptly returning assignments and giving students feedback regarding their work. She dealt with inappropriate behavior by brief verbal correction of students or short private conferences with individuals inside the classroom. Often, she would simply mention what the student should be doing if all the rest of his or her work was finished. Ms. Harmony made extensive use of telephone contacts with parents to inform them of their children's progress and particularly to identify when a student was not completing assignments satisfactorily. She did this frequently during the first few months of the school year, with long-lasting results.

◆ *Example 6–3: A Token Exchange System*   Mr. Young used a variety of strategies, some simple and some elaborate, for encouraging appropriate behavior in his third-grade class. Throughout the year, he used a system in which the class as a whole earned blue chips for good behavior and red chips for poor behavior. When a monthly goal for the number of blue chips was reached, the class was rewarded with a treat or special privilege.

Goals and rewards escalated during the course of the year, beginning with a class party at the end of the first month and culminating in a field trip to a state fair. During each day, blue chips were dropped into a container for various appropriate behaviors—two for good behavior during the time a visitor was in the room, ten for each satisfactory cleanup, one for each student who at the end of the day had completed his or her individual contract work, and so on. Red chips were dropped into the container for excessive noise, throwing trash on the floor, bad behavior on the way to lunch, or other transgressions. Shaking the can that contained the chips was often used to signal that there was too much talking or misbehaving and that failure to get quiet would result in another red chip. At the end of the day, red chips were counted, and an equal number of blue chips were deducted from the blue chip collection.

In addition to the chip system, Mr. Young complimented good workers aloud, sometimes let best-behaved or best-prepared students line up first, put names of cooperative students on the board under a "Super People" title, and awarded happy faces to students who did all of their work that day.

◆ *Example 6–4: Another Token Reward System* Every Friday, Mrs. Smith used a special incentive system with her fourth graders. She cut out small strips from colored paper and used these as tokens for good behavior during the day. Good behavior was described ahead of time to students the first few times Mrs. Smith used the incentive system. At the end of an activity, she would pass out a strip to each student who had been attentive or on-task; if the activity took awhile to complete, she would give out strips during the activity. This would be accompanied by feedback about what was being rewarded: "I really appreciate how attentive everyone is being during this lesson." Or "Boys and girls, you are working so well on the assignment, I just know we are going to have a very good day." Or "I really like how everyone worked hard and cooperated during the group assignment, thank you very much." During the last thirty to forty-five minutes of the day, the teacher let the students trade in their strips for different treats during an afternoon party. During the party, Mrs. Smith would provide an activity, such as a game or a short videotape of a children's program or cartoon, or she would read a story. The children enjoyed and looked forward to this end-of-week activity, and it assisted Mrs. Smith in obtaining very good effort and participation during her regular Friday academic activities.

Mrs. Smith also used special award certificates for individual students (booklets of certificates that can be copied can be purchased in school supply stores). These certificates were especially impressive because each was signed by the principal as well as by Mrs. Smith. Students were recognized for outstanding effort, improvement, or accomplishment. The certificates were awarded both publicly and privately.

✖ PROBLEM 6-1

MISBEHAVIOR IN A THIRD-GRADE CLASS

Ms. Greene's third-grade students never seem to settle down for very long. Regardless of whether the children have been assigned independent work or are supposed to be paying attention to a presentation, some degree of commotion or noise is always present. During the first few days of school, the class seemed well-behaved and was seldom out of order, and almost all the children were cooperative and did their work. Gradually, however, more and more inappropriate socializing, loud talk, call-outs, and other interruptions occurred, even from previously quiet students.

During Ms. Greene's presentations to the class, students are frequently inattentive, and she is able to complete lessons only with difficulty. Sometimes, she even stops lessons short because the children are so difficult to control. At times, the only way she can restore a semblance of quiet is to start writing names on the board and assigning detention. However, even that tactic doesn't work for long because so many students are inattentive that the list of names gets very long and not being on the list becomes something of a social stigma.

During a recent reading-group period, three students talked continuously while Ms. Greene was working with one of the small groups. Two other children wandered around the room and a half-dozen others made frequent trips to the drinking fountain, restrooms, and hamster cages.

What has gone wrong in this class? How might Ms. Greene attempt to gain better cooperation from her students?

Communication Skills for Teaching

$\mathbf{T}$hroughout this book, we have emphasized classroom management's preventive and instructional aspects. Not all problems can be prevented, however, and sometimes unobtrusive handling of inappropriate behavior during instruction is not sufficient. The approaches described in this chapter provide additional means for dealing with problems that persist. The example below illustrates such a situation.

> During the past several days, Debra and Diane have been increasingly inattentive in Ms. Harris' fifth-grade class. Their off-task behavior has included whispering

with other students and each other, teasing boys seated nearby, and displaying exaggerated boredom with class discussions. Ms. Harris first asked the girls to stop bothering the class, and when that had no effect, she moved the girls to different seats. However, Debra and Diane continued to disrupt by passing notes and calling out loudly to one another.

We will not second-guess Ms. Harris by wondering whether she had communicated expectations clearly or had taken action promptly enough: Let us suppose that she had, in fact, practiced good preventive management skills, but the students misbehaved anyway. No strategy works all the time! What options are now available to Ms. Harris to deal with the situation? Possible approaches include the following:

- ◆ Ignore the problem and hope it goes away.
- ◆ Refer the students to the principal.
- ◆ Call the students' parents and ask for their help.
- ◆ Apply a consequence, such as detention or some other punishment.

Each of the above approaches has advantages and limitations. For example, ignoring the problem requires little effort and might work if the students are mainly seeking teacher attention. The description does not, however, suggest that this is a likely reason for the behavior, and ignoring may only allow it to intensify and spread to other students. Referral has the advantage of demanding little of the teacher's time, at least in the short run; it also temporarily removes the disruptive students, and it can have deterrent value. However, it may do nothing in the long run to deal with the problem the students are causing in the class, and although referral may sometimes be a reasonable approach to serious misbehavior, it can easily be overused.

A telephone call to parents sometimes works wonders and is usually worth a try. However, parents cannot always stop misbehavior. They do not, after all, accompany their child to your class, nor do they control the cues that are eliciting the misbehavior. Punishing the students by assigning detention or withholding some desirable activity or privilege is another possible reaction. Punishment, as will be discussed in Chapter 8, can stop misbehavior, at least temporarily, and it can deter other students. But punishment can have the disadvantages of creating hostility or resentment and of trapping the teacher and students in a cycle of misbehavior–reaction that leads to power struggles. By itself, punishment does little to teach the student self-control and responsibility.

Because each of these approaches has limitations, you need additional means of coping with problems. This does not mean that other approaches such as ignoring, referral, applying consequences, or involving parents will be supplanted. It does mean that communication strategies should be added to your repertoire to deal with problems that cannot be corrected with minor interventions and to help students learn to take responsibility for their own behavior.

In addition to being helpful in dealing with students whose behavior is creating a problem for the teacher or for other students, communication skills can be used to assist students who are themselves experiencing problems. Teachers frequently become aware of students' problems caused by factors both inside and outside the classroom. Sometimes, teachers can help these students by being good listeners and by encouraging them to consider alternate ways to solve problems or to adapt to difficult situations.

We use the label *communication skills* for the set of strategies described in this chapter to emphasize that the approach focuses on communicating clearly and effectively with others to help bring about a change in their behavior, in their thinking, or in the situation that has caused the problem. But communication also means being open to information, so teachers also need to be good listeners and try to understand the student's (or parents') concerns and feelings. To become an effective communicator, three related skills are needed:

1. **Constructive assertiveness:** This includes describing your concerns clearly, insisting that misbehavior be corrected, and resisting being coerced or manipulated.

2. **Empathic responding:** This refers to listening to the student's perspective and reacting in ways that maintain a positive relationship and encourage further discussion.

3. **Problem solving:** This component includes several steps for reaching mutually satisfactory resolutions to problems; it requires working with the student to develop a plan for change.

The three elements are derived from a variety of sources, including Gordon's *Teacher Effectiveness Training*, Gazda's *Human Relations Development: A Manual for Educators*, Glasser's *Reality Therapy*, Alberti's *Assertiveness*, Zuker's *Mastering Assertiveness Skills*, and other standard references. These books are included in the bibliography. The treatment of communication skills in this chapter is intended to be an introduction; if you are interested in further reading, we suggest you refer to one or more of the cited books.

Although this chapter's treatment of assertiveness, empathic responding, and problem solving focuses on their use with students, the skills are helpful when dealing with parents—especially during parent conferences—and other adults. Thus, the skills described in this chapter have a variety of applications and will improve your effectiveness in handling many classroom and school-related situations.

FOR REFLECTION

Most teachers are sensitive to, or self-conscious about, some aspect of their image or background. Height, weight, appearance, content knowledge, inexperience, marital status, and acceptance or respect are among the areas that may be a source of insecurity or concern. Because teaching is such a public event, and because students are astute observers of teachers' reactions, teachers often reveal much of themselves in their reactions when their students find the right "button" to push. Think about an area that represents a source of insecurity to you. Consider how your communication with students may be affected if a student "pushes" that button. ■

CONSTRUCTIVE ASSERTIVENESS

Assertiveness is the ability to stand up for one's legitimate rights in ways that help ensure that others cannot ignore or circumvent them. The adjective *constructive* means that the assertive teacher does not deride or attack the student. Assertiveness can be thought of as a general characteristic or attribute that we use in a wide variety of settings or as a set of skills that are more situation specific. Some individuals are assertive in a variety of settings (e.g., interacting with strangers, on the job, at parties, in school, etc.), whereas others lack assertiveness in many social situations.

However, even if you are not generally assertive, you can learn to use assertive behaviors while you are teaching. In fact, doing so may generalize to other situations as you become more confident of your skills. People who are very unassertive (e.g., feel extremely nervous whenever they are expected to lead a group; are unable to begin conversations or to make eye contact with others; accede to inappropriate demands readily; are unable to ask others to respect their rights) will find teaching uncomfortable and will have particular difficulty with discipline. Such people can help themselves in several ways, especially by reading about assertiveness and practicing some of the skills, preferably in situations that are not too uncomfortable, until they begin to develop more confidence. It is also possible to obtain professional help, such as from a counseling center, or to enroll in a course or workshop on assertiveness training. A good training program will usually include cognitive restructuring to reshape negative thought patterns that interfere with appropriate social interaction, anxiety-reduction exercise, and skills training and practice to develop more effective behaviors.

The elements of assertiveness include:

◆ A clear statement of the problem or issue

◆ Unambiguous body language

◆ Insistence on appropriate behavior and resolution of the problem

Assertiveness is not:

- Hostile or aggressive
- Argumentative
- Inflexible
- Wimpy, wishy-washy, doormat behavior

Assertiveness lies on a continuum of social response between aggressive, overbearing pushiness and timid, ineffectual, or submissive responses that allow some students to trample on the teacher's and other students' rights. Assertiveness skills allow you to communicate to students that you are serious about teaching and about maintaining a classroom in which everyone's rights are respected.

We will now consider aspects of constructive assertiveness that have special importance for teachers.

Stating the Problem or Concern

Student misbehavior usually causes problems for teachers by making it difficult to conduct lessons, by slowing down activities, by subverting routines that help a class run smoothly, and by distracting other students from their work. When misbehavior persists, it is time for the teacher to let the student know what the problem is, from the teacher's point of view. Sometimes just a simple description of the problem may result in students' changing their behavior because they become more aware of it and begin to monitor it better. Stating the problem has two parts: (1) identifying the student behavior and (2) describing its effects as in the following examples:

"Loud conversations in the library corner distract other students."

"Please raise your hand so that I can call on you."

"Wandering around the room disturbs the class."

"Calling other students names causes hard feelings."

By focusing on the behavior and its effects, you can reduce the potential for student defensiveness and keep open the opportunity for achieving a satisfactory resolution to the situation. Conducting the conference privately (e.g., after class or during a conference period) when possible will lessen the potential for embarrassing the student in front of peers and will reduce the likelihood of a confrontation or power struggle that challenges the teacher's authority. Sometimes you will be forced to act immediately when a private conference is not an option.

Notice that the problem descriptions do not label students or their behavior; that is, students are not accused of being bad, rude, and annoying or behaving in an inconsiderate and stupid manner. Such labeling, whether for a student or the student's behavior, should be avoided because it impedes behavior change by suggesting that a student's behavior is a permanent characteristic that the student might accept as valid. Notice also that statements rather than questions are used. Quizzing students (e.g., "Why are you talking?" "Do you think that you should be calling someone that name?") invites defensive, sarcastic, or oppositional responses and can result in arguments.

Body Language

Constructive assertiveness with students needs the visual reinforcement of appropriate body language in three areas. The first is making eye contact when addressing the student, especially when describing the problem and when calling for behavior change. Note that there is a difference between eye contact that communicates seriousness and resolve and an angry glare that emits hostility. Breaking eye contact from time to time relieves tension. A second area of assertive body language is maintaining an alert posture and body orientation toward the student (but not so close as to threaten the student). Maintaining an erect posture and facing the student communicates your attention and involvement in the conversation. A third area is matching your facial expressions with the content and tone of your statements (e.g., not smiling when making serious statements).

Obtaining Appropriate Behavior

Assertiveness requires that the teacher not be diverted from insisting on appropriate behavior. Students may engage in diversionary tactics in several ways: by denying involvement, by arguing, and by blaming others (including the teacher). When dealing with such tactics, remember: There are many reasons, but no excuses, for misbehavior. Although it is possible that others contributed to the problem, the student needs to accept responsibility for his or her own behavior. It is important to listen carefully to and understand the student's point of view, but in the end, if the student's behavior is interfering with your ability to teach, the behavior must change. Thus, if a student begins to argue or to deny responsibility for the behavior, avoid being sidetracked; the bottom line is that the student's behavior is not acceptable, whatever the reason for it.

Being an assertive teacher means that you let students know your concerns and wants in a manner that gets their attention and communicates your intent to carry through with consequences and to deal with the situation until it is resolved. It is not necessary that you lose your sense of humor or treat students impolitely. A little humor can reduce tension, and treating students with courtesy models the kind of behavior you expect of them. Developing a level of assertiveness that is comfortable for you and understanding how your behavior is perceived by others are important; working through the activities at the end of the chapter will help.

EMPATHIC RESPONDING

Another important communication skill is the ability to respond empathically to students. This skill shows you are aware and accepting of the student's perspective, as well as willing to seek clarification of it when necessary. Empathic responding helps keep the lines of communication open between you and your students so that problems can be understood and resolved in mutually acceptable ways. Such skills are especially appropriate when a student seems excessively concerned, under stress, or otherwise upset. As a teacher, you need to be able to respond in a manner that helps students deal constructively with those emotions or at least avoids further discomfort or distress. Empathic responding can also be used as a part of the problem-solving process when dealing with students who must change their behavior. In such situations, students may be resistant and express negative feelings; the teacher's empathic response can then help defuse these reactions and increase acceptance of a plan for change.

Empathic responding complements constructive assertiveness. Whereas assertiveness allows teachers to express their wants, empathic responding solicits and affirms the student's viewpoint. The use of empathic responding skills does not imply that misbehaving students are entitled to "do their thing" without regard for others; rather, the purpose is to understand and take into account the student's views to reach a satisfactory solution. If the teacher shows some openness toward the student's perspective, there is a better chance that the student will make a commitment to change. Conversely, a teacher who shows no interest in the student's feelings is more likely to encounter defiant behavior and an unwillingness to cooperate or to accept responsibility.

Compare the following two episodes.

Episode A

STUDENT: I'm not staying. You can't make me.

TEACHER: You'll have to stay after school. You haven't completed your work.

STUDENT: No, I can't stay.

TEACHER: That's life. If you don't serve your time now, it's doubled. That's the rule.

STUDENT: (Angry) I'm leaving.

TEACHER: You'd better not.

STUDENT: I'm going! (Student leaves.)

In the above episode, the teacher's response does nothing to resolve the situation. It's likely that the student is aware of the consequences of skipping detention, so the argument only provokes a confrontation, which the student wins, at least temporarily, by leaving.

Another way to handle the situation is illustrated below.

Episode B

STUDENT: I'm not staying. You can't make me.
TEACHER: It's true, I can't. It's up to you.
STUDENT: I can't stay.
TEACHER: Staying after school is a problem for you?
STUDENT: I have to be at home right away.
TEACHER: So it would be a problem for you to get home late.
STUDENT: Right, we're going somewhere after school today.
TEACHER: That's a difficult situation. Would you like to talk about what you could do?
STUDENT: Okay.

In Episode B, the teacher avoids arguing with the student and instead acknowledges the student's concern and invites further discussion. The student responds to the teacher's approach by stating his or her concern more explicitly. Notice that the teacher's role in this conference is that of listener or helper rather than opponent. Notice, too, that the teacher does not offer to solve the student's problem by dropping the detention penalty. Instead, the student is led to consider what options are available. Of course, there is no guarantee that the situation will be resolved to everyone's satisfaction. But the approach at least offers the possibility of resolution, and it avoids the confrontation that occurred in Episode A. Further, it maintains the student's responsibility for dealing with the situation rather than giving the student yet another excuse for avoiding responsibility.

Empathic responding has several advantages. It provides the teacher a means of dealing with strong student emotions without taking responsibility for solving the student's problems. At the same time, the strategy helps defuse emotionally charged situations. Often, intense feelings are transient and will persist only when fed by an intense response. By not reciprocating with similar emotional intensity, the teacher avoids fueling the fire. Also, the calm, empathic teacher serves as a good model for constructive problem solving.

Empathic responding has two components: listening skills and processing skills.

Listening Skills

Listening skills acknowledge or accept the student's expression of feeling or ideas. At a minimal level, the listener merely indicates attention. Sometimes, an interested look will encourage the student to continue speaking. Other examples of nonverbal listening behaviors are nodding, making eye contact with the speaker, and other body language that communicates openness to discussion. Verbal encouragement is indicated by utterances such as "Um hm," "I see," "Go on," "That's interesting," and the like. At other times, a little more encouragement may be needed. A child who expresses feelings of rejection or discouragement and who needs reassurance may respond to a friendly touch, a pat on the shoulder, or a hug. Beyond this level of response, the teacher can invite more discussion with statements such as, "Tell me more," "I'm interested in hearing your ideas about this," "Would you care to comment?" "What do you think?," and "You've listened to my opinion. I'd like to listen to yours."

Processing Skills

Processing skills allow you to confirm or clarify your perception of the student's message. Consider the following interchanges and identify the one that would be most likely to lead to further discussion:

STUDENT:	I can't do this assignment.
TEACHER (A):	You're having difficulty?
TEACHER (B):	Come on, try harder—you'll get it done.
STUDENT:	(Tearful) I hate Angela. She's not my friend any more.
TEACHER (A):	It's upsetting to lose a friend.
TEACHER (B):	Don't be silly. She's your best friend. Just tell her you're sorry.

In these interchanges, the A responses are more accepting of the student's feeling, whereas the B responses ignore the student's emotional tone and tend to block further communication. The B comments are judgmental and suggest a solution without obtaining enough information about the situation and without giving the students the opportunity to deal with their own problems.

To process student comments, you can repeat or summarize what the student says. If the student has given multiple messages or a confusing array of statements, select what seems to be most important and paraphrase it. This paraphrase can simply be stated back, or you can "reflect" or "bounce back" the paraphrase as a question. Whichever you do, the student usually will either acknowledge the correctness of your perception or else offer clarification or elaboration. Consider the following interchange from a short afterschool conference:

STUDENT:	I hate this place. School is stupid!
TEACHER:	Would you like to talk about it?
STUDENT:	I just don't like it here.
TEACHER:	There's something about school that bothers you.
STUDENT:	(Crying) Yes. Sean and Billy laugh at me.
TEACHER:	(Puts arm around student) You feel sad because they're making fun of you?
STUDENT:	Yes.
TEACHER:	Can you tell me about that?
STUDENT:	They call me stupid and dummy.
TEACHER:	It hurts a lot to be called those names. Are you worried that they really think that about you?

STUDENT:	No. I'm not dumb.
TEACHER:	You're not, and I'm glad you don't think so. I don't think so either. Would you like to talk about what to do when someone calls you a name or makes fun of you?

In this example, the teacher uses a variety of responses with an unhappy student and progresses to the point where the student can express, at least partially, some of the basis for the feelings. The teacher can then offer to help the student learn how to deal with the problem. Although it is not realistic to expect that major problems will usually be resolved via a single empathic interchange with a teacher, it is not unusual for the sharp edge of negative emotions to be blunted and for the conversation to end on a positive note. At the least, the student will know that an adult cares enough to listen, and the teacher will be in a better position to guide the student in the future.

The skills of empathic responding—both listening and processing—have been presented in the context of interactions with an individual student, but they are also helpful when problems arise in group settings. In particular, using these tactics helps prevent teachers from responding defensively when students react emotionally or express a problem during class. They also "buy time" for the teacher to consider alternatives for dealing with a problem. In addition, listening and processing skills are useful for leading group discussions.

Although empathic responding skills are very helpful in some situations, they are not intended as the primary means of dealing with students who are acting out, breaking class rules, or interfering with other students. Such misbehavior needs to be dealt with using approaches discussed in Chapters 6 and 8 and in the other sections of this chapter. However, listening and processing can be used to support these other measures.

Another limitation in the use of these skills is that of finding the right time and place to use them. It would be awkward, to say the least, to respond empathically to every expression of emotion or opinion during class activities. Such reactivity would cause slowdowns and would undermine your students' attention to lessons. How frequently and in which circumstances you choose to use these skills will depend on a variety of factors, including opportunities, your goals and values, and how competent you feel. At the least, you should develop your skills so you are able to respond empathically in situations where the use of the skills would be helpful. Doing so effectively requires practice and observation, and working through the activities at the end of the chapter will help.

PROBLEM SOLVING

Problem solving is a process that is used to deal with and to resolve conflicts. Conflicts arise between teachers and students because different roles give rise to different needs and because individuals have different goals and interests. In a crowded classroom, diverse paths can cross, and individuals can find themselves at odds with one another. If conflict arises, teachers need a way to manage it constructively so that teaching and learning can continue in a supportive classroom climate. An effective means of accomplishing this is the problem-solving process in which the teacher works with the student to develop a plan to reduce or eliminate the problem. Steps in the problem-solving process include (1) identifying the problem, (2) discussing alternative solutions, and (3) obtaining a commitment to try one of them. Depending on circumstances, problem solving may also include attempts to identify the causes of the problem and may specify the consequences of following or not following the plan. Because it generally requires more than a brief intervention, problem solving is usually conducted during a conference with the students it concerns. Often, the skills of constructive assertiveness and empathic responding are helpful in reaching a workable agreement for solving the problem.

Problem-solving conferences are usually reserved for chronic situations that have not yielded to simpler remedies. Action needs to be taken to stop the behavior because allowing it to continue would interfere with your ability to teach, with other students' opportunities to learn, or with the student's long-term functioning in your class or school. Consider the following examples:

1. Brad likes to be the center of attention. Whenever you ask a question, he calls out the answer without raising his hand and with no regard for the fact that you have already called on another student. Although you have reminded him of correct behavior and have tried to ignore his call-outs, the behavior continues to interfere with your class discussions.

2. Alice and Alicia never seem to clean up materials, supplies, or their work areas when they have finished a project or assignment. They resent your reminders and insistence that they observe class procedures, but unless you monitor them closely, they avoid all responsibilities. Lately, they have been arguing and complaining whenever they are asked to complete a task. Their foot-dragging seemed trivial at first, but it has become a constant source of irritation.

3. Terrence has skipped his last three arithmetic assignments, even though you allowed ample time in class to work on them. He seems to have a lackadaisical attitude about academic work, and he uses his time in class for goofing off whenever he can get away with it. Twice last week, he was kept in from recess to work on his missing assignments, but he did not finish them, and he resented the loss of his midmorning break. During the previous grading period, he had several unsatisfactory grades on his report card, and skipping assignments is sure to prevent his making satisfactory progress in learning arithmetic skills.

Each of the above examples illustrates a situation that has reached a stage at which a problem-solving conference might be useful. In each case, routine interventions have not changed the student's behavior; in each case, more of the same teacher response is likely to result in a continuing power struggle or in a deterioration in the student's ability to behave constructively.

What is evident in the three examples is that the students are not accepting responsibility for their behavior. It may be that what is needed is a stronger consequence (i.e., a penalty) that is clearly tied to the misbehavior. In fact, this strategy can be an alternative discussed with the student during a problem-solving conference. But until the student makes a commitment to change the offending behavior, the use of punishment will probably be perceived as coercive and controlling rather than as a natural consequence of the behavior and thus may do little or no good. It also appears that the basis of the problem in each of the three examples is not totally clear. Why won't Brad wait his turn? Why can't Alicia and Alice follow simple clean-up procedures? Is Terrence having difficulty understanding the content, or is some external problem the source of his reluctance to do his work? Giving the students a chance to discuss their situations might provide insights that would lead to better solutions. It would also permit the teacher and students to become more aware of each other's perceptions and possibly prevent the development of additional problems.

Steps in a problem-solving conference are described below.

STEP 1: *Identifying the problem.* You can begin the discussion by stating the purpose of the meeting and asking the student to express his or her viewpoint. Obtaining the student's views will give you useful information for later steps, and it will also enable you to gauge the student's degree of cooperation and understanding of the situation. An alternative opening is to describe the problem yourself and ask the student for a reaction; this alternative is especially needed when dealing with young children, with students having limited verbal skills, and with evasive and dissembling students. Unless the student's attitude is cooperative, you will need to be assertive in expressing your concerns. As explained earlier, this can be done by describing, without labeling, the behavior of concern and the problem it is causing. You may also need to stress that the problem will not be allowed to continue and that something must be done to solve it.

Glasser (1975) recommends asking students to evaluate whether their behavior is helping or hurting them or has good or bad effects. The logic is that a student who understands and admits that a behavior has negative consequences will be more likely to participate in the search for and commitment to a solution. A student who denies responsibility or who sees no harmful effects seldom makes a meaningful commitment to change. It may be helpful to ask such a student what might happen if the behavior continues.

During this initial phase of the conference, students may react defensively or emotionally, and they may try to avoid responsibility by blaming others, arguing, citing extenuating circumstances, and so forth. When such behavior occurs, you must decide if the student's reactions are primarily for the purpose of evading responsibility or if they have some validity. If the latter is the case, then you can use listening and processing skills to respond. This communicates willingness to hear the student's point of view and may increase subsequent cooperation. By modeling such desirable behavior, you encourage its use by the student. A disadvantage of using empathic responding during this phase of problem solving is that the student's excuses, arguments, and extenuating circumstances may simply be a means of avoiding responsibility. Because you do not want to get sidetracked from the issue that brought the student to the conference in the first place, be sure to return the focus to the main problem once student concerns have been expressed. When the problem has been identified and agreed on, the conference can move to the next step.

STEP 2: *Selecting a solution.* One way to begin this phase is to invite the student to suggest a solution to the problem. If the student is unable to do so, then you can offer one. Whenever possible, it is best to have two or more alternatives so that options can be compared and the most desirable one chosen. Frequently, the student's solution will be stated negatively, focusing on simply ending an undesirable behavior. Although this is a step in the right direction, it is best to include a positive focus as well by suggesting a plan for increasing desirable behavior. Thus, you should be ready to work with the student's ideas and also to suggest modifications.

If you are the one who suggests a solution, seek the student's reaction to check whether the plan is understood and accepted. Also, evaluate the plan's appropriateness: Is it realistic? Will it significantly reduce the problem? Does it call for changes in other students or in the classroom environment, and are such changes feasible? Can it be evaluated readily? Occasionally, a student may try to avoid responsibility by proposing a solution that places the burden for change on the teacher or on other students; for example, to design more interesting lessons or to get other students to "leave me alone." Consider such changes to the extent they are appropriate and reasonable but don't allow a student to shift responsibility to others—unless, of course, that is where responsibility for the problem lies. A reasonable response is, "Yes, such changes would help, but what will you contribute?" Once a mutually agreeable solution is reached, you are ready for the third step.

STEP 3: *Obtaining a commitment.* In this step, the teacher asks the student to accept the solution and try it for a specified period, usually with the understanding that it will be evaluated afterward. The student's commitment can be given orally or in written form, as in a "contract." Sometimes, contracts are printed with an official-looking border, seal, and script, with space for student and teacher signatures and for listing contract terms and consequences if the plan is or is not followed.

Whether consequences are specified in case the plan is not followed will depend on the severity of the problem and whether it is a first conference or a follow-up for a broken contract. Some teachers like to give students a chance to correct their behavior without resorting to penalties, the rationale being that long-range cooperation is better when the teacher uses the least controlling or coercive approach. However, if the student is not making a reasonable effort to comply with the plan, or if the misbehavior is dangerous or too disruptive to be allowed to continue, spelling out the consequences may be needed to get the student's attention and to communicate the seriousness of the situation: "You will need to choose between following our agreement or discussing your behavior with our principal, Mrs. Steele, and your parents."

If the plan fails to solve the problem, you'll either need to follow through with whatever consequence was stipulated, or else you'll need to work with the student to alter the plan to produce a more workable solution. A major consideration is how much time and energy you can or should devote to pursuing the plan versus using a referral, a detention, or some other consequence available in your school. You might also consult with a counselor, an assistant principal, or another teacher before taking further action to get another perspective on the problem.

When problem-solving conferences fail to make progress (e.g., the student does not make a sincere commitment to a plan or simply does not cooperate), the teacher should evaluate his or her assertiveness and empathic responding skills before concluding that the problem-solving approach does not work with that student. Poor assertiveness skills—hostile, critical, or attacking behaviors—and their opposites—timid, tentative responding—will interfere with the problem-solving process. An excessively assertive, hostile style reflects a reliance on the teacher's power and cuts off communication. An unassertive, timid style abdicates authority and is easily ignored; the teacher is not seen as credible, and students simply will not believe that he or she will insist on correct behavior or will follow through with consequences. A constructively assertive teacher, however, captures the students' attention and communicates seriousness of intent in changing the situation. Empathic responding communicates a willingness to listen to the student's point of view and permits the teacher to clarify and react to a student's statements without closing off further discussion. Such skills are especially needed during problem-solving discussions because they allow the teacher to deal constructively with defensive student behavior. They also help to clarify solutions as they are discussed and improve the chances of obtaining a sincere commitment to change.

When you use these skills, be patient and give them a chance to work. Often, teachers use a problem-solving approach after a situation has become chronic or for behavior that has been established over a long time. In such cases, you cannot expect miracles; change may occur only gradually and imperfectly. However, problem-solving conferences can be helpful in many cases and should be a component of your set of management and discipline skills.

Examples of problem-solving conferences are presented in Case Studies 7–1, 7–2, and 7–3. In addition, exercises on problem solving are presented in activities at the end of the chapter.

A NOTE ON TALKING WITH PARENTS

As we have already mentioned, constructive assertiveness, empathic responding, and problem solving can be useful strategies in your interactions with students. They can also be effective in working with parents. Think about the following suggestions in your interactions with parents or when holding parent conferences.

- ◆ Approach parents as team members. Both you and the parents want what's best for the child; the point of a conference is to find ways to work together.

- ◆ Parents who had difficulty in school themselves may be intimidated by schools and teachers. This may come across as avoidance, anger, or defensiveness. Be respectful, open, and nonthreatening.

- ◆ Respect parents' knowledge of their children.

- ◆ Show your appreciation for parents' efforts to rearrange work schedules to meet with you. Use the time wisely by being prepared and organized.

- ◆ Stick to descriptions of behavior rather than characterizations of students (e.g., "Abigail calls other children names," rather than "Abigail is mean.")

- ◆ Whenever possible, document your concerns. For example, if you feel a student's work is sloppy, have samples available to show parents. If the student isn't turning in assignments, give them the assignment sheet with due dates.

For more information on working with parents, see readings at the end of this chapter.

FURTHER READING

Berger, E. H. (1995). *Parents as partners in education: Families and schools working together* (4th ed.), Englewood Cliffs, NJ: Merrill/Prentice-Hall.

> *This is a useful handbook for understanding important aspects of home–school relations. It provides a comprehensive look at parent–school partnerships and offers practical suggestions to aid collaboration between teachers and parents. It includes topics such as diverse families, the exceptional child, programs to enrich parent–school involvement, and communication necessary for partnerships.*

Miller, P. W. (1981). Silent messages. *Childhood Education, 58* (1), 20–24.

> *The author contends that if students and teachers are to communicate effectively in today's schools, they must possess the ability to send and receive verbal and nonverbal messages accurately. The article discusses six forms of nonverbal communication such as intonation, expression, eye contact, touch, dress, and spatial distance.*

Puro, P., & Bloome, D. (1987). Understanding classroom communication. *Theory into Practice, 26* (1), 26–31.

> *Teacher and student classroom communication occurs at explicit and implicit levels. These forms of communication create social contexts for learning both academic content and social processes. These concepts are important to understanding how meanings are created in classroom settings.*

Woolfolk, A. E., & Galloway, C. M. (1985). Nonverbal communication and the study of teaching. *Theory into Practice, 24* (1), 77–84.

> *The authors consider how nonverbal behaviors affect communication processes in classrooms. Reciprocal influences between teachers and students shape the patterns of interaction and the nature of classroom behavior.*

SUGGESTED ACTIVITIES

ACTIVITY 7-1: DEVELOPING ASSERTIVENESS SKILLS

The purpose of this activity is to provide situations for practicing assertiveness skills. For each situation described below, prepare an assertive response. Use the following sequence of steps with each situation until you are comfortable with the approach. Then, combine the steps so you have the experience of responding to situations.

STEP 1: Write out a statement that describes the problem clearly or that insists your rights be respected. Compare and discuss your statements with other participants. Revise your statement if you wish.

STEP 2: Use role playing to portray the situation, with you as teacher and someone else as the student. During the role play, try to use appropriate body language (including eye contact and facial expression) to support your intervention.

STEP 3: Get feedback from observers regarding your use of assertiveness skills. Use the Assertiveness Scales to assess your own behavior, and check out your perceptions by comparing your self-ratings to those of observers. Be sure to discuss any discrepancies and any problems you experienced enacting an assertive role. Repeat Step 2 until you feel comfortable with your handling of the situation.

It is not necessary to continue the role play to a complete resolution of the situation. The purpose is only to provide experience in enacting assertive behaviors. The person playing the student role should respond as naturally as possible.

◆ *Situation A.* Scott has been sliding by lately, doing the minimum and barely passing. At the end of class today, he asks you if it would be all right to turn in his project a few days late. He knows that you have already given similar permission to two other students who had difficulty obtaining needed materials.

◆ *Situation B.* Alyson and Maria are supposed to put the equipment away, but they have left much of it strewn about the gym. Now, they are heading for the door in anticipation of the end-of-recess bell.

◆ *Situation C.* Victor has not been working on his assignment. You caught his eye but he looked away, and he has continued to talk to nearby students. As you move around the room checking other students' progress, he begins to make a paper airplane.

◆ *Situation D.* As you walk down the hallway, you hear two students trading insults ("Your mama! . . ."). The students are not angry yet, just fooling around, but several other students are gathering, and you think they may encourage the two students to fight.

◆ *Situation E.* As you begin class, you observe Daphne eating a Twinkie, in violation of the rule prohibiting food in the room. When she sees that you notice her, she stuffs the Twinkie into her mouth and gets another one out of the package.

◆ *Situation F.* During your current events discussion, Susan and Kris trade notes and laugh noisily. You sense that other students' attention is being captured by the duo's antics, and you begin to be annoyed by having to compete for class attention.

◆ *Situation G.* When you were absent yesterday, your fourth-grade class gave the substitute teacher a difficult time; according to the note she left for you (with a copy sent to the principal!), many students refused to work at all, four or five students left for the bathroom and didn't return until lunchtime, and a paper and spitwad fight raged most of the afternoon. As the morning bell rings, you enter the room to greet your class.

ACTIVITY 7-2: RECOGNIZING LISTENING RESPONSES

Each of the following dialogues depicts a statement and a variety of teacher responses. In each case, decide which one is closest to a listening response; i.e., invites further discussion or best reflects the idea or feeling. Check your accuracy against the key in the Appendix.

1. *Student:* School stinks.

   a. Don't use that type of language.
   b. You seem upset about school.
   c. Come on, things aren't that bad.
   d. That attitude will get you nowhere.

2. *Student:* I can't understand fractions. Why do we have to learn this stuff?

   a. You'll need it to get into college.
   b. Just keep at it. It'll make sense after a while.
   c. Something isn't making sense to you?
   d. Would you like to come in for extra help after school?

3. *Student:* I don't want to sit near those boys any more.

   a. Sorry, but seats have been assigned.
   b. If they're bothering you, I can move you.
   c. Can you handle this on your own?
   d. What is the situation?

4. *Parent:* My child is very upset and needs more help or she won't be able to pass. She says she doesn't understand anything.

   a. Please go on. I'd like to hear more about this.
   b. She needs to pay closer attention in class.
   c. She's very anxious, but actually she'll do just fine. She only needs to review more before tests.
   d. Most students find my explanations to be quite clear. Perhaps she isn't listening.

5. *Teacher next door:* My class is going to drive me up a wall. They have been impossible lately!

   a. Have you ever considered being more assertive with them?
   b. I know, everyone in this wing can hear them.
   c. They are really a handful!
   d. You think they're bad, you should have my group.

ACTIVITY 7-3: PRODUCING EMPATHIC RESPONSES

You will need to work with a colleague during this activity. Take turns role playing the student and the teacher. The person role playing the teacher should practice empathic responding skills, and the student should try to behave as naturally as possible. Note that it is assumed that the dialogue is occurring at a time and place that permits this type of interchange and that the teacher is interested in allowing the student to describe the problem. These assumptions will not always be true, of course—you could not deal with these issues in the middle of reading groups, for example, nor will you always have the time to deal in this way with every student problem. In this exercise, you should avoid giving solutions for the student's problem; instead, concentrate on using listening and processing skills to encourage the student to talk about the situation and think through the problem.

   ◆ *Situation A.* Monica is an average student with poor writing skills. With tears in her eyes, she approaches you after class with an assignment you have given an unsatisfactory grade. "I thought that I did okay on this."

   ◆ *Situation B.* David, a bright student, offers you some advice: "This class would be a lot more interesting if we didn't have to do all these worksheets. Couldn't we choose our own work sometime?"

   ◆ *Situation C.* While the rest of the class is at work on an assignment, Barry closes his book, throws away his assignment sheet, and slinks down in his seat disgustedly.

◆ *Situation D.* For the second time this week, SueAnn has not turned in an assignment. Last week, she "forgot" to bring her homework twice. Later, you remind SueAnn that assignments are important. "I don't care," she responds.

◆ *Situation E.* Armand, a new student, has been having trouble making friends. Lately, he has been getting into arguments with some of the more popular boys, and he has been teasing a few girls, apparently to gain attention. However, he has not succeeded in breaking into the social scene. After class one day he says to you, "I wish I could go back to my old school."

ACTIVITY 7-4: PROBLEM-SOLVING EXERCISES

Use role playing to practice the problem-solving steps (identify the problem and its consequences, identify and select a solution, obtain a commitment to try it out) with the situations described below. In those situations in which the student is mainly experiencing the problem, assume that the teacher's initial listening response is received positively by the student so there is a basis for continuing the discussion and for the teacher to assist the student in thinking through a solution. In cases in which the student's behavior is affecting the teacher's ability to teach or interfering with other students' rights, the student may initially be reluctant to participate in this type of discussion, and the teacher will need to use assertiveness skills to overcome this resistance. In addition to the situations listed below, you can also use some of the situations presented in Activities 7–1 and 7–3 for additional practice.

◆ *Situation A.* Bob and Ray are noisy and distracting when they clown around and vie for other students' attention. Reminders and penalties have only fleeting effects on their behavior. Therefore, you decide to have them come in for a conference.

◆ *Situation B.* David is good-natured as long as no demands are placed on him. However, when reminded that class time is for learning and for working on assignments, he becomes defiant and insists that it is his right to do whatever he wishes, as long as he "don't hurt no one."

◆ *Situation C.* Lucy is a bright student but often turns in work late; frequently it is incomplete. She is able to pass your tests, however, and she could easily be a top student if she were prompt and better organized. Recently, you sent her parents a progress report because of missing assignments, and Lucy and her mother have come in for a conference to discuss the situation. Her mother wonders whether you will allow Lucy to make up the missing work to avoid making failing grades.

ACTIVITY 7–5: DIALOGUE ANALYSIS

Discuss the following three vignettes. To what extent did the teachers use the problem-solving steps as well as constructive assertiveness and empathic responding? Were they appropriately used? What other approaches might the teachers have tried for dealing with these problems? What are their advantages and disadvantages?

VIGNETTES

The three examples illustrate the use of a problem-solving conference for the three problem situations described earlier in this chapter.

DIALOGUE 7-1: BRAD

TEACHER: Brad, I asked you to stay to talk with me because of a problem we've been having during discussions. Often, when I ask a question, you call out the answer without waiting to be called on. Do you agree that this is happening?

BRAD: I guess so.

TEACHER: Can you tell me why this is a problem?

BRAD: I suppose it doesn't give others a chance.

TEACHER: That's absolutely right. I have to be able to find out whether other boys and girls understand what we are discussing.

BRAD: What if they don't know?

TEACHER: You mean, if nobody raises a hand or tries to answer?

BRAD: Yeah, then can I answer?

TEACHER: Do you suppose that some people might need more time to think about what they are going to say?

BRAD: I guess so. But it's boring to just sit and wait for someone to think if I already know it.

TEACHER: It is difficult to wait and be patient. But I must be able to teach the whole class and to conduct the discussions for everybody. Can you think of any way that we could handle this so that I can call on others when I want to and you can still have your fair turn?

BRAD: I suppose I could raise my hand.

TEACHER: That would be a big help. I would really appreciate that. I think you have some good ideas and should have plenty of chances to answer. Brad, how often would you like to speak during our discussions?

BRAD: I don't know. (*Pauses.*) Three or four times, I guess.

TEACHER: That would be fine. How about if I guarantee you four times during each discussion? You keep track of the times you answer, and I'll call on you when your hand is raised. If I don't call on you sometime, you know you'll get your chances later.

BRAD: Okay.

TEACHER: How about our trying this for the rest of the week, and then we'll talk again and see if it solves our problem?

BRAD: Okay.

DIALOGUE 7-2: ALICE AND ALICIA

TEACHER: Girls, I asked you to stay for this conference because I've been having to take more and more of my time to get you to clean up and to keep work areas neat. I wonder what you both think about this problem.

ALICE: I don't know.

ALICIA: I don't think we're so bad about it.

TEACHER: It has become very frustrating to me. Do you remember that I had to remind you and wait for the jobs to be done?

GIRLS: Yes.

TEACHER: Whose job is it to pick up materials and put things away?

GIRLS: Ours.

TEACHER: Do you think we can find a way for those jobs to get done? (*Girls nod affirmatively.*) Do you have any suggestions?

ALICIA: I could just do it without being asked.

TEACHER: Okay. That is a good idea. Do you have any other suggestions?

ALICE: We could ask someone to help us.

TEACHER: That is an interesting idea. Do you know someone who wants to clean up your things?

ALICE: I don't know. Probably.

TEACHER: Would you like to help someone else clean up or put things away?

ALICIA: Sure, it'd be fun.

TEACHER: How about you, Alice?

ALICE: Okay.

TEACHER: Well, then I have an idea. How about if I let you both be my room helpers this next week. As soon as you finish your own cleanup then you can help me with jobs that I need to have done. How would that be?

GIRLS: Yeah!

TEACHER: Okay. Let's try this out. Tomorrow, when you have cleaned up, let me know. Then I'll tell you what you can do to help me. How does that sound?

GIRLS:	Sure! Okay.
TEACHER:	I'm glad we had a chance to plan this, because now I have two room helpers and we will have our problem solved.

DIALOGUE 7-3: TERRENCE

TEACHER:	I have noticed that you did not turn in the last three arithmetic assignments. What seems to be the matter?
STUDENT:	That work is too hard!
TEACHER:	You weren't able to do the work.
STUDENT:	No. I can't do it.
TEACHER:	When I was going around the room during seatwork, I noticed that you were able to do some of the problems, but then you stopped working.
STUDENT:	That's 'cause I couldn't do them any more!
TEACHER:	I see. That's pretty frustrating. Do you know, that happens to other people, too. (*Student shrugs.*) Even teachers. Did you know that even teachers sometimes don't know what to do next?
STUDENT:	No.
TEACHER:	Even me. (*Student smiles.*) Do you know what I do when I can't figure out how to do something?
STUDENT:	You ask somebody?
TEACHER:	Right! Does that give you any ideas about what to do when you don't know what to do?
STUDENT:	Ask somebody.
TEACHER:	Sure. If you get stuck, then ask. Do you know who you can ask?
STUDENT:	You.
TEACHER:	That's right. And you can also ask anyone at your table if I am busy and you need help right away.
STUDENT:	Okay.
TEACHER:	Did you finish your arithmetic problems today?
STUDENT:	No. I need some help.
TEACHER:	Why don't you get your paper from your desk and let's see what the problem is. . . .

ASSERTIVENESS ASSESSMENT SCALES

When using the following scales, note that a midrange rating represents an appropriate degree of assertiveness. When rating your own or another teacher's behavior as either nonassertive or hostile, circle the descriptive term that best reflects the basis for your judgment or write a note on the scale if the descriptors don't adequately capture your perception.

	Nonassertive	Assertive	Hostile
	1 _____ 2 _____ 3 _____ 4 _____ 5		
Eye contact	Teacher avoids looking at the student.	Teacher maintains eye contact with student.	Teacher glares at student; stares student down.
	1 _____ 2 _____ 3 _____ 4 _____ 5		
Body language	Teacher turns away, gestures nervously, trembles.	Teacher faces student; alert posture but not threatening. Gestures support statements.	Teacher crowds student, points, shakes fist threateningly.
	1 _____ 2 _____ 3 _____ 4 _____ 5		
Message	Obsequious, self-denigrating; excuses student behavior; pleads with student.	Clearly states the problem or insists that the behavior stop. Makes own feelings known, may use humor to relieve tension.	Name calling, labeling, blaming, threatening, being sarcastic, preaching, lecturing.
	1 _____ 2 _____ 3 _____ 4 _____ 5		
Voice features	Tremulous, whiny, hesitant, broken, or too soft.	Appropriate volume, natural sounding, varied for emphasis	Voice too loud; shouts, yells.
	1 _____ 2 _____ 3 _____ 4 _____ 5		
Facial features	Smiles inappropriately; nervous twitches and tics.	Expression suits message.	Excessive affect; contorted, disgusted, enraged expression.

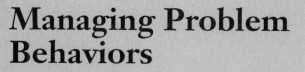

Managing Problem Behaviors

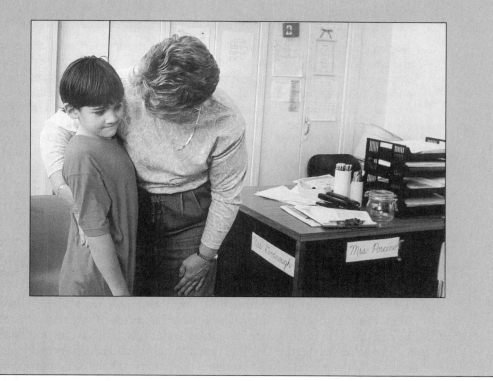

In this chapter, we describe a series of strategies for dealing with problem behaviors you may encounter in your classroom. Although previous chapters described preventive measures as well as tactics that can be used to manage inappropriate behavior, it will be helpful to consider the full range of approaches that can be used. We hope that you will not encounter problems, especially serious ones, in large numbers. But as you work with students, you will undoubtedly face difficult situations that must be resolved to preserve the climate for learning or to assist a student in developing behaviors more compatible with group life and learning.

The aim of this chapter is to pull together and organize a wide array of possible strategies from which you can select. By having a broad array of approaches to draw on, you will be better able to choose one that fits specific conditions. Having some alternatives in mind is very useful too, in case your first plan doesn't work.

FOR REFLECTION

Teachers' reactions to problem behaviors such as those described in this chapter are often affected by the adult models they observed and the type of discipline they received as children, both at home and at school. Recall your early experiences in this area and consider their implications. To what extent do these earlier models provide a positive guide for managing problems of varying severity? Would the strategies that were effective for you be equally appropriate or effective for the varied kinds of students you may teach? Where do you need to add to or modify your approach? ■

We hope this chapter's concern with behavior problems will not be taken as a grim comment on the teacher's role. In particular, the extensive list of strategies in this chapter should be considered within the context of the other chapters in this book. We have advocated generally a positive, supportive climate with heavy reliance on preventive measures. Within that framework, however, we must be ready to deal with problems when they arise. With a variety of strategies at hand, we can tailor our approach to fit the situation, keeping interruptions to the instructional program to a minimum and at the same time promoting positive student behavior.

This chapter's focus is on problem behaviors rather than problem students. Only a small percentage of students exhibit maladaptive behaviors with such consistency and to such a degree that they warrant being labeled emotionally disturbed or behaviorally disordered. Most students do, however, behave inappropriately on occasion; we think it is much more constructive in the long run to deal with the student's behaviors and help students learn how to behave rather than impute internal causes for the behavior and assume the student is restricted in the capacity to make good choices.

On occasion, problem behaviors result from stressors (e.g., abuse, a death in the family, parental unemployment, serious illness, or divorce) the student is experiencing at home or elsewhere. If a student's behavior changes, or if inappropriate behavior persists after reasonable attempts to deal with it have been made, a discussion of the situation with a school counselor, social worker, parent, or guardian is in order. Sometimes the student's previous teacher might provide additional information. When you talk with the child about what is happening, use listening skills (see Chapter 7) to try to understand the situation. Be empathic but help the child understand that acting out will not help the problem. By all means, follow up if you discover that a situation outside the classroom is affecting the child's behavior.

WHAT IS PROBLEM BEHAVIOR?

The concept of problem behavior is broad. Rather than enumerate all the possible misbehaviors that might occur in classrooms, it is more manageable to think of categories.

Nonproblem

Brief inattention, some talk during a transition between activities, small periods of woolgathering, and a short pause while working on an assignment are examples of common behaviors that are not really problems for anyone because they are of brief duration and don't interfere with learning or instruction. Everyone is the better for their being ignored. To attempt to react to them would consume too much energy, interrupt lessons constantly, and detract from a positive classroom climate.

Minor Problem

This includes those behaviors that run counter to class procedures or rules but that do not, when occurring infrequently, disrupt class activities or seriously interfere with student learning. Examples are students calling out or leaving seats without permission, reading or doing unrelated work during class time, passing notes, eating candy, scattering trash around, and excessive social talk during independent work or group work. These behaviors are minor irritants as long as they are brief in duration and are limited to one or a few students. We would not give them much thought except for two reasons: Unattended, they might persist and spread; if the behaviors have an audience, not to respond might cause a perception of inconsistency and potentially undermine an important aspect of the overall management system. Moreover, if students engage in such behavior for an extended period of time, their learning is likely to be adversely affected.

Major Problem but Limited in Scope and Effects

This category includes behaviors that disrupt an activity or interfere with learning but whose occurrence is limited to a single student or perhaps to a few students not acting in concert. For example, a student may be chronically off-task. Another student may rarely complete assignments. Or a student may frequently fail to follow class rules for talk or movement around the room or may refuse to do any work. This category also includes a more serious, but isolated, violation of class or school rules; for example, an act of vandalism or hitting another student.

Escalating or Spreading Problem

In this category, we include any minor problem that has become commonplace and thus constitutes a threat to order and the learning environment. For example, many students roaming around the room at will and continually calling out irrelevant comments make content development activities suffer; social talking that continues unabated even when the teacher repeatedly asks for quiet is distracting to others; and talking back and refusal to cooperate with the teacher is frustrating and may lead to a poor classroom climate. Frequent violations of class guidelines for behavior will cause the management and instructional system to break down and interfere with the momentum of class activities.

GOALS FOR MANAGING PROBLEM BEHAVIOR

Several types of goals need to be considered. We need to judge short-term and long-term effects of any management strategy we choose. In the short term, the desired results are that the inappropriate behaviors cease, and the students resume or begin appropriate behaviors. In the long run, it is important to prevent the problem from recurring. At the same time, we must be watchful for potential negative side effects and take steps to minimize them. Effects on the individual student or students causing the problem as well as the effect on the whole class should also be considered.

> Joel is talking and showing off to a group of students during independent work. The teacher could squelch Joel by using a sarcastic put-down or a strong desist but chooses instead to redirect Joel's behavior and stand close by until he is working on the assignment. The put-down or strong desist might get quicker results in the short run, but it may lead to resentment or even conflict if Joel tries a rejoinder. Redirection and proximity control take a little more effort but do not have negative side effects. In addition, they offer more support for appropriate behavior.

The ideal strategy is one that maintains or restores order in the class immediately without adversely affecting the positive learning environment; in addition, an ideal strategy would prevent a repetition of the problem and result in the student or students subsequently behaving appropriately in similar situations. In practice, classrooms are busy places, and we rarely have sufficient time to mull over the various options and their effects whenever a problem arises, especially in the midst of a crisis. If only there were a "pause" button on classroom events! The need for prompt reaction should not, however, deter us from evaluating the results of our efforts and from seeking alternative approaches, especially when our initial efforts do not meet with success. It will, therefore, be useful to have a repertoire of strategies to apply to various problem situations.

MANAGEMENT STRATEGIES

In this section, we present useful strategies for dealing with a variety of classroom behavior problems. The first several strategies can be utilized during instruction without much difficulty, require little teacher time, and have the great virtue of being relatively unobtrusive. Thus, they have much to recommend them because they do not give undue attention to the misbehavior, and they do not interfere with the flow of instructional activity. As we move down the list, we encounter strategies that are more direct attempts to stop the behaviors and to do so quickly; however, the strategies have more negative features: They demand more teacher time, they may have unintended consequences on students, or they interrupt class activities. A general principle that is helpful in selecting a strategy is to use an approach that will be effective in stopping the inappropriate behavior promptly and that has the least negative impact. An implication is that minor problems should usually be dealt with by the use of limited interventions. As problems become more serious, the limited interventions may be ineffective in quickly ending the disruptive behavior and thus a more time-consuming or intrusive intervention may be required.

It should be emphasized that most elementary schools have prescribed procedures to deal with certain types of major problems and sometimes even minor ones. For example, teacher responses to events such as fighting, obscene language, stealing, vandalism, and unexcused absence are likely to be directed by school (or district) policies. Therefore, the beginning teacher must learn what policies are in force and follow them. When no specific policy is established for particular problems or when teachers are given latitude in their response, the alternatives listed later in the chapter will be helpful in guiding teacher action.

It is a given that preventive measures are more desirable than reactive ones. Thus, the contents of earlier chapters have mainly been devoted to setting up the classroom environment to eliminate the need for frequent recourse to major interventions. Notwithstanding such efforts, responsive strategies still will be needed. However, when teachers find themselves frequently using major interventions to deal with minor problems, it is time to reevaluate their expectations and their overall management and instructional plan and make needed modifications. To this end, reviewing suggestions for management presented in prior chapters and perhaps using the checklists to provide focus could result in changes that would help reduce the problems. Teachers should also be sensitive to the possibility that the source of the problem lies in frustration with content that the student does not grasp or with tasks that the student lacks skills to perform. When the problem is one of a poor fit between student capabilities and academic demands, the source must also be addressed by developing more appropriate class activities and assignments or by giving the student more assistance.

If you have a special education student whose behavior is causing a problem, you may find it helpful to discuss the situation with a special education teacher and ask for suggestions. In particular, ask the teacher if the student has a special discipline program as part of an individualized education plan (IEP). Sometimes, such a plan will specify particular ways to respond to the student or give useful alternative strategies. Even if no specific discipline plan is included in the IEP, you may be able to obtain helpful ideas for working with the student.

We have compiled classroom strategies that have a wide range of application, but the list is certainly not exhaustive. Readers interested in additional sources for ways of coping with specific problems may find the book by Stoner, Shinn, and Walker (1991) helpful. Also, suggestions for managing problems that have reached a crisis level are provided in Pitcher and Poland (1992). Many of the recommendations in the latter book are for school-level administrators or school psychologists, but there is much of value to teachers as well.

Minor Interventions

USE NONVERBAL CUES

Make eye contact with the student and give a signal such as a finger to the lips, a head shake, or a hand signal to issue a desist. Sometimes, lightly touching a student on the arm or shoulder will help signal your presence and have a calming effect.

GET THE ACTIVITY MOVING

Often student behavior deteriorates during transition times between activities or during "dead" time when no apparent focus for attention is present. Students leave their seats, talk, shuffle restlessly, and amuse themselves and each other while waiting for something to do. The remedy is obvious: Move through the transition more quickly and reduce or eliminate the dead time. This entails planning activities so that all materials are ready and adhering to a well-conceived lesson plan. Trying to catch and correct inappropriate student behaviors during such times is usually futile and misdirected. Just get the next activity under way and direct students to the desired behaviors.

USE PROXIMITY

Move closer to students. Combine proximity with nonverbal cues to stop inappropriate behavior without interrupting the instruction. Be sure to continue monitoring the students at least until they have begun an appropriate activity.

USE GROUP FOCUS

Use group alerting, accountability, or a higher participation format (see discussion in Chapter 5) to draw students back into a lesson when attention has begun to wane or when students have been in a passive mode for too long and you observe off-task behavior spreading.

REDIRECT THE BEHAVIOR

When students are off-task, remind them of appropriate behavior. "Everyone should be writing answers to the chapter questions," "Be sure your group is discussing your project plan," "Everyone should be seated and quiet unless you have been given permission to leave your seat or talk." If only one or two students are engaged in inappropriate behavior, a private redirection will be less likely to interrupt the activity or to direct attention toward the incorrect behavior. A redirection strategy that works well with younger children is the use of group and individual public praise for appropriate behavior. For example, if several students are talking and inattentive at the beginning of a new activity, the teacher should identify students who are behaving correctly: "I see many students who are sitting quietly ready to begin. . . . I really appreciate the boys and girls who are ready for our next activity. John is listening, Donica is being very quiet. Oh, good, Demetrius, Richard, and Corby are ready. . . ." In most cases, off-task students quickly come around.

PROVIDE NEEDED INSTRUCTION

Especially during individual work or group work, off-task behaviors may reflect poor comprehension of the task. Check student work or ask brief questions to assess understanding; give necessary assistance so students can work independently. If many students can't proceed, stop the activity and provide whole-class instruction. Next time, be sure to check comprehension before starting the independent work activity.

ISSUE A BRIEF DESIST

Tell the student(s) to stop the undesirable behavior. Make direct eye contact and be assertive (see Chapter 7). Keep your comments brief and monitor the situation until the student complies. Combine this strategy with redirection to encourage desirable behavior.

GIVE THE STUDENT A CHOICE

Tell the student that he or she has a choice: either to behave appropriately or to continue the problem behavior and receive a consequence. Be sure to describe the desired behavior. Telling a student to "behave appropriately" does not communicate clearly what the desired behavior should be. For example, suppose a student has refused to clean up properly after completing a project: "You may choose to clean up now; if not, then you are choosing to stay in during recess until your area is clean." To a student who continues to distract nearby students: "You may choose to work quietly on your assignment at your seat, or you will need to sit in the time-out area to do your work." The purpose of stating the consequence as a choice is to emphasize the student's responsibility for his or her behavior. Also, making the consequence clear increases the chance of the student choosing to self-regulate.

Use an "I-Message"

An I-message is a statement that describes the problem and its effects on the teacher, the student, or the class; it may also include a description of the feelings produced by the problem. The formula for an I-message is:

◆ When you (state the problem)

◆ Then (describe the effect)

◆ And it makes me feel (state the emotion).

For example, to a student who constantly calls out comments, the teacher might say, "When you talk without permission, it interrupts the lesson, and I get frustrated and resentful." It isn't necessary, of course, to follow the formula exactly; the main idea is to communicate clearly what the problem is and why it's a problem (e.g., "It's very distracting to me and to others when you wander around the room during seatwork.") The I-message can be combined with a brief desist or with redirection. A rationale for using an I-message is that students often act without much awareness of the effects their behavior has on others, and they will change if they realize they are causing someone a problem. Also, by communicating directly with the student about the effects of the behavior, the teacher implies that the student is capable of controlling the behavior, if only he or she understands its effects.

Moderate Interventions

These strategies are more confrontational than the limited interventions described above and thus have greater potential for eliciting resistance. In cases in which the student's behavior has not become especially disruptive, it is desirable to use a minor intervention or to issue a warning to the student before using these interventions. Doing so will permit the student to exercise self-control and may save the teacher time and effort.

Withhold a Privilege or Desired Activity

Students who abuse a privilege (e.g., being allowed to work together on a project, sitting near friends, or freedom to move around the classroom without permission) can lose the privilege and be required to earn it back with appropriate behavior. Sometimes, teachers allow quiet talking during independent activities, and removing this privilege can be an effective way to limit unproductive social behavior. Other teachers allow a class to choose a favorite activity or a short period of free time on one or more days each week as incentives. Time lost from such activities can then be a strong deterrent to inappropriate behavior at other times. Although withholding a privilege is a form of punishment, it usually has fewer side effects than punishment that requires directly applying an aversive consequence.

ISOLATE OR REMOVE STUDENTS

Students who disrupt an activity can be removed to some other area of the room, away from other students. It is helpful to have a carrel with sides or at least a desk at the back of the room facing away from other students to discourage eye contact from the time-out area. If no suitable place is available, the student may need to have time-out in the hall outside the door, although not if your school has a policy prohibiting this because of the problem of adequately supervising the student.

Time-out is a variation on the preceding consequence in that it takes away the student's privilege of participating in the activity. It is a good idea to allow excluded students to return to the activity in a short time, as long as their behavior in time-out is acceptable. Some teachers prefer to let the student retain some control over the return, using a direction such as, "You may come back to the activity in five minutes if you decide that you can follow our class rules." Other teachers prohibit the student from returning until the activity is completed or until they have a brief conference with the student.

A problem with time-out is that some students may find it rewarding. They receive attention when it is administered, and it allows them to avoid an activity they dislike. When this occurs, you should switch to another strategy. Another problem is that a student may refuse to go to the time-out area. Usually this is a temporary problem; if you are firm, ignoring the student's protests and continuing with the activity, the student will go eventually. One way to move a recalcitrant body is to offer a choice: "You can either take time-out or you take a walk to the principal's office. It's your decision."

Time-out has another risk. Its use clearly identifies a student as someone who is excludable, and it may result in implicit labeling by the teacher, by other students, or by the excluded student. If used frequently with an individual student, it may cause resentment and anger. Therefore, be sure to provide opportunities for the student to resume full participation in the class and use other strategies to promote appropriate behavior at the same time.

USE A PENALTY

Sometimes, a small amount of repetitious work is required as payment for inappropriate behavior. For example, in physical education, students may be required to run an extra lap or do push-ups. In math, students may work extra problems. The advantage of this type of consequence is that it can usually be administered quickly with a minimum of teacher time and effort. A disadvantage is that the task is being defined as punishing, and therefore the student's attitude toward the content may be negatively affected. Another problem with the use of penalties is that their ease of use can lead to overuse, detracting from the overall climate.

ASSIGN DETENTION

Another penalty commonly used is to require that the student serve a detention, either at lunch, during recess, or sometimes before or after school. Because of the logical relation between the problem and the consequence, this penalty is often used for misbehaviors that involve time (e.g., extended goofing off and time wasting; behavior that interferes with instruction or student work time). Other common uses of the penalty are for repeated rule violations and for frequent failure to complete assignments. You may need to supervise the detention in your room, or your school might have a detention hall with an assigned monitor. The time in detention need not be lengthy, especially for misbehaviors that are not severe or frequent; a ten or fifteen minute detention is often sufficient to make the point.

An advantage of detention as a penalty is that it is disliked by most students, and they want to avoid it; at the same time, it is administered away from other students in the class and thus does not give undue attention to the behavior. Also, it is a common punishment, so extensive explanations and unusual procedures aren't needed. Finally, the teacher can sometimes use a little of the detention time to hold a conference with the student and perhaps work out a plan for improving the situation.

A disadvantage of detention is that it does take teacher time, especially when the teacher must supervise it. Even when the school has a D-Hall, the teacher still will need to write a referral. Another disadvantage is that students might be able to avoid detention, at least in the short run, simply by not showing up. Thus, the teacher or the school must have a backup plan, such as doubling the time; moreover, records must be kept and often additional time will be required to deal with such students.

"My mom told me to tell you that I was the educational challenge you were told about in college."

Reprinted by permission of Heiser Zedonek.

USE A SCHOOL-BASED CONSEQUENCE

If your school has a prescribed consequence for particular problem behaviors, and you are allowed some latitude in its administration, you should consider utilizing it after you have not had desired results with other strategies. For example, some schools have a system of referral to the principal, who then deals with the student. Often, a first referral consequence is limited to detention or to a warning, with subsequent referrals resulting in a parent conference. It is necessary to apprise the administrator of the basis for the referral and to discuss what outcome is desirable. An advantage of this approach is that it does not require much teacher time. A disadvantage is that the usefulness of this strategy is dependent on others for its effectiveness; also, extensive and frequent external support for handling in-class problems is not a realistic option in most schools.

More Extensive Interventions

When students do not respond to minor or moderate interventions and their behavior continues to disrupt classroom activities and to interfere with their own and others' learning, one or more of the strategies described below can be helpful in reducing the inappropriate behaviors and allowing the teacher to re-establish a focus on learning.

USE PROBLEM SOLVING

Because problem solving was described extensively in Chapter 7, it will not be discussed in this chapter. However, the next two strategies, which share features with problem solving, are sufficiently unique to warrant a separate presentation.

Use a Five-Step Intervention Procedure.   Jones and Jones (1995) recommend following five steps when dealing with disruptive student behavior.

STEP 1: Use a nonverbal signal to cue the student to stop.
STEP 2: If the behavior continues, ask the student to follow the desired rule.
STEP 3: If the disruption continues, give the student a choice of stopping the behavior or choosing to develop a plan.
STEP 4: If the student still does not stop, require that the student move to a designated area in the room to write a plan.
STEP 5: If the student refuses to comply with Step 4, send the student to another location (e.g., the school office) to complete the plan.

The use of the five-step intervention process requires a form for the plan (Figure 8–1). When the approach is introduced to the students, preferably at the beginning of the year, the teacher explains its purpose and how to fill out the form. Role playing the use of the five steps is recommended, both to teach the procedures and to provide a positive model of their application. It will be helpful to laminate a couple of examples of appropriate plans so that students have models.

Advantages of this approach include its emphasis on student responsibility and choice. Also, a graduated response to the problem allows the teacher to intervene nonpunitively at first and thus provides a means of settling the matter quickly

---

CHOOSE TO BE RESPONSIBLE

Name _____ Date _____

Rules we agreed on

1. Speak politely to others.
2. Treat each other kindly.
3. Follow teacher requests.
4. Be prepared for class.
5. Make a good effort at your work and request help if you need it.
6. Obey all school rules.

Please answer the following questions:

1. What rule did you violate? _____

   _____

2. What did you do that violated this rule?_____

   _____

3. What problem did this cause for you, your teacher, or classmates? _____

   _____

4. What plan can you develop that will help you be more responsible and follow this classroom rule?_____

   _____

5. How can the teacher or other students help you?_____

   _____

I, _____ , will try my best to follow the plan I have written and to follow all other rules and procedures in our classroom that we created to make the classroom a good place to learn.

FIGURE 8–1   Problem-Solving Form

From Vernon F. Jones and Louise S. Jones, *Comprehensive Classroom Management: Creating Positive Learning Environments for All Students,* Third Edition. Copyright © 1995 by Allyn and Bacon. Reprinted with permission.

with a minimum of disturbance to the ongoing activity. The steps are simple and straightforward, which will promote consistency in their use by the teacher; students, in turn, will be aided by the structure and predictability of the approach.

A disadvantage of the system is that movement from Step 1 to Step 5 can occur very rapidly, and intermediate strategies may be necessary to avoid excessive reliance on sending students out of the classroom. In addition, some students, especially in early primary grades, will have difficulty writing an acceptable plan by themselves. Finally, setting up the system and, later, meeting with students to discuss their plans and monitoring implementation require at least a moderate investment of time.

Use the Reality Therapy Model.   William Glasser's (1975, 1977) ideas have been widely applied in education. Some of his recommendations for dealing with disruptive or maladaptive behaviors in a classroom setting are presented on the next page.

The essential features of using a Reality Therapy strategy when working with an individual student include establishing a caring relationship with the student, focusing on the present behaviors, getting the student to accept responsibility, developing a plan for change, obtaining a commitment to follow the plan, and following up. Glasser believes strongly that students choose behavior depending on their perceptions of its consequences. Most students will choose appropriate behaviors when they believe these will lead to desirable outcomes, and they will avoid behaviors they perceive will lead to undesirable consequences. Glasser's plan can be put into effect using the following steps.

STEP 1: *Establish involvement with the students.* If students believe the teacher cares for them and has their best interests in mind, they will be more likely to follow the teacher's guidance when evaluating and changing their behavior. Teachers can show commitment to and caring for students in numerous ways: commenting favorably to the students about their work; being friendly; and showing an interest in different students' activities, family, likes and dislikes, and hobbies. Teachers can also get involved by demonstrating school spirit, joking, being a good listener, and taking time to talk with students about their concerns. The best time to establish involvement is before a student becomes disruptive, but even if a student has begun to exhibit problem behavior, it is not too late to begin. When a teacher makes a special effort to have two or three friendly contacts a day with such a student, it can be helpful in creating a more positive climate for change.

STEP 2: *Focus on behavior.* When a problem has occurred, Glasser recommends that a brief conference be held with the student. The initial concern should be to determine what the problem is. To this end, the teacher should ask only questions about "what happened" or "what's going on" and avoid trying to fix blame. Even if the teacher knows exactly what the problem is, it is wise to obtain the student's perspective.

STEP 3: *The student needs to accept responsibility for the behavior.* This means the student acknowledges that he or she did engage in the behavior. No excuses are accepted. Admitting responsibility is difficult, especially when there are so many other handy things to blame, but in the end, it is a form of denial to try to assign responsibility elsewhere when it was the student who engaged in the behavior. Of course, it is possible that more than one individual is responsible for the problem, but that should not be an excuse for irresponsibility.

STEP 4: *The student should evaluate the behavior.* If students have difficulty perceiving their part or they minimize it, Glasser suggests asking, "Has the behavior helped or hurt you? Has it helped or hurt others?" The teacher may need to point out the negative consequences of continuing to misbehave. Unless the student sees that the behavior will lead to negative consequences and that changing it will produce desirable consequences, there isn't much reason to expect a change.

STEP 5: *Develop a plan.* The teacher and student need to identify ways to prevent the problem from recurring and what new behaviors are needed. The plan can be written as a contract.

STEP 6: *The student must make a commitment to follow the plan.* Progress will be limited at best if students do not seriously intend to make a change. It may help if the teacher makes clear the positive and negative consequences of following or not following the plan. The plan needs to be do-able in a reasonable time.

STEP 7: *Follow up and follow through.* If the plan doesn't work, it should be modified with the student; if a negative consequence was called for in the plan, it should be used. Glasser also proposes several additional steps beyond the classroom if a student continues to be a problem. For example, use of in-school suspension could be a consequence of continuing misbehavior; before the student is allowed to return to the classroom, an acceptable plan would need to be agreed on. Only after several failed attempts to obtain a change should the teacher refer the student to the principal.

The Reality Therapy approach to dealing with individual discipline problems has several positive aspects. It is a systematic way for teachers to deal with many kinds of individual student problems, and it provides a simple, yet effective, process for getting right at the issues and avoiding being sidetracked by fault finding, conning, or excuse making. Research on the effects of this aspect of Reality Therapy is generally supportive (Emmer & Aussiker, 1990) for applications to individual students.

Use Peer Mediation/Conflict Resolution

Another approach for solving conflicts between students in the classroom falls in the category of peer mediation and conflict resolution. Both of these approaches involve students in the process of arriving at an understanding of why the conflict occurred, how it might be resolved, and how it can be prevented in the future. Students who serve as peer mediators are taught how to help their peers deal with disagreements that cause conflict. Students learn how to mediate a discussion between peers who are at odds and help them arrive at a consensus. For example, if two students are arguing over who owns a calculator, they could enlist the help of a third party, a peer mediator, to help them solve the dispute. As a part of this approach, students are also taught specific strategies for helping them communicate disagreements or problems with their peers in a constructive way. Readings at the end of this chapter provide more information on this approach.

Conference with a Parent

Sometimes, a telephone call to a parent can have a marked effect on a student's behavior, signaling to the child that accountability for behavior extends beyond the classroom. Parents react best if they don't feel they are being held responsible for their child's behavior in school (after all, they aren't there), so don't put the parent on the defensive. Describe the situation briefly and say that you would appreciate whatever support the parent can give in helping you understand and resolve the problem. Acknowledge the difficulty in rearing children as well as in teaching them. Be sure to use listening skills (see Chapter 7) during the conversation and be alert for information that might help you determine an appropriate strategy for dealing with the student. Have your grade book handy so you can give the parent specific information about the student's progress, if the information is requested or needed.

Rather than a phone conference, you might need to schedule a face-to-face conference with a parent. Sometimes, but by no means always, when such conferences are arranged, it is because a problem has become severe, and other school personnel (e.g., a counselor or principal) may need to be present. If you have initiated the meeting, brief the others and plan your approach ahead of time.

The chief drawback to parent conferences is the time and energy they require. The effort is frequently worth it; although not every conference is successful, many times the student's behavior will improve. Another potential problem is identifying beforehand what strategy would be best to follow with the parent. Occasionally, parents overreact and punish children excessively. As the year progresses, you will get to know parents better and be able to gauge the probable effects of your call or conference.

Individual Contract with the Student

When a student's inappropriate behavior has become chronic or if a problem is severe and must stop immediately, try an individual contract. You will need to discuss the nature of the problem with the student, including the student's perspective on it. Then you and the student can identify appropriate solutions and agree on which course of action to take. Typically, the contract specifies changes the student will make, but it might also call for the teacher to alter some behavior or activity. You should also make clear what consequences will occur if the plan is not followed, and you can also identify an incentive to encourage the student to follow through with the contract. The plan and consequences are written down and signed by the student. Contracts can also be used with other strategies (see the Five-Step Plan and the Reality Therapy sections).

SPECIAL PROBLEMS

Children sometimes behave in ways that require stronger measures than those described in the preceding sections. Behaviors include rudeness toward the teacher, chronic avoidance of work, fighting, other aggressive behavior, and defiance or hostility toward the teacher. Although these behaviors are not pleasant to contemplate, they are an inevitable result of close contact with up to thirty students for long periods of time. Fortunately, few teachers encounter these behaviors in large numbers. Regardless of their frequency, it is wise to be aware of ways to cope with them if they occur.

Before discussing each type of problem, general guidelines applicable to aggressive behaviors will be considered. Consider coping with these behaviors in two phases: the immediate response and a long-range strategy. At the time the behavior occurs, your immediate concern will be to bring it to a halt with the least disruption possible. Because these behaviors are annoying and can arouse your anxiety or anger, be careful not to exacerbate the problem. By staying calm and avoiding overreaction, rather than becoming overbearing or dictatorial, you are more likely to bring the situation to a successful conclusion. Thinking about ways to handle disruptive behavior ahead of time and consulting with more experienced teachers will help you to act rather than react. You may tell the student how you feel, but by avoiding an argument or an emotional confrontation you will be in a better position to deal with the student and his or her problem.

Long-range considerations are to prevent a recurrence of the behavior and to help the student learn a more constructive means of dealing with others. Preventing a recurrence of the behavior is best accomplished by (1) finding out what triggered the incident and resolving the cause if possible, and (2) by having a predictable classroom environment with reasonable and consistently used rules, procedures, and consequences. Aggressive behavior rarely occurs in such classrooms. Helping these students acquire better behavior may require much individual attention from you over a period of time. The extent to which this goal is feasible is, of course, limited by many factors, including your time constraints and the severity of the student's problem. In dealing with students who have chronic problems, you may need consultation and assistance from the student's parents, the school counselor, a special education resource teacher, or the principal. Suggestions for handling different types of behavior follow.

Tattling

Although tattling is often not a disruptive behavior, it can nevertheless become a problem when it becomes a common practice. Most teachers in the early grades develop standard policies for dealing with tattling and apply these when it happens. In deciding how you will handle it, keep in mind that tattling is usually a bid for attention; students who do this are usually seeking attention from the teacher. If tattlers are successful in getting you to intervene with the alleged misbehavior, other students are likely to follow suit. It is usually sufficient to remind tattlers of what they are supposed to be doing at that moment and have them return to it. It is also probably prudent for you to follow up and check out the situation for yourself. One question asked of tattlers is often enough to discourage manipulative tattling. This is, "What have you done to solve this problem?" This provides children with your attention, but it communicates your expectation that only problems they are unable to resolve by their own efforts need to be reported to you.

Rudeness toward the Teacher

Rudeness may take the form of back talk, arguing, crude remarks, or gesturing. Although this kind of behavior may trigger your anger, it is best to maintain a low-key professional manner in your response. In this way, you can model the kind of behavior you expect from students, and you will be more effective in interacting with the student in question. Frequently, the student is using such behavior as a means of getting attention from you or from peers, so avoid overreacting or being trapped into a power struggle. To some extent, your response will depend on the degree of rudeness and on how public it was. In borderline cases, the student may not even realize that a comment was offensive. A reasonable first reaction is to inform the student that the behavior is not acceptable, possibly referring to a general classroom rule such as "respect others" or "be polite." If the incident is repeated or if the original comment was intentionally rude, conferring with or penalizing the student may be necessary. Should disrespectful behavior occur that disrupts the class or that persists, the student may need to be isolated from other students or sent to the school office and not allowed to return until he or she agrees to behave appropriately. Most schools have a standard policy for dealing with extreme cases, and you will be able to rely on whatever procedures have been established.

Chronic Avoidance of Work

You may have students who frequently do not complete assigned work. Sometimes they will not complete assignments early in the school year; more often, a student will begin to skip assignments occasionally and then with increasing regularity until he or she is habitually not completing them. This behavior can be minimized by a carefully planned accountability system (review Chapter 3 for details). How-ever, even in classrooms with a strong accountability system, some students may still avoid work.

It is much easier and better for the teacher to correct this problem before the student gets so far behind that failure is almost certain. To be in a position to take early action, you must collect and check student work frequently and also maintain good records. When you note a student who has begun to miss assignments, you can talk with him or her, seeking further information to help identify the problem and then take corrective action. If the student is simply unable to do the assigned work, you should provide appropriate assistance or modify the assignments for that student. If the student feels overwhelmed by the assignments, break them up into parts whenever possible. Have the student complete the first part of the assignment within a specific time (perhaps five or ten minutes), then check to see that it has been done. A bonus of a few minutes of free time at the end of the period can be offered for completion of the portion within the time limit or for working steadily without prodding. Sometimes, you can provide a list of assignments for the student to check off. This can serve as a self-monitoring device and can provide a sense of accomplishment.

If ability is not the problem, in addition to talking with the student, the fol-lowing procedures can be used. Call the student's parents and discuss the situation with them. Often the home can supply the extra support needed to help motivate the student. A simple penalty of requiring that the student remain after school until assignments have been completed can prove effective. If the student rides a bus, you won't be able to use the procedure, of course, without making special arrangements with the parents. Any time the child is likely to be detained for more than a few minutes, alert the parents ahead of time. Another procedure that can be used when the parents are cooperative is for the child to take home daily a list of incomplete assignments and all books or materials needed to complete the work.

Be sure not to soften the negative consequences of repeated failure to com-plete work by giving students higher grades than they have earned. To do so teaches them to avoid responsibility. Provide added incentives for good effort and com-pleted work. Set up a reward system (see Chapter 6) that encourages students to do their best.

Fighting

Fighting is less likely to occur in classrooms than on the playground, in the cafete-ria, or in some other area of the school. In the elementary grades, you can usually stop a fight without undue risk of injury. (If for some reason you cannot intervene directly, alert other teachers and administrators so that action can be taken.) When you do intervene, first give a loud verbal command to stop. This alone may stop the fight; it will at least alert the combatants that a referee has arrived. Instruct a student in the group of onlookers to go immediately for help; be specific about where the student should go. Separate the fighters; as you keep them separate, instruct the

"... and suddenly there were teachers all over the place!"

© 1968 by Bill Knowlton. Reprinted from *Classroom Chuckles* published by Scholastic Book Services.

other students to leave, to return to their play, or to their classes. Without an audience before which the fighters need to save face, you are more likely to be able to keep them apart until help arrives or until you can get them to a different location.

Your school will undoubtedly have a procedure to deal with fighting; you should carry it out. Students may be questioned by the principal, who may call the student's home, arrange a conference, and determine the next step.

If school policy leaves the teacher with wide discretion in following up on such incidents, decide on your procedures. It is generally best to arrange a cooling-off period. If you cannot find someone to supervise your class, let the fighters wait in separate areas or in the school office. Older children can cool off by writing their version of how the fight started. If you do not know what started the fight, try to find out from uninvolved students. As soon as you have an opportunity, meet with the offenders and get each one's point of view. The conference should focus on the inappropriateness of fighting and the need to resolve problems in ways other than accusations or personal criticism. Help each student understand the other's point of view so they have a basis for better communication. Finally, stress the importance of cooperativeness and friendliness toward one another. During the next day or two, watch for any indications of residual hostility. If the issue seems not to have been resolved, follow up by contacting the children's parents, discussing the matter with your principal, or talking with the students again.

Other Aggressive Behavior

Aggressive behavior toward other students is not confined to open fighting. Name-calling, overbearing bossiness or rudeness toward other students, and physically aggressive but "playful" pushing, shoving, or slapping are examples of other forms of aggressive behavior found in the classroom. Such behavior should be treated as is rudeness toward the teacher. Tell offending students that such behavior is not acceptable, even if they are just "fooling around." It can easily escalate. Refer to whatever class rule fits the situation, such as "Respect others." Give no more than one warning and then assess whatever penalty is appropriate. Students engaged in such behavior should be separated and seated apart if they give any indication of intending to persist.

If you have a student who persists in verbal or physical aggression despite consequences, you may need to solicit the help of the school counselor or school psychologist. Students who are consistently aggressive may have learned this as the primary means of getting their needs met and may need direct instruction with positive reinforcement in more appropriate techniques and social skills. Other students with this pattern of behavior may be carrying a great deal of anger that has nothing to do with school but which is easily aroused. These students may need additional help from the counselor or school psychologist. Sometimes, it is helpful to ask these students how you might help them stay calm or stay out of situations that set them off. If they are distressed over their own lack of control (and this is often the case), perhaps you can help them identify things they can use as cues so they can seek your help or go to a cooling-off spot before their behavior escalates out of control. Establishing a private signal between the two of you can be helpful for the child to use when needing help or a time away and for you to use if you see the student getting tense. Helping students recognize that you are for, not against, them is important. It is just as important for you to remember that despite your efforts and their good intentions, change is likely to be slow and difficult and not to lose patience or confidence in them.

Defiance or Hostility toward the Teacher

Defiance or hostility is understandably threatening to teachers. The teacher feels, and rightfully so, that if he or she allows the student to get away with it, the behavior may continue, and other students will be more likely to react in the same way. The student who has provoked a confrontation, usually publicly, feels that backing down would cause a loss of face in front of peers. The best way to deal with such an event is to try to defuse it by keeping it private and handling it individually with the student, if possible. If it occurs during a lesson and is not extreme, deal with it by trying to depersonalize the event and avoid a power struggle: "This is taking time away from the lesson. I will discuss it with you in a few minutes when I have time." If the student does not accept the opportunity you have provided and presses the confrontation further, instruct the student to leave the room and wait in the hall. After the student has had time to cool off, give your class something to do and discuss the problem with the student.

When discussing the incident, remain objective. Remember—act, don't react. Do not engage in arguments with the student. Point out that the behavior was not acceptable, state the consequence clearly, and implement it. Listen to the student's point of view and respond to it. If you are not sure how to respond, say that you will think about it and discuss it later. However, you should still administer the penalty.

In an extreme (and rare) case, the student may be totally uncooperative and refuse to keep quiet or leave the room. If this happens, you can escort the student from the room yourself or, when dealing with a student who is older or larger, send another student to the office for assistance. In most cases, however, as long as you stay calm and refuse to get into a power struggle with the student, the student will accept the opportunity to cool down.

A FINAL REMINDER: THINK AND ACT POSITIVELY

In this chapter, many of the strategies for dealing with problem behaviors involve some form of punishment. This is especially the case for the strategies in the moderate and extensive categories. A drawback to punishment is that, by itself, it doesn't teach the student what behaviors should be practiced. Consequently, it is important for teachers using one of these approaches also to communicate clearly about those behaviors that are desired. That is, the focus should remain on teaching appropriate behaviors. Furthermore, a classroom in which the main consequences are negative will not have a good climate. Thus, teachers using strategies in the moderate and extensive categories more than occasionally should try to incorporate additional incentives or a reward system into their overall classroom management to help mitigate the effects of using punishment. After correcting students' behavior, the teacher who supplies a generous helping of warmth and affection will reassure them that they have been restored to good grace.

FURTHER READING

Curwin, R. L. (1995). A humane approach to reducing violence in schools. *Educational Leadership, 52* (5), 72–75.

> *The author advocates dealing with inappropriate behavior in ways that do not exclude students nor punish them. Instead, students should be taught alternative appropriate behaviors and treated with respect. Examples are provided to illustrate recommendations.*

Cutona, C., & Guerin, D. (1994). Confronting conflict peacefully: Peer mediation in schools. *Educational Horizons, 72* (2), 95–104.

> *Problem behavior that pits student against student can escalate to threaten schoolwide climate and safety. These behaviors often frustrate teachers and are difficult to resolve through adult intervention alone. This article describes the use of peer mediation to resolve conflicts. Examples of such programs are also presented along with an analysis of their benefits.*

Johnson, D. W., & Johnson, R. T. (1994). Constructive conflict in the schools. *Journal of Social Issues, 50* (1), 117–137.

> *Learning how to handle conflict constructively is a major accomplishment that eludes many adolescents and children (not to mention adults). This article describes the peer mediation approach to handling conflict along with championing the use of cooperative strategies and structured controversy. Procedures involved in classroom-based and schoolwide peer mediation programs are carefully described along with their rationale and supporting research.*

Shrigley, R. L. (1985). Curbing disruption in the classroom—Teachers need intervention skills. *NASSP Bulletin, 69* (479), 26–32.

A sequence of strategies is set forth for dealing with various mild and moderate disruptions. The strategies, which are consistent with many of those presented in this chapter, are easily applied in classroom settings, providing useful alternatives for handling problem behavior.

Zakariya, S. B. (1987). Fair, unfailing discipline is the least schools owe to delinquent kids. *American School Board Journal, 174* (2), 23–29.

Teaching students whose behaviors are delinquent or disruptive is often complicated by the absence of consistently enforced consequences in schools as well as in the community. The author recommends a number of ways to strengthen school discipline, and she illustrates them with descriptions of programs in place in school systems across the country.

SUGGESTED ACTIVITIES

1. Review the descriptions of problem types presented at the beginning of the chapter. Decide which interventions would be best suited for each type. Given several alternative interventions for any type of problem, how would you decide which to use?

2. Within each type of intervention—minor, moderate, or extensive—are there any that you distinctly prefer? Do you reject any? Discuss your reasons for liking or disliking particular approaches.

3. Listed below are several problem behaviors. Decide on a strategy for dealing with each and also an alternative response if your first approach does not produce good results. Indicate any assumptions you are making about the teaching context as you choose your strategy.

   ◆ *Situation 1.* Ardyth and Melissa talk and pass notes as you conduct a class discussion. Several other students whisper or daydream.

   ◆ *Situation 2.* Desi and Bryce talk constantly. They refuse to get to work, and they argue with you when you ask them to open their books.

   ◆ *Situation 3.* Joe manages to get most of his work done, but in the process he is constantly disruptive. He teases the girls sitting around him, keeping them constantly laughing and competing for his attention. Joe makes wisecracks in response to almost anything you say. When confronted, he grins charmingly and responds with exaggerated courtesy, much to the delight of the rest of the class.

   ◆ *Situation 4.* When someone bumped into Marc at the drinking fountain, he turned around and spit water at the other child. Later, Marc ordered a boy who was standing near his desk to get away, and he then shoved the boy. On the way back from the cafeteria, Marc got into a name-calling contest with another boy.

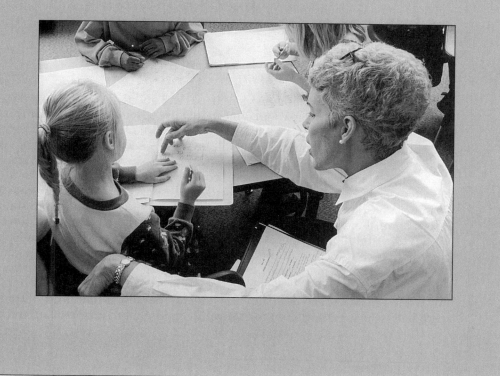

C H A P T E R 9

Managing Special Groups

Although the classroom management principles and guidelines discussed in previous chapters of this book apply to most classroom settings, classroom management is also affected by the characteristics of students making up the class. The ages, academic ability levels, goals, interests, and home backgrounds of students have an impact on their classroom behavior. Consequently, adjustments in management and instructional organization practices are sometimes needed to meet the needs of different groups of students. Among the students that frequently present some special challenges are students who are working below or well above grade level, students who are academically or physically disabled, and students whose English language skills are limited. Often, a classroom includes all of these types of students, which presents a special challenge to a teacher. Meeting the needs of students with such diverse needs and abilities requires special effort.

This chapter presents information and suggestions that, combined with the principles in previous chapters, will help you organize and manage classes with a range of student achievement or ability levels, groups of students with below-level skills, and students with special needs in the classroom.

ASSESSING ENTERING ACHIEVEMENT

To identify the extent of differences in needs and ability levels (i.e., the degree of heterogeneity) in your classroom, you should use several sources of information. These sources include tests you administer, your own observation of each student, and indicators of performance available in each student's file, including assessments obtained from prior teachers, samples of the student's work, and standardized achievement test information. Of course, if you have a student identified as having special needs, you will consult with the resource teacher. Be cautious about forming a hasty impression of a student's abilities based on only one source of information. Furthermore, you must guard against the possibility of forming a negative self-fulfilling prophecy—forming low expectations of some students and communicating these to students, causing them to achieve below their potential.

Because of the importance of reading, language arts, and mathematics skills in the elementary school curriculum, these subjects will be the major focus of your initial assessment. As you evaluate your students, be alert to indicators of study and work habits such as the ability to follow directions and to maintain attention to a

"I'm an underachiever. . . . What's *your* racket?"

© 1968 by Bill Knowlton. Reprinted from *Classroom Chuckles* published by Scholastic Book Services.

task. Children with poor skills or who are highly distractible may require special consideration in your room arrangement, in planning for instructional activities, and in monitoring.

When obtaining information about entering reading and math skill levels, special attention must be given to those students for whom you lack information. Typically, these will be students who have transferred from another school district. You must also be careful about the assessment of children for whom existing information is not consistent. It is especially important to assess such children individually by listening to them read and checking their vocabulary and word attack strategies and by testing to identify their math skills. Consult with other teachers or other professionals or both for help in selecting suitable assessment procedures if you do not already have them.

It is best to delay individual student assessment until several days after the beginning of school. During such testing, it will be difficult for you to monitor your class, and you may also have to leave students too long in seatwork. By delaying testing, you will have a chance to observe the students first, and the students will become better acquainted and more comfortable with you before they are tested. If you do individual testing, plan enough work to keep your class busy. When several students need to be assessed individually, space the testing over several days.

IDENTIFYING SPECIAL GROUPS

For the purpose of classroom instruction, it is important to determine the range of entering achievement in basic skill subjects, the degree to which individual students are unable to work effectively with the grade-level curriculum, and other special needs of your students. Other characteristics such as student interests and backgrounds can also affect learning and instruction and should be considered whenever possible as you plan instructional activities and set goals.

Information on student ability levels can be used to identify small groups for instruction, to pair students for peer tutoring, or to create cooperative groups for learning activities. Each of these types of activities requires special planning and management considerations.

STRATEGIES FOR INDIVIDUAL DIFFERENCES

In the next sections we describe strategies frequently used to adjust for individual differences and examine management concerns associated with these.

Team Teaching

Teachers at the same grade level frequently form teams to deal with heterogeneous student populations. Students can then be reassigned to different teachers on the team for instruction in one or more subjects. This allows teachers to form relatively more homogeneous subgroups than would be possible using only students initially assigned to their individual classrooms. For example, two or three students whose entering reading skills are extremely low might be grouped for reading instruction with similar students from other classrooms. At the same time, students at the highest level in the classes might be combined into a single group and taught by another teacher on the team. This arrangement permits instruction for these students to be targeted closer to their skill levels than if the students remained in their original classes. Still, it is important that these students participate in groups with mixed ability levels in some activities.

Team approaches to student heterogeneity can be applied to a variety of subjects but are most common in reading and mathematics instruction. If ability grouping will be used, teaming should be considered whenever the range of student ability is too great to be accommodated by three groups in reading and by two groups in mathematics. Although extreme heterogeneity within a class could theoretically be accommodated by forming more groups, to do so is usually not practical because it would place excessive demands on teacher planning and would reduce the amount of time each group receives for instruction. Because teaming requires careful planning and cooperation, the following items are important to consider.

COORDINATION OF SCHEDULES

The teachers on the team must establish compatible schedules for the subjects being team taught. If teachers deviate from the schedule without warning, children from other classrooms may be kept waiting with nothing to do, and everyone will be thrown off schedule.

STUDENT MOVEMENT

Because some students will be going from one room to another, they must be taught what procedures and behavior to use during transitions. A teacher should accompany children in transit between rooms, at least until they have learned the routine.

REMINDING STUDENTS WHAT THEY ARE SUPPOSED TO TAKE WITH THEM

Sometimes children have trouble remembering their materials. When they do not bring the appropriate materials, they may be sent back to their classrooms, losing valuable instructional time and sometimes disturbing students in both rooms. If students will need different sets of materials on different days, all teachers involved should be notified so they can help students remember what will be needed and when, perhaps by posting a list of materials to take or by reminding students as they prepare to leave the room.

RULES AND PROCEDURES

Students coming to you from another teacher's class will not know your expectations for their behavior. Therefore, you will need to discuss rules for conduct in your room and the procedures needed for small-group work and seatwork. Do this when you first meet with your new students. Monitor them carefully until good behavior becomes established. If possible, plan rules and procedures with other members of the team to establish a common set of expectations. Consistency across settings will simplify the task of teaching students to behave correctly.

MAINTAINING RESPONSIBILITY FOR WORK

In addition to rules for conduct and procedures for behavior, care must be taken to keep students responsible for their work. This may be more difficult to do in a team-teaching situation than with the students in your regular class because the full range of incentives, penalties, and parental contact may be limited. Also, you will not be able to supervise the students at other times of the day when they might have an opportunity to work on assignments (and when, ideally, you would check work and provide supplementary instruction). For these reasons, several steps should be followed to keep students accountable:

1. When you meet with students each day, check their work before you dismiss them and give students whatever feedback they will need to complete the work successfully.

2. Be clear about your expectations for work, other requirements, and your grading criteria.

3. Return graded papers promptly. Don't let these materials accumulate.

4. Be certain that students, especially younger children, realize that you are responsible for checking their work and assigning a report card grade.

5. Contact parents if children begin to skip assignments in your class. Don't rely on the homeroom teacher to do this.

Modifying Whole-Class Instruction

In some subjects, the use of small groups for instruction will not be feasible or even desirable. Limited time, the problem of ascertaining individual differences on relevant entering skills, and greater procedural complexity may make small-group instruction less efficient than whole-class instruction. When used for subjects such as science or social studies, whole-class instruction can be modified to accommodate extremes in student abilities and interests. A number of simple modifications and cautions should be considered.

INTERACTIVE INSTRUCTION

Try to involve all the students in presentations, discussions, and recitations. Do so by making a conscious effort to call on all students, not only those who are eager to respond. Students with a special ability or an obvious interest in a topic can be encouraged to complete special projects and to organize their ideas in oral reports to the class. These opportunities will allow the students to advance their understanding and receive recognition.

SEATING ARRANGEMENTS

Students who need closer supervision or more than the usual amount of explanation should be seated near the front of the room (or wherever you usually conduct whole-class presentations). Their proximity to you will enable you to check for understanding more readily and make it easier to monitor their behavior and progress.

DIRECTIONS

Communicating instructions and directions to a highly diverse class requires care. Be certain you have all students' attention and provide both oral and written directions when feasible. Some students have difficulty following a long series of verbal directions. Break directions into student-manageable chunks and provide visual cues. The use of questions to verify comprehension and careful monitoring will also be helpful. Be certain to check with those students who frequently have problems following directions. If you have seated them near you, you will be able to provide them with added assistance as needed.

ASSIGNMENTS

If you give the same assignments to all the students in a highly heterogeneous class, the work may be much too easy for some students and much too difficult for others. Consider giving assignments in two parts: a basic assignment for all students to complete and a second, more difficult part that is assigned to some students or that can be completed for extra credit. When assignments are the same for everyone, the students will complete them with different degrees of proficiency and speed. In such cases, use a grading or credit system that, at least in part, emphasizes individual student progress rather than competition among students. Enrichment or extra-credit material for students who finish classwork early should be work related and should not distract other students. Avoid free-time activities that are so attractive that slower-working students feel deprived or attempt to quit or rush through their work. Set up a system for giving credit, feedback, or recognition for completion of enrichment activities. If you allow students to read when they finish work, be sure to provide supplementary reading materials at a variety of reading levels.

Supplementary Instruction

Sometimes, students' needs in some subject areas cannot be well-met in a regular classroom. For example, a student's skills may be so deficient in reading or math that he or she cannot profit from small-group instruction; even the lowest group may be too far beyond the student's current level. Or a student may be so distracted by the stimulation of twenty-five or thirty students in a regular classroom that he or she cannot focus on assignments long enough to complete them. Such students may fall behind in their performance, even though they possess average or above-average ability. Students whose first language is not English may need intensive help that cannot be provided in the regular instructional program. Finally, some students may possess special talents that programs for the gifted can more fully develop. In all of these cases, supplementary programs may be available. The term *pull-out* is sometimes applied to these programs because the students are taken out of the regular classroom for part of the school day to receive special instruction. You will need to check to see if a student is enrolled in a pull-out program that is intended to supplement or to replace his or her regular classroom instruction. This will have important implications for your planning. Examples of pull-out programs include the following:

◆ Special education: This is usually available in a resource room. Students with learning disabilities and other conditions that interfere with learning or adjustment in a regular classroom setting receive instruction (usually reading or math or both) for part of the day. These students return to the regular classroom for other instruction.

◆ Title I programs: These are special programs established in schools that serve students from lower-income families. Students with deficits in academic skills receive supplementary instruction from special teachers.

◆ Enrichment programs: Programs that provide enrichment in particular subjects are often established for students who have special talent in the area. These programs frequently use community resources, parents, or other volunteers as well as the regular teaching staff to provide programs during school hours or after hours.

The aspect of supplementary programs that has a major impact on your classroom management plan will be the removal of students from your classroom during the time that regular instruction is proceeding. Thus, scheduling must be carefully planned so the pull-out students do not miss essential instruction and so the other students' instructional program is not interrupted. Transitions out of and back into your classroom can become a major headache if they are not handled well.

COORDINATING TIMES WITH OTHER TEACHERS

As soon as schoolwide schedules are set for lunch periods and activities such as music, art, and physical education classes, plan a schedule with the other teachers that will be as convenient as possible for everyone. If a number of students leave for special reading instruction, arrange with the reading teacher to have these students leave in a group at a time when you will be meeting with a reading group in your class. If several students will be pulled out for special instruction in a subject such as mathematics, you will probably want to schedule your math instruction for the rest of the class at that time.

STAYING ON SCHEDULE

When class schedules involve pull-outs and drop-ins, it is especially important for teachers to stay on schedule so that students can be where they need to be at appropriate times. Have a large clock placed where everyone can see it. If you have trouble remembering to look at the clock, enlist the aid of the students in prompting you. Older students should eventually assume responsibility for their own schedules. You may want to post a list of times when different students are supposed to leave to remind both you and the students. You can also set a timer as a reminder.

HAVING SOMETHING FOR DROP-IN STUDENTS TO DO WHILE WAITING FOR INSTRUCTION

Sometimes, a teacher is not quite through with one group when it is time for another group to meet. Students who are working at their desks in the teacher's room should have enough activities to keep them busy. However, drop-in students sometimes arrive early and have nowhere specific to sit other than in the small group. You will need a procedure for dealing with these students so that small groups and seatworkers are not distracted. Some teachers tell students to take an empty seat while waiting. Other teachers set aside a waiting area on a small rug or at a table. While there, students can get a copy of their textbook or workbook and begin reading the next lesson or do other constructive activities.

GETTING RETURNING STUDENTS INVOLVED AGAIN

After receiving instruction outside the room, some pull-out students may tend to dawdle or seem confused about what they are supposed to do when they return to the room. The best way to avoid confusion is to establish routines so that students always know what to do when they return. It is a good idea to post assignments or give students a list of assignments to help them remember. If you are working with a small group when some students return, give the small group something to do and go to the returning students to be sure they get back on task. Student helpers could also be given the responsibility for explaining the assignment or activity to individual returning students.

ACTIVITIES WHEN SUPPLEMENTARY INSTRUCTION IS NOT HELD

Sometimes the special teacher will be absent or the special class will not be conducted for some other reason. When this occurs, it is important to have something for these students to do while you carry on with regular instruction. In some cases, students may be included in regular class activities. In other cases, you will have to provide special activities. If possible, meet regularly with the other teachers so you will know what students are working on and be able to assign appropriate activities. Have free-time or enrichment activities set aside to accommodate varying levels of ability. It is important to monitor these students and give them something meaningful to do; otherwise, valuable learning time is lost, and they may become bored or disruptive.

IN-CLASS AIDES

Sometimes, teachers are fortunate enough to have parents or other adult volunteers, teacher aides, or university education students to help out in their classrooms. These aides may be assigned to help with a particular subject or be available to help with any subjects. Other aides may help with materials and administrative tasks and have little contact with the children. If you have one or more aides, there are several things you will need to do to promote smooth functioning in your classroom. You should be specific in informing the aide of his or her responsibilities for teaching or working with students and for disciplining students. You will probably want aides to enforce your rules consistently when they are in charge of students. If you must leave the room, inform students that the aide will be in charge of the class and will enforce the rules as you do. If the aide will be working with individual students or small groups, you will need to make available a space that will not cause distractions for the rest of the class, particularly if you are instructing simultaneously. Students should be told whether and when they may go to the aide for help.

CONTENT MASTERY CLASSROOM

A special form of supplementary (pull-out) program that has recently become widely used is the Content Mastery Classroom. This program designates one or more teachers, at least one of whom is trained in special education, to work with students identified as needing supplemental instruction. The Content Mastery Classroom is one to which students may come from their own class for extra help on assignments, new material, and so forth or to have extra time to spend on tests. In many school districts, both a general education and a special education teacher are available in the CMC to help students, but in some places this is solely a special education option. An advantage of CMC, compared to a resource or self-contained class, is that it allows the integration of special education students in regular education classrooms but provides support for them when they need more help. Also, the regular education teacher, who may have thirty other students, does not have to provide as much supplemental instruction. Another advantage is that students may go as needed when they feel the need for extra help.

It will be important to coordinate with the CMC teacher(s) about which students may go to the CMC and when and what kind of information and materials they will need to take with them. For example, for younger students, a laminated assignment card may be helpful, with your name and grade level printed on it; when a student is to go to CMC, you might write a brief description of the help the student needs, page numbers in the text the student will take, and the time the student leaves your room. It is also possible, however, that the CMC teacher will have tested routines for getting information about the students' assignments, etc., and that you can use these.

When you have one or more special-needs students who use CMC regularly, you will need to provide assignments ahead of time (e.g., weekly) so that appropriate planning may be done by the CMC teacher. When students take your tests in CMC, be sure you have discussed your expectations for assistance ahead of time. Because the CMC teacher will have worked with your students individually, this teacher may have suggestions for adapting instruction or management that will aid you in teaching the student. Similarly, because CMC teachers will have had substantial training and experience in working with students with special needs, you may be able to benefit from their suggestions. The CMC teacher may be reluctant to give unsolicited advice, so be sure to ask if you have questions about how best to work with particular students.

"About this time of year, I start thinking of them in the past tense."

© Martha Campbell. Reprinted by permission of Martha Campbell.

INCLUSION

Inclusion programs for students with special needs provide support to enable them to participate in as many regular education activities as possible. Typically, a special education teacher will work with regular education teachers of designated students, both to help modify assignments and written material as specified on the students' Individual Education Plans (IEPs) and to provide assistance within the classroom itself. Scheduled planning meetings between the special education and the regular education teacher are crucial to the success of any inclusion program. Only by knowing exactly what activities are planned by the regular education teacher can the special education teacher know how to provide support for the student.

On some occasions, the special education teacher may need to be in the regular classroom, such as when students are working on assignments or class projects. At other times, the special education teacher may provide copies of modified assignments. Both the timing and nature of the special education teacher's participation in class, as well as the extent of lesson modifications, will need to be specified during planning sessions. Case Studies 9–1 and 9–2 at the end of this chapter illustrate how regular education teachers can accommodate special-needs students in the classroom.

Individualized Instruction

When each student receives instruction, is given assignments at a level established by careful assessment of entering skills, and is encouraged to progress at whatever pace his or her abilities and motivation allow, the instructional program is said to be individualized. Some educators consider individualized instruction to be the best means of coping with heterogeneity because it offers, at least in principle, instruction tailored to the needs of each child. However, individualized instruction is difficult to implement. It requires (1) careful and continuous assessment of individual pupil progress, (2) management of time so that all students receive adequate interactive instruction from the teacher, (3) sufficient resources, including materials suitable for all ability levels in the class, and (4) time for the teacher to plan and develop appropriate activities. The absence of one or more of these features will make it difficult to mount an effective instructional program. Also, teachers who wish to implement such programs should do so gradually, allowing themselves adequate time to develop the necessary resources. Because of these difficulties, we regard the first strategies for coping with heterogeneity and low-achieving students to be the modification of whole-class instruction, supplementary instruction, and team teaching. Only when these strategies are not adequate should individualized instruction be necessary.

When individualization of instruction is used for one or more subjects, you should anticipate a number of management problems and take action to prevent them or at least minimize their impact.

TRANSITIONS

Students engaged in individual rather than group activities will generally finish at different times. If the next activity is also an individual activity, many individual transitions will occur throughout the period of instruction. This can cause confusion and lost time. Some students may not know what to do; others may delay starting the next activity. More efficient transitions can be effected if the teacher is alert to help students who are between activities. Assignments must be posted or written somewhere so that students will know what to do next. The teacher can also have students bring completed work to be checked to provide structure during the transition and to be certain that students know how to get started on the next activity.

STUDENT MOVEMENT

Movement between locations of activities is more difficult to manage when students complete or start them at varying times. Because the teacher is frequently working with one or a few students at a time, less supervision of movement is possible, and students may begin to wander around, waste time, and distract other students. Student movement should be regulated by procedures that make clear when and for what purpose students may move around, converse with other students, or be out of their seats. Identifying the reason for excessive wandering or out-of-seat behavior can be helpful in remedying it. If students have completed their work satisfactorily and have nothing to do, more challenging work or enrichment is appropriate. If students quit working because they are not able to do the assignment, additional instruction, assistance, or modified assignments are in order.

MONITORING STUDENT BEHAVIOR

Different expectations for students in different activities, along with a variety of simultaneous activities, make monitoring student behavior during individualized instruction difficult. Also, the teacher often instructs individual students or performs other tasks associated with individualized instruction (such as assessment), thus adding to the complexity of monitoring. To overcome these problems, the following key behaviors should be practiced:

◆ Know what all students are supposed to be doing at any given time so that you can support their efforts and prevent problems.

◆ Be sure students know what they are expected to do and what conduct is appropriate in different activities.

◆ Be alert for students who are having difficulty getting started or completing an activity so that you can provide help. Don't get overly engrossed with helping one or a few students and don't wait until students quit working or become disruptive before providing assistance.

◆ Circulate among the students and look at their work periodically. Scan the room frequently to detect early signs of frustration or task avoidance.

◆ Usually, a few students will require more supervision than others. When possible, be sure these students are seated where you can observe and assist them readily.

ENCOURAGING STUDENT RESPONSIBILITY FOR WORK

The use of an individualized instruction program does not guarantee that students will accept responsibility for completing assignments and participating in learning activities. In fact, some students will take advantage of the more complex instructional arrangements and limitations on the teacher's monitoring capability to avoid responsibility and to expend minimal effort. To avoid these problems, give clear directions for assignments and other activities. Many teachers prefer to review directions with students at the beginning of the period devoted to the individualized instructional activities. A basic set of activities can often be listed on the chalkboard and reviewed, or students can be given activity or assignment folders that list what is to be done. Such a folder can also be used to check off completed work. This system helps both the teacher and the students keep track of progress. Setting time limits for work on one activity before proceeding to the next will help students pace their efforts.

Students should expect their work to be checked frequently. If they get accustomed to simply completing one activity and starting a new one without feedback, their performance will deteriorate. The teacher should develop monitoring procedures that include periodic progress checks and evaluation and feedback on completed assignments and other work. It is also important to review overall student progress and decide whether the pace and scope of work are adequate. Some teachers prefer weekly or biweekly reviews and a short conference with individual students for this purpose.

Sometimes, the teacher's role in individualization diminishes to the point where almost all the teacher's time is devoted to making assessments, giving assignments, keeping records, and checking. When this occurs, students receive little interactive instruction from the teacher and do little except complete worksheets. The teacher's diminished instructional role may be partly due to the incorrect perception that because instruction is individualized, the teacher can only instruct one student at a time. In fact, it is far more efficient if the teacher presents information and conducts recitations with groups of students, supplementing these group lessons with individual instruction for students who require extra help.

CONTRACTS

These are often used with individual instruction. Contracts usually include a list of assignments or activities to be completed by a student during a fixed period of time, such as a day or a week. Contracts also may specify the goals or objectives, materials, and incentives associated with completing the contract. Use of a contract has a number of advantages. It is a good way to communicate assignments and objectives, it enables students to suggest modifications they would find helpful or interesting, and the student's signature on the contract can increase motivation for completion within the agreed-on time period.

Additional Strategies

STUDENT COOPERATION: HELP FROM PEERS

Another method for coping with extreme heterogeneity and for dealing with low achievers is to use students to help other students. Examples of such peer helping arrangements include the following:

◆ Students work in pairs, reading and listening to each other read. "Reading with a buddy" can be part of contract work.

◆ Certain students are assigned as monitors to help other students when the teacher is busy with group or individual instruction.

◆ When the teacher is busy with small-group instruction, students who need help are encouraged to get assistance from another student before interrupting the teacher.

◆ Group leaders are assigned to each learning station to answer questions and set up materials.

◆ A capable, mature student is assigned as a helper for another student who needs frequent assistance. The helper's responsibilities are to answer questions and explain directions.

◆ Students may be permitted to help or seek help from a neighbor on some seatwork activities.

When using students as helpers, recognize the potential for excessive noise, poor attention to the task, or excessive reliance on the helper by the helpee. Also, not all students are amenable to this type of arrangement or work well together. These negative effects can be averted by communicating clearly what is and is not permitted and by monitoring the helping arrangements and relationships to be sure no undesirable side effects develop. As is true for all of the variations from regular instruction patterns, gradual introduction of new arrangements will give the best opportunity for managing their implementation and for correcting problems.

COOPERATIVE GROUPS

For many activities, using small groups with mixed-ability levels or diverse backgrounds or both provides a good opportunity for all students to help and to learn from each other. Researchers such as Robert Slavin (1995) have shown that working in mixed-ability teams can benefit both higher and lower achieving students in many subject areas. Benefits of cooperative groups include increased student achievement, positive race relations, mutual concern among students, and increased student self-esteem.

Effective use of cooperative student groups requires several components: mixed-ability (or background) groups, a reward structure that provides for individual as well as group rewards, and well-chosen activities. To ensure that all students play active roles, the selection of appropriate cooperative groups entails careful assignment of students to groups or teams rather than letting students choose their friends and assignment of student roles within the groups. Most of the cooperative group designs call for a mixture of high achieving (or high ability), average achieving, and lower achieving students or students with special needs. In some types of cooperative group activities, each student is expected to learn or be responsible for a certain amount of lesson content, to instruct the rest of the group in that content, and to learn from the rest of the group members the content for which they are responsible. In other types of cooperative group activities, the groups work together to complete a task and ensure that all group members have learned the content. Each member of the group is required to participate.

An essential component of cooperative groups is the reward structure. An effective reward structure typically includes a combination of individual and group rewards. Each individual in the group must feel that his or her performance will be rewarded individually for effort and performance compared against others of similar levels. In addition, rewarding the group's performance encourages the interaction of group members working toward a common purpose.

Good suggestions for beginning to use groups are provided by Holubec (1992), listed in the Further Reading at the end of this chapter. For teachers beginning to use groups, Holubec recommends a gradual introduction of group-based activities. For example, a teacher might have students work in pairs on small tasks of short duration until they learn how to work together. Initial group activities should be accompanied by discussions with the students about how to work in groups to create positive expectations and to help students learn appropriate roles. As students gain more experience and skill in group work, more types of group activities can be added. Depending on the type of content being taught, students can work as partners to practice spelling or vocabulary. They might also review for tests, work on assignments, summarize alternate sections of reading material, check and correct assignments, and explain answers to questions or solutions to problems.

After a period of time in which students engage in different forms of group activity, they may be ready to tackle more complex and sustained activities in larger groups (e.g., four students). Groups might, for example, develop a group project or report, construct displays or models, or prepare demonstration, performances, or presentations. Such activities may have numerous components and take several days or weeks to complete. Managerial concerns that should be addressed include determining ways to structure the task so that each group member can make a contribution, devising a means of assessing both individual and group performance, developing procedures for absent students, and monitoring student work and behavior to identify problems that require teacher attention.

Time, study, and practice are needed to develop the skills and knowledge for successful group learning activities. Attending workshops on the approach, observing in classrooms, and reading relevant references (Johnson & Johnson, 1994; Slavin, 1995) will be good preparation. Review related materials on groups in Chapters 2, 4, 5, and 6 and Case Study 4–2, which illustrates one teacher's approach to using groups at the beginning of the year.

Peer Tutoring

Peer tutoring provides an opportunity for each student to have access to one-on-one assistance, particularly when the teacher is unavailable to provide assistance. This can be done during class by pairing students at similar levels to work together or by asking a student who has achieved a certain level or learned a concept to work with another student who has not. The student who receives assistance benefits from individualized instruction. The helper, or peer tutor, benefits from planning for and explaining the concept.

To use peer tutoring effectively, certain management issues must be addressed. You must decide when tutoring is and is not acceptable. There may be some subjects for which peer tutoring is not appropriate. For instance, you may not be assured that the potential peer tutors have sufficiently learned the concept to be able to provide assistance.

You will also want to decide where tutoring will occur. Some teachers provide a special location within the classroom where peer interactions are less likely to interrupt other classroom activities or disturb students who are working unassisted. Others may allow students to work quietly side-by-side at their desks.

If you use peer tutors, you must teach students to be peer tutors. Potential peer tutors should be shown how to model behaviors, instructed in how to ask questions to assess the other student's understanding, and counseled on interpersonal behaviors. For long-term peer tutors, you may want to provide a brief training during class or after school. Other directions can be given as part of the overall instructions for an activity.

WORKING WITH SPECIAL NEEDS STUDENTS

This section deals with students who have special needs, either because they are physically or mentally challenged or because they have background characteristics such as language proficiency that affect their classroom performance.

Recent research on students with special needs because of physical or mental disabilities has shown the benefits of providing instruction to these students in the least restrictive environment. As a result, more and more students with special needs are being served in the regular classroom with some outside help from specialized teachers. Meeting these students' needs presents special challenges to teachers with a classroom full of children. Fortunately, research has provided specific guidelines to help teachers work with these students in ways that promote their peer acceptance and their self-esteem as well as their academic achievement. Following are suggestions for planning instruction for students with different types of special needs.

Students with Learning Disabilities

Although there is still no consensus for a concise definition of learning disability, certain characteristics are commonly seen. A primary feature is more difficulty with and lower achievement in certain academic areas than would otherwise be expected based on these students' overall ability levels. Other common problems experienced by these students are disorganization and a disconcerting tendency to forget something they seemed to understand thoroughly just a short time earlier. Accompanying these difficulties is a natural sense of frustration and the risk of developing a generalized attitude of anger or hopelessness along with a negative view of themselves.

Learning disabled students generally respond well to a positive and structured approach with predictable routines. They may forget steps in even familiar routines, however, and require much patience and repetition. These students need more help than others in learning to identify and pay attention to relevant cues. Point out cues and relevant directions and have students repeat directions out loud to be sure they understand what to do. Place a special emphasis on what is correct rather than on what they are doing wrong. Model the appropriate behavior or actions to ensure they are transferring positive learning rather than reinforcing negative learning. Avoid trial and error activities where they may spend too much time doing the wrong thing, thus adding to their confusion.

Overlearning is important for these students, especially because of their retention problems. Remember that it is more helpful to distribute numerous short practices of tasks over a period of time than to have fewer long practices. These students benefit from a wide range of multisensory experiences in learning concepts. These experiences help learning disabled students to overcome problems they have because of lack of experience with their environments. Be aware that although social praise may help motivate, it may also interfere with development of independent decision-making skills. Use praise sparingly, gradually reducing it to enhance internal motivation and satisfaction.

Students with learning disabilities often develop behavior problems. They may benefit from keeping their own record of specific behaviors including completion of assignments. This helps them to build a sense of control over themselves and their environment.

Students with Emotional or Behavioral Problems

Remembering that students with a diagnosed emotional disturbance are usually different from others merely in the degree of emotionality rather than in the type of feelings they have may relieve some potential anxiety in working with these students. Any psychological report available can be helpful (it must, of course, be treated confidentially), both in shedding light on why students are having such problems and in providing recommendations for working with them successfully. The school psychologist and special education teacher can also help you understand and support these students. It is likely that a behavior management plan has been developed through the special education services, so being familiar with this and clear on how to follow it may prevent problems from occurring. If behavior is a serious issue, it is advisable to overlook minor inappropriate behavior, reinforce acceptable behavior, and reduce known stressors. This may include adjusting your expectations if the student is having an especially bad day. A positive, supportive, structured, and predictable environment is of key importance to help the student feel safe and accepted.

If you have students who tend to have temper outbursts or become easily or violently frustrated and angry, reinforce all attempts they make toward self-control. Learn to recognize any behavioral cues that may precede an outburst so you can anticipate and intervene to prevent their losing control. Maintain a balanced perspective, remembering that it is more important that they get through the day without an outburst than that they follow instructions exactly or complete assignments errorlessly. Sometimes, if you think problems are developing, but before they escalate, it is helpful to allow the students to change their activity momentarily to defuse the situation (e.g., "Would you be willing to take this note to the office for me?" or "Why don't you get a drink of water and then we'll work this out together?"). Offering structured choices can also be helpful, especially with students who have a strong need to control and who often appear noncompliant and oppositional (e.g., "Would you prefer to do the odd-numbered problems or the even-numbered?" or "Would it be helpful for you to work awhile in the study carrel, or do you think you can concentrate well enough at your own desk?").

Work with your principal, counselor, and other teachers to devise a plan to carry out if students with emotional problems have a tantrum or explode in your classroom. These students may need to be removed from the classroom to a safe time-out place; they will need to be supervised as they cool down. Students with emotional or behavioral problems often do not know why they lose control and are frequently embarrassed and remorseful afterward. These students generally do not understand how their feelings relate to what has happened and have not learned to discern the subtle changes in themselves that trigger such outbursts. Learning to anticipate and divert these feelings in an acceptable manner is often their greatest need.

After any kind of violent outburst, when both you and the student have regained your composure (and it may take longer for one than for the other), it is important that you reestablish your relationship with the student. Other than attempting to learn from each incident to prevent future occurrences, it is best to leave each incident behind and not focus on past failures.

One crucial reminder: When students lose rational control and are verbally or physically abusive or violent, it is rarely personally directed at you, even though it may sound and feel that way. If you have learned about the backgrounds and histories of these students, logic will tell you that you have merely been a handy target, not the root cause of their pain or rage. Logic and feelings do not always coincide, however. Having someone listen to you and give you support and feedback when dealing with extremely volatile students is essential to your ability to continue to be supportive for these students.

Students with Attention Deficit and Hyperactivity

Broad characteristics of students with attention deficit and hyperactivity include distractibility, a short attention span, impulsiveness, an inability to organize, and a high level of physical movement. As distracting as these behaviors are, it is important to remember that they are not deliberate. Even for the most highly motivated children it is difficult, and it takes a long time for them to learn ways to compensate for or control these problems. A low-key approach with much predictability and structure is almost essential to enable these students to function successfully. Frequent communication with parents, often daily, is necessary to ensure that school and home techniques and expectations are compatible.

Techniques that have been found to have the greatest degree of success in working with these children include:

- Be sure you have their attention before giving oral instructions.

- Give brief and clear instructions, preferably one step at a time.

- If instructions involve a series of steps, have these written in sequence; teach these students to complete one step before going on to the next. Having them mark off each step as they complete it helps them to keep track and see progress.

- Monitor them closely as they begin a new assignment or activity; be willing to explain directions again.

- Adjust the amount of work required within a time period compatible with their attention span. The amount may gradually be increased as their ability to concentrate increases.

- Remind them that accuracy is more important than speed and that they need not be the first to finish or to speak up. Reinforce neatness and accuracy; when feasible, do not penalize messiness or errors. When accuracy is an issue, reinforce effort.

◆ Retrieve completed assignments, as they often lose completed work before turning it in.

◆ Show them how to use window cards as frames to help focus attention on a specific area, problem, line of print, or paragraph. Teach them to use their fingers as pointers so they stay focused on the page or line.

◆ Organize the daily schedule so that stimulating or exciting activities come after, rather than before, activities requiring concentration.

◆ Develop a plan so they can move around every few minutes; for example, by bringing up their papers after they have completed part of the assignment (e.g., a few math problems, a paragraph).

◆ Find a spot with few distractions and offer the option of doing independent work there.

◆ Prepare several low-pressure, low-risk activities for times when they need to spend a few minutes regaining control or relaxing.

◆ Teach them relaxation techniques such as deep breathing, tensing and relaxing muscles, etc., to relieve tension during long periods or tests.

◆ If students receive medication at school, establish a cue or routine to help them remember to go to the nurse at the proper time. Monitor this until they have assumed the responsibility successfully.

◆ Express your confidence in them and their ability to learn new concepts and skills.

Students Who Are Deaf or Hearing Impaired

Students with serious hearing loss may be able to function in regular classes if some crucial modifications are made. If you have one or more students who are deaf or hearing impaired, it will be helpful to consult regularly with a teacher specializing in auditory handicaps about students' needs and techniques that will benefit. If assistive devices are available (e.g., FM auditory systems, caption decoders for videos), the specialist can show you how to use them.

It is usually best to seat these students near the center of the room and close to the front. It is always wise to face the students when speaking, using the overhead projector rather than the chalkboard. As you talk, this will enable them to see your face while you are writing. Have the room well-lighted so these students can see your lips and face to lip-read. Take care not to stand in front of windows or a bright doorway while talking; the glare behind you will make your face difficult to see.

Often, these students miss out on important information, being able to catch only portions of words or phrases. Because understanding is more complex than just hearing or responding to a name and because these students are often reluctant to ask you to repeat, be ready to repeat and rephrase important information or instructions. When possible, provide written back-up as well. The amount of new content vocabulary introduced routinely may be overwhelming, so the support of the auditory specialist in introducing vocabulary may be necessary for these students to succeed in the regular classroom. Content Mastery, a special form of supplementary program described earlier in this chapter, may be utilized to reteach, especially written language assignments.

During classroom discussions, these students will need you to restate other students' questions and responses, because the deaf or hearing impaired students will probably not be able to lip-read these. It will also be helpful to check for understanding frequently during guided practice. They will require close monitoring as they begin written work. If note taking is required, ask a student with legible handwriting to take notes using carbon paper or to provide a copy to students needing help. Deaf or hearing impaired students cannot take notes and lip-read at the same time. During films, the narration and placement of actors may make it impossible to lip-read at all. The specialist may be a helpful resource in locating captioned versions of the videos you plan to use. You might also assign a buddy to cue deaf or hearing impaired students when it is important to watch the teacher, to locate information in the text being discussed, and so on.

Increasingly, deaf and hearing impaired students are assigned interpreters to accompany them to regular classes. Again, a consultation with the specialist on your campus for deaf or hearing impaired students will be helpful to make clear what the role of the interpreter is to be. Interpreters may assist with oral or sign language interpretation and provide a "communication bridge" between teacher and student. As such, they relay information both from the teacher to the student and vice versa, but they do not typically function as a teacher assistant in the classroom. Their role is to devote their skills to supporting their assigned deaf or hearing impaired student to ensure this student's success.

Students Who Have Visual Impairments

Students who are blind or who have severe visual impairments may be able to function well in regular classes with your help. Suggestions for adaptations of teaching methods and materials should be available in the student's functional visual assessment written by a teacher of these students. The following suggestions may provide direction in accommodating the needs of these students.

1. Remember to verbalize anything that is written on the chalkboard, overhead projector, or chart paper.

2. Allow students to use a tape recorder or to have fellow students make copies of their notes for parents to read aloud at home. Large type, dark print, and good contrast are easier to see.

3. When possible, use tactile models and hands-on activities along with verbal descriptions to demonstrate concepts; these students often miss gestures, facial expressions, and details in demonstrations.

4. Encourage students to ask for help; if in doubt about how you can help them, ask them directly and do not hesitate to discuss their vision problems with them.

5. Remember that students with partial vision may tire more quickly, in part because of the concentration and effort required to perceive material close to their eyes. Frequent changes in the focus of activities may alleviate this.

6. Seat these students with their backs to the windows. Glare on materials, on someone who is speaking, or on the chalkboard or other displays will seriously impede their ability to see at all.

7. Allow these students to walk up to the chalkboard or other displays as needed.

8. Students with visual impairments may have limited knowledge of spatial relationships and directionality. They may miss social cues and thus need assistance in peer interactions and personal adjustment.

Students with Limited English Proficiency

There are many students in our schools for whom English is not their first language. Some of these students have acquired sufficient English language skills to perform successfully in English-only classes. Other students have not acquired a sufficient level of skill in speaking, understanding, reading, or writing English, and they need additional assistance to participate successfully in school activities.

Some students need bilingual classes in which school content is presented in their native language, with a specified amount of time daily spent learning English. Other children know enough English to benefit from being in a class with a bilingual teacher; here, the content is presented in English, but the teacher is able to explain in the students' primary language when necessary. For many students, English learning occurs in conjunction with content learning in a regular classroom, ideally with the aid of an English-as-a-Second-Language (ESL) certified classroom teacher and with instruction in English for a portion of the day.

Although children who speak virtually no English will probably have a bilingual or an ESL teacher for most of the day, they often attend such subjects as P.E., music, and art without support of the bilingual teacher. If you find that you have students who speak little or no English in your class, here are suggestions to help you communicate with them.

1. Find out from the bilingual or ESL teacher which children understand some English and which ones understand none, so your expectations will be fair and realistic.

2. Learn what the children prefer to be called and be sure to pronounce their names correctly.

3. Learn key words in the children's native language, such as "listen," "yes," "no," "please," "good," "stop," "look," and "thank you."

4. Rather than relying on someone to translate for you, use your creativity in communicating, speaking naturally, and using phrases and many gestures.

5. Reinforce key points with visual aids and demonstration when possible and by repeating in clear and concise words.

6. Because these children are not accustomed to processing English, assume they will not understand what is said and ask the bilingual or ESL teacher to encourage them to pay close attention when they are with you to see if there are words or phrases they can understand or learn.

7. Consider assigning peer "buddies," who are outgoing and warm, to communicate what you cannot and to let you know when the students need your help when they are reluctant to ask.

8. Keep in mind that a long receptive period, during which they will respond with gestures or nods before they feel confident enough to speak any English words, is normal for students with limited English proficiency.

9. Be careful not to ignore or marginalize these students; include them in class activities as much as possible. For example, assign them to cooperative small groups with their peers. They may not be able to participate fully at first, but the interactions with their peers are important.

TEACHING LOWER ACHIEVING STUDENTS

Many teachers feel they need help in organizing instruction to teach successfully the students who are on a low academic level. Whether you have a class with only a few low achievers or one with many students whose entering skills are far below grade level, you will need to give special attention to the instructional needs of these students.

In many cases, students who are achieving substantially below grade level come from disadvantaged or low socioeconomic backgrounds. Research has shown that these students may not benefit from the same teaching strategies that work with average or high-achieving students who have learned how to learn early in life. In addition, techniques that are good instructional practices with all student populations are especially important when teaching low-achieving students.

Active Instruction

Research has shown that students at a low academic level make more progress in basic skills when their teachers provide structured classroom activities with close teacher supervision and lots of active, teacher-led instruction. Large amounts of class time spent in unstructured or free-time activities should be avoided, as should situations calling for frequent student self-direction and self-pacing. It is especially important for lower-achieving students to have many opportunities to interact with the teacher during instruction, and to answer teacher questions and receive feedback about their work. Low-achieving students should be seated where they can easily be monitored and given assistance.

Organizing and Pacing Instruction

When teaching lower-achieving students, you can encourage more student learning and better classroom behavior if you break instruction into small segments or short activities with frequent assessments of student understanding. Avoid activity plans that require students to attend to a presentation or to work for twenty-five or thirty minutes at a stretch on the same seatwork assignment. Instead, use two or more shorter cycles of content development and work samples in each lesson, as described in Chapter 5. There are two distinct advantages of using several cycles instead of one when teaching lower-ability students. One advantage is that it is easier to maintain student involvement. Also, by carefully monitoring the first seatwork/classwork exercise, you can easily observe whether students are able to complete the assignments, which in turn makes it easier for you to pace instruction appropriately and give ample feedback to students.

In planning lessons, keep in mind that especially with lower-ability students it is better to cover material very thoroughly than to cover a lot of material quickly. Plan for plenty of practice and repetition and keep your lesson plans flexible enough to allow for reteaching. This does not mean, however, that assignments for lower-level students should be limited to routine, repetitious, and uninteresting work. On the contrary, assignments and class discussion should provide opportunities for all your students to think, be creative, and organize and apply what they know. At least some of the questions lower-ability students encounter in written and oral work should give them practice with these higher level operations.

Plan introductions of new content very carefully. Clear communication is important in all classes, but it is especially important when teaching lower-achieving students. Careless, overly complex communication is likely to result in student confusion, frustration, and misbehavior. Follow the guidelines for clarity discussed in Chapter 7, paying careful attention to the amount of information presented at one time, appropriate vocabulary, and the use of concrete or specific examples to illustrate new concepts. Check for student understanding frequently. Avoid overlapping many procedural directions. Get students' attention, then present directions in a step-by-step fashion, waiting for students to complete each step before going on to the next.

Remedial Instruction

For learning to occur, all students (and especially lower-achieving students) must be provided with instructional materials and tasks at which they can succeed. Lower-achieving students often require remedial instruction. When beginning a new unit, you may find that some students do not have prerequisite skills. Or after teaching a lesson, you may realize that several students have not mastered the new material. Both of these situations require that you provide remedial instruction. Two considerations are crucial: You must build time for remediation into your classroom activity plans, and you must get instructional materials that are appropriate for the students who need remediation. Talk with your instructional supervisor, a resource teacher, or other teachers to obtain instructional materials that your low-ability students will be able to complete successfully.

Building Positive Attitudes

Even in lower elementary grades, lower-achieving students are more likely to have developed a poor self-image or poor attitude toward school. By the upper elementary grades, lower academic level students have often fallen two or more grade levels below average for their grade and age group. Some may have failed one or more grades in previous years. Because of their frequent failure in school in the past, some of these students will have become very discouraged; they may react by giving up easily or by fighting back. These reactions may be evidenced in the extremes of apathy, shyness, belligerence, or clowning in class. Especially in earlier grades, these students may perceive classroom events as arbitrary or mysterious. They do not expect to understand or to succeed in schoolwork, and maintaining their attention for long periods of time may be difficult, particularly when they encounter demanding or frustrating tasks.

As a teacher of lower-achieving students, an important part of your task is to improve these students' self-images and expectations of accomplishment. There are several steps you can take. First, remember that it is important for these students to finish their work and not give up. This may require that you shorten assignments for some or provide students with extra time and encouragement to finish their work. Be careful, however, that the extra time lower-achieving students are given to finish assignments does not prevent them from participating in interesting and worthwhile activities with the rest of the class. Constantly being denied participation in show-and-tell, art activities, interest centers, and recess will not contribute to an improved self-image. A better approach is to provide materials and assignments that lower-achieving students are able to finish in the available time.

Class discussions are opportunities for students to display their knowledge. Because teachers' questions and students' answers are heard by everyone, the teacher's handling of discussions often communicates expectations about student performance. The way lower-achieving students are treated during class discussions can have effects on their attitudes and achievement. Staying with students until they answer a question, giving them time to answer without being interrupted, providing constructive feedback to wrong answers, and helping students improve their answers are all ways that you can help low-achieving students succeed.

A warm, supporting, and accepting classroom climate will benefit lower-achieving students, but be thoughtful in your use of praise. Research suggests that praise is more helpful when it is specific and contingent on good work or good behavior or both. Don't make the mistake of frequently rewarding lower-achieving students with vague or general praise or praise for wrong answers or sloppy, incomplete work. This kind of teacher behavior may confuse students or convey the message that you don't expect much from them. Be alert for opportunities to give slower students deserved and specific praise.

TEACHING HIGHER-ACHIEVING STUDENTS

Higher-ability students may present special challenges in heterogeneous classes. The need to keep these students productively involved in learning activities requires that they be challenged at the appropriate level and be given sufficient activities to avoid boredom or disruption of the rest of the class.

Research has shown that higher-ability students learn more when they are challenged. The level of success on activities can sometimes be lower than that needed for students with less ability; that is, they may not become as frustrated if they do not perform with an extremely high level of success. Effective teachers of higher-ability students tend to work at a faster pace than normal with these students, and they introduce more variety in their teaching methods and materials.

It bears noting that not all of your high-ability students will function in your classroom in the same way. Some high-ability students may also be high achievers; these students are often a joy to work with. High achievers may be well-socialized, independent workers who have developed positive attitudes toward school and learning. Some high-ability students, however, may appear very different. They may be highly creative, highly divergent, gifted thinkers who approach every problem you present in your classroom differently from their peers, or they may create behavior problems. You must be careful not to confuse compliant behavior with academic ability.

The ability, creativity, and divergence of students who are gifted should be nurtured and encouraged, but this may be difficult in a heterogeneous classroom. Classrooms with more open-ended assignments, where each student may pursue a project or a problem to the extent of his or her ability, may provide more support for divergent thinkers and may help to avoid behavior problems which arise out of boredom or frustration with the limitations of highly structured assignments.

Have resource materials available for these students to use for bonus questions or extra projects. Develop a file box of index cards with a variety of ideas for projects. Include extra or bonus questions on all assignments and tests and encourage these students to attempt these. If your classroom or school library has a computer, check out programs from your educational service center or public library that provide enrichment to areas you are covering in class. Involve these students in activities that can benefit others, such as peer tutoring, peer counseling, school improvement projects, etc. Encourage your higher-ability students to keep up with current events (as appropriate for their age) and to write their questions or opinions to the newspaper or to people in the news.

Higher-ability students can contribute greatly to the learning environment in your classroom. Their contributions to class discussions and activities may encourage creativity and divergent thought in your other students. Your response to them, as well as to the other special groups that will make up your class, will signal to all students their range of abilities, interests, and skills is welcomed and appreciated.

FURTHER READING

Buzzell, J. G., & Piazza, R. (1994). *Case studies for teaching special needs and at-risk students.* Albany, NY: Delmar Publishers Inc.

> *This book contains more than twenty cases written by teachers chronicling their experiences with teaching students with special needs. The cases cover the full range of physical, mental, and emotional disabilities and provide grounding for analysis and problem solving.*

Holubec, E. J. (1992). How do you get there from here? Getting started with Cooperative Learning. *Contemporary Education, 63* (3), 181–184.

> *Cooperative Learning groups are a favorite method for teachers to use to accommodate diversity among learners. This article presents many good ideas for "easing into" the use of this approach. The author also discusses common problems that may be encountered when groups are first used.*

Kronberg, R., Jackson, L., Sheets, G., & Rogers-Connolly, T. (1995). A toolbox for supporting integrated education. *Teaching Exceptional Children, 27* (4), 54–58.

> *Including special needs students in the regular education classroom requires that special educators, regular educators, and administrators work together to develop new conceptions about roles and responsibilities. This article suggests a framework for thinking about how all participants should cooperate, and it also describes numerous activities and strategies to further this goal.*

Students with special needs [Special issue]. (1996). *Educational Leadership, 53*(5).

> *This theme issue contains helpful articles about the challenges in educating students with special needs. The authors deal with such issues as preventing learning disabilities through early intervention programs (Slavin), teaching English language learners (Gersten), holistic approaches to teaching students with Attention Deficit Disorder (Armstrong), and identifying and developing special talents (Feldhusen).*

Tomlinson, C. A. (1995). *How to differentiate instruction in mixed-ability classrooms.* Alexandria, VA: ASCD.

> *This book is a helpful guide for teachers who want to accommodate student diversity in their classrooms. The author describes differentiated instruction, suggests how to plan for it and how to manage it, and provides guidelines for assessing student progress. The appendix describes several strategies for accommodating diverse learners and gives rationales and guidelines for the use of each.*

SUGGESTED ACTIVITIES

I. Read Case Studies 9–1 and 9–2 to see two teachers' strategies for working with special needs students.

2. Problems 9–1 and 9–2 describe two situations that elementary teachers frequently encounter. Use ideas presented in this chapter to identify strategies that could be used in these situations. Check your ideas with the suggestions in the Appendix.

CASE STUDY 9-1

ORGANIZING READING INSTRUCTION FOR LOW ACADEMIC LEVEL STUDENTS

Mr. Bartolo is beginning his second year as a first-grade teacher in an urban elementary school that serves a predominantly Hispanic population. His twenty-six students present a variety of challenges—a wide range of reading levels, several students with limited English proficiency, students who receive supplemental instruction from the resource teacher, and one student who has been diagnosed with attention deficit hyperactivity disorder.

In his first year of teaching, Mr. Bartolo used the recommended reading basal series with small, homogeneous groups of students. He has followed this format for the first six weeks of his second year, but he is especially concerned with the progress of two students in the classroom. The first student, Jason, is one of four students in the highest reading group. Jason has above average academic abilities, but has difficulty getting along with his classmates. The second student, Juan, is one of five students in the lowest reading group. Juan's family immigrated from Puerto Rico at the beginning of the school year, and he speaks limited English.

Mr. Bartolo is familiar with peer tutoring, and he knows that several of his colleagues utilize it in their classrooms. After discussing peer tutoring with a colleague and with the boys' parents, he decides to implement this strategy with Jason and Juan. Mr. Bartolo hopes that the tutoring arrangement can strengthen Jason's social skills and help Juan's reading.

Before the peer tutoring begins, Mr. Bartolo knows that he must work with Jason and Juan to teach them strategies for comprehension and decoding unknown words during their small-group reading instruction. Other skills necessary for peer tutoring such as listening, sharing, and problem solving have been emphasized during the first six weeks of school. In addition to these skills, Mr. Bartolo schedules extra time to practice the peer tutoring with Jason and Juan. After several practice sessions, Jason and Juan begin the tutoring without Mr. Bartolo's assistance. He continues to monitor and intervene as necessary, and he sees signs of improvement in the boys.

Along with the small-group instruction and limited implementation of peer tutoring, Mr. Bartolo modifies students' assignments as necessary. This includes making audio tapes of books, shortening assignments, providing one-on-one instruction, and designing literacy projects for heterogeneous cooperative groups. Mr. Bartolo is confident that his students' reading comprehension has improved this year. He is thinking of expanding the peer tutoring to include every student in his class next year. What things should he consider?

CASE STUDY 9-2

SUPPORTING STUDENTS WITH AUDITORY DISABILITIES IN THE CLASSROOM

Ms. Chin has a lively class of twenty-four second graders, two of whom have severe auditory impairments. Bobby wears hearing aids that require Ms. Chin to wear an FM power pack so he can hear what she is saying. Sally has a cochlear implant, but she has virtually no hearing. Both children use sign language; Bobby speaks to some extent. An interpreter follows them throughout the day, sitting or standing near the teacher during instruction and signing. The interpreter stays near them during independent work periods to translate and sign any teacher instructions that may be out of the children's line of vision.

During the first week of school, and before Bobby and Sally began attending Ms. Chin's class full-time, she explained hearing impairments to the class so they would understand. A specialist for the auditorily impaired showed the students the FM equipment, let them hear through it, and played a tape to demonstrate what sounds were like for those with hearing loss. Ms. Chin also spoke with the class about the interpreter's role, emphasizing that all the students were to look at the teacher, not the interpreter. She marked a place on the carpet with masking tape as "Sally's spot," because Sally needed to be at the front and center of the room to see the teacher and the interpreter during rug time.

Ms. Chin learned basic signs herself and began using these while speaking to the class. Above the alphabet letters at the top of the chalkboard, she posted hand signs for each letter. She found that several children quickly picked up signing and began communicating with Sally and Bobby with signs, words, and gestures. The school also has a "Sign Club," through which the entire student body learns five new signs a week.

During center time, Ms. Chin usually places the FM power pack in the middle of the table for Bobby. She has taken care to let both Bobby and Sally sit near children with whom they have made friends, because this eases their problems with communication. Many of the activities are already structured to be hands-on, a preferred means of learning for auditorily impaired students. Ms. Chin does not use phonics approaches with Sally and Bobby, because even with Bobby's partial hearing he misses distinctions among the "ch," "sh," "th," etc. sounds. Ms. Chin works closely with the special education teacher, who also teaches Bobby and Sally for part of the day, to coordinate and reinforce what they are learning. Ms. Chin also communicates often with Bobby's and Sally's parents so they too can reinforce what the children are learning in school.

The teacher keeps a signing manual in her classroom and when she starts a new unit, she sends vocabulary words home along with the signs for any words that are unusual, so she, the interpreter, the special education teacher, and the parents will be consistent in using the same signs. Bobby and Sally learn vocabulary words both orally and through signs. Several other manipulatives are available to help these students learn such as a number line, shapes, and puzzle boards.

PROBLEM 9-1

TEAM TEACHING

Mr. Miller and two other fourth-grade teachers use team teaching for math instruction. Shortly after lunch each day, some students from the other teachers' classes come to Mr. Miller's room while some of his students go to the other two teachers' rooms. Mr. Miller has grown dissatisfied with the arrangement because he feels that too much of his teaching time is wasted while groups change rooms, get organized, and get ready to work. Sometimes, early-arriving students disrupt lessons. At other times, stragglers hold up the rest of the class. Students frequently arrive without the materials they need for that day. While Mr. Miller answers questions and deals with problems, students begin chatting and wandering around. When Mr. Miller is ready to start the lesson, he has trouble getting students settled down to work. What can Mr. Miller do to make teaming work more smoothly?

PROBLEM 9-2

A HETEROGENEOUS CLASS

Ms. Ortiz feels that her class this year is more difficult to teach than any she has had in her four years of teaching third grade. Of twenty-six students in class, seven are beginning the school year functioning at first-grade level or below in reading. Five of these seven are also far behind in mathematics concepts; the other two are on grade level. Three students in the class have advanced reading and mathematics skills, whereas others are nearer to grade level. Ms. Ortiz is frustrated in her attempts to meet the needs of the slowest students while challenging the brighter students. She now conducts four reading groups. What strategies might Ms. Ortiz consider?

Appendix: Answer Keys for Chapter Activities

CHAPTER 1

Activity 1

The room arrangement shown in Figure 1–2 could contribute to classroom management problems in a number of ways:

- When the teacher presents information to the whole class from the area near the main chalkboard, students on the other side of the room will be quite distant from the chalkboard and the teacher. This will make it difficult for them to see some of the material written on the chalkboard, and it will be more difficult for the teacher to monitor these students. At the same time, the teacher's range of movement is restricted to a relatively small area, and there is no place to store materials needed in whole-group presentations.

- Traffic lanes are clogged or blocked, especially near the bookshelves, computer, and en route to the bathrooms and the pencil sharpener.

- The small-group table in the center of the room is too near student desks. Not only might the arrangement cause distractions for students seated at their desks, but there is no place at the table where the teacher can sit and easily see everybody in the room.

- The teacher should consider using a low bookcase to avoid blocking the view of the center. Because of the location of the bookcase, the center may be difficult to monitor.

- Some students have their backs to the chalkboard and to the main presentation area.

- When the teacher assists individual students at their desks, he or she will have difficulty seeing students in several places in the room.

- The isolated desk near the girls' restroom door is a source of potential problems. Not only does it block the path to the door and to the computer, but a student seated at the desk would be distracted by and be a distraction to students coming and going from this area. Also, the location of the desk makes it difficult for the teacher to monitor a student seated there.

◆ The student sitting at the desk against the teacher's desk might be distracted if the teacher worked with other students at the desk. Also, this desk is far from the main instructional area.

CHAPTER 3

Case Study 3-4

DIAGNOSIS

The continuing confusion of Mr. Ambrose's students about due dates, directions, and completion of work suggests that although he may have planned plenty of activities for the students, he may not be explaining requirements clearly or checking for understanding frequently enough. In addition, students are not receiving feedback about their progress or the quality of their work, nor are there any apparent rewards or penalties connected with work completion or lack of it. Having students hold papers until the next day may result in many of them being misplaced and in further delay in receiving feedback about the correctness of the work.

SUGGESTIONS

Mr. Ambrose can begin to improve his situation by trying the following strategies:

◆ Each assignment should be explained carefully and in detail in addition to being posted on the chalkboard. Students could also be encouraged to keep an assignment book or some other record of daily assignments in particular subjects. In addition, Mr. Ambrose could keep a record of the assignments in a folder so that students could refer to it if needed or check on assignments they missed while they were absent. Keeping several days' assignments posted on the chalkboard may be confusing unless these are clearly marked.

◆ While giving directions and explanations, Mr. Ambrose should be aware of signs of confusion or inattention. He should also be sure to go over sample questions, problems, or exercises with the class, use a standard format for student headings on papers, and use routines whenever possible to avoid constantly having to re-explain or give new directions.

◆ Mr. Ambrose should also have students begin assignments under his direction. He can do a small part of the assignment orally, then question students to check their understanding until he is sure they can work independently.

◆ He should circulate around the class and monitor student progress rather than sit at his desk doing paperwork. He should allow students to come to his desk for help only after they have tried the assignment. Then he should allow only one student at a time to come up. When several students need help, he should circulate around the class again rather than encouraging "come-ups."

◆ Assignments should be checked and collected as they are completed. If they are too complex to be checked immediately, Mr. Ambrose should check for completeness and return incomplete work to the students to finish. It may be helpful to set aside one or two specific times each day to review each student's progress on assignments. That way, students will know they are accountable, and Mr. Ambrose can more easily identify problems that students are having with work. In addition, he will be able to identify students who are having difficulty and need extra help before they get too far behind. Students who fail to turn in assignments should be given assistance and direction promptly.

◆ Students can be encouraged to set goals by helping them keep records of their scores on assignments in particular subjects. Mr. Ambrose may be able to boost motivation by encouraging the students to set a class goal of improved completion rates or overall student averages and may then provide a treat or a special activity as a reward.

CHAPTER 5

Problem 5-1

In organizing her students' day, Ms. Kendall must plan to accommodate both "school givens" of time and space and "pupil givens" of numbers and abilities. Before developing her daily schedule, Ms. Kendall must first check the school's master schedule to learn what times have been assigned to her class for lunch, recess, music, art, physical education, etc. In planning around these time constraints, she must consider how many students will be in the class, the range of their ability levels, and the size of the classroom. She must take into consideration both student attention patterns throughout the day and student attention spans within the day. As students tend to be more alert in the morning and less alert after lunch, she will want to schedule academic subjects accordingly. Also, she will need to provide a variety of activities, with none lasting too long. Room size, however, will determine the number of centers and individual study areas available.

On the first day of school, Ms. Kendall's plans should include the following: greet the students; give a brief introduction of herself and her class; explain the areas of the room and procedures needed for the first week; begin a presentation and discussion of class rules, procedures, and consequences; direct a student get-acquainted activity; provide whole-class, uncomplicated academic activities; allow time to complete administrative tasks; have constructive "time fillers" ready for use if needed.

CHAPTER 5

Problem 5-2

The following suggestions for Mr. Hart could improve his students' performance during independent work.

◆ He should make sure everyone understands instructions before starting groups. Explanation alone may not be sufficient; students should be questioned, and they should repeat key directions. Mr. Hart can also write the directions on the chalkboard. Students should be told what will be checked and when.

◆ If independent work includes silent reading, reading comprehension questions can be listed on the board so that students have a focus for their reading and know what they will be accountable for when they are called to the reading circle.

◆ Students may need help pacing themselves. The teacher can show them on the clock how much time the first assignment should take or set a timer to signal when they should be finished with a particular assignment.

◆ To have time to get the independent work group started, Mr. Hart can give the first reading group a getting-ready activity to complete before he joins them. This will enable him to monitor all out-of-group students at the beginning of the activity to be sure they have made a good start.

◆ After working with the reading group for a while, the teacher can give these students a short activity to do on their own while he checks on the progress of out-of-group students and answers their questions. When out-of-group students are wasting time and in danger of not completing other necessary activities, their papers can be marked to show each student's progress on the first assignment. They can then start on their next assignment, but they should be required to finish the first assignment at home or later in class.

◆ Students should not be allowed to interrupt the teacher with questions during small-group instruction. Students should be told to skip troublesome parts until the teacher can talk to them, or student monitors can be assigned the responsibility of giving assistance to children who need it.

◆ A visual signal, such as a sign or a flag, can be used to inform students when they may approach the teacher with questions and when they may not.

◆ A "help" list for the class may be established. Children can sign the list if they want to talk to the teacher when he is busy. The teacher needs to be conscientious about checking the list and going to the children as soon as possible (e.g., between reading groups).

◆ Students need to know what they may and may not do once their assignments have been completed. They should be given free-time enrichment activities or provided with a good set of interesting materials for free reading.

CHAPTER 5

Problem 5-3

Apparently, this type of instruction is new for Ms. Jackson's class, so students will need to learn a new set of procedures. They may be accustomed to highly directed lessons, and they may not have had much science instruction. Ms. Jackson will need to explain the procedures for a discovery lesson, including how to work on your own and with a partner and the purposes for this science lesson. She should make sure she has everyone's attention before beginning the explanation. She should start by introducing the lesson and its purposes and demonstrating appropriate uses of the cups. She must make clear at the beginning what uses of the cups she sees as inappropriate.

Ms. Jackson must consider how to create a balance between overdirecting students and leaving them too much on their own. She should work through questions like those in Checklist 5 to focus on her purposes for this lesson and which aspects of it are new to her students. For example, what kind of product does she expect from her students? Will they demonstrate their findings, write a lab report, apply their findings to another situation? If pairs or groups work independently, what will they do if they finish at different times?

Ms. Jackson needs to develop a system for distributing and collecting materials to minimize the time the teacher is unavailable to circulate and provide assistance. For example, she could appoint one student from each group as "Materials Manager" and set up a central place for that student to pick up cups for the group.

CHAPTER 5

Problem 5-4

See how many examples of Kounin's concepts you can find in the following description.

As he is about to begin class after lunch, Mr. Case makes eye contact with two students who are exchanging notes; the students quickly get out their class materials. (**Withitness.**) "Let's begin by working some of the exercises at the end of the chapter; you will need a piece of paper with a heading." As students begin to get out their materials, Mr. Case calls out, "Oops, I forgot to tell you to bring money for tomorrow for the field trip. How many of you will be going?" (**Thrust.**) After a brief discussion, students finish getting out their materials. Mr. Case says, "We'll go through these exercises orally, but I also want you to write the answers on your papers as part of today's classwork. I'll come around later and check your answers. (**High participation format and accountability.**) Now, who can answer the first question? Hands please. Tyrone?" Mr. Case conducts the lesson by calling on various students, some with hands up, others seemingly at random from the nonvolunteers. (**Group alerting.**) About halfway through the exercises, a student enters the room and says that he is new to the school and has been assigned to the class. Mr. Case goes to his desk, sits down, and says, "OK, come here. I'll check out some of your books to you. (**Lack of overlapping.**) I wish the school office wouldn't send children in the middle of the period. Where are you from anyway? That's a nice shirt you are wearing." (**Stimulus boundedness.**) After finishing with the student and sending him to a seat, Mr. Case leaves his desk and says to the class, "Now where were we? Oh, yes, question 7. Say, where did Kim and Lee go? I didn't give them permission to leave." (**Lack of withitness.**) After several more minutes, Mr. Case calls a halt to the activity and says, "Now, I'd like us to discuss the test coming up this Thursday. Let's make sure that you are all clear on what will be on the exam and what you will need to get ready for it." After a pause, he adds, "I almost forgot. Get your questions from before and look at the next to the last one. We need to add an important point that was left out. . . ." After finishing the item, Mr. Case turns the topic back to the upcoming test. (**Flip-flop.**) "Now, where were we. Oh, yes. I need to show you some items that will be similar to those on the test. Here's one." He writes it on the chalkboard, then pauses: "Well, I don't want to give away the test, do I?" Without discussing the test further, he turns to another topic. (**Dangle.**) "Just wait until you hear about the video tape we will be viewing tomorrow. I borrowed it from another teacher, and she said that her students thought it was one of the most interesting, exciting stories they had ever seen!" (**Group alerting.**)

CHAPTER 5

Case Study 5-1

DIAGNOSIS

Although Ms. Lake has planned interesting presentations, her students seem to be floundering during the follow-up activities. A large part of Ms. Lake's problem lies with poor instructional clarity, poor sequencing of activities, and unclear directions. Students' poor showing on the five-item test suggests that related content from the previous week had not been understood. The twenty-minute presentation contains several indicators of poor clarity, including presenting information out of sequence, backtracking, inserting extraneous information, and moving from one topic to another without warning. In addition, the assignment does not support the content development activity. The assignment is made without checking for understanding, and the directions are vague and indefinite.

SUGGESTIONS

Ms. Lake would achieve more success with her class if she concentrated on the following items:

◆ Information should be presented systematically; plan the lesson sequence and stick to it; state major goals and objectives; pace the lesson so that adequate time is available to cover major points; and avoid vagueness by being specific and using familiar words.

◆ Ms. Lake should review her procedures for keeping students responsible for work, especially in the areas of communicating work requirements and giving directions clearly. She should be sure that step-by-step directions are given for complex assignments, and she should ask students to repeat directions if there is a possibility they do not understand them.

◆ During content development activities, frequent work samples should be obtained and other checks on student comprehension used. With this information, available instruction can be adjusted as needed.

◆ The amount of information being presented in any one lesson should be considered carefully. It might be better to present less information and leave sufficient time to check classwork prior to assigning students homework.

◆ Complex lessons should be broken down into smaller parts, and later concepts should not be presented until primary ones are mastered.

◆ If some students still do not seem to understand after a presentation and discussion, the teacher can meet with them in a small group to review the presentation and answer questions. If one or two students consistently have difficulty, they can be seated near the teacher's desk so it is easier to work with them.

◆ During the independent work portion of lessons, the teacher should circulate to check student progress and to make sure that assignment directions are being followed.

CHAPTER 6

Problem 6-1

DIAGNOSIS

Ms. Greene has failed to communicate and reinforce her expectations for classroom behavior and to establish rules and procedures that deal with the problem areas in her classroom. She apparently did not stop inappropriate behavior when it first began occurring; as a result, what could have been a good start during the first weeks of school has deteriorated into a difficult situation. At this point, even the well-behaved students are misbehaving, and her only deterrent has lost its effect.

SUGGESTIONS

Ms. Greene should decide what kinds of behavior she expects of her students with regard to general conduct as well as procedures they should follow in particular activities. She should then develop new rules and procedures where they are needed and clarify and reteach those that were part of her original plan but are no longer effective. For example, she could set aside specific times for students to get drinks, use the restroom, sharpen pencils, or visit the class pets.

In addition, she should select a time—perhaps a Monday or the day after a school vacation—to introduce or to review and reteach the rules and procedures to her class. She should also explain to the students the rationales for the desired behaviors and perhaps rehearse complex ones so she can give students feedback about especially important behaviors. She will certainly want to review with the students about when they are allowed to whisper quietly. Because students have acquired poor classroom talk habits, they may need visual cues such as stop or go signs to remind them when they must work quietly and when they may whisper or talk in classroom voices. She can also help students learn when it is appropriate to talk quietly and when it is not by alerting them about class noise level and encouraging them to monitor it themselves.

Ms. Greene should review procedures for working in small groups with the students. She may need to adopt the following practices:

◆ Use shorter independent work periods, breaking up activities in the groups more often.

◆ Help students pace themselves by setting a timer to signal when work should be completed.

◆ Tell students ahead of time what work will be checked and when. Remind them they will be questioned about their assignment when they come to the reading circle.

◆ Make sure that students in the first group understand their assignment by checking for understanding and having them do an example or two before calling for the second group.

◆ Monitor the out-of-group students for appropriate behavior while working with the reading group.

◆ After sending one group back to independent work, don't call the second group until the work of the other students has been checked and help given when needed.

Once the rules and procedures are introduced—or reintroduced—to the class, Ms. Greene should:

◆ Monitor the class with the goal of anticipating and preventing misbehavior before it occurs and noting appropriate behavior.

◆ Make sure that students have enough work to do and that they understand and are able to complete activities. Students should also know what specific things they can do when they have finished their assigned work.

◆ Structure time for student movement and activity.

◆ Make statements that pace students through their work, such as: "You should now be working on problems 2 through 5. No one should be talking," or "After I've checked your paper you may go to the listening center."

◆ Reward academic performance and other desirable classroom behavior regularly, using stars, happy faces, displays of student work, pats on the back, smiles, etc.

◆ Be certain that stated consequences for inappropriate behavior are related to the misbehavior and that they can be carried out consistently. Positive consequences as well as negative ones should be communicated to students.

CHAPTER 7

Activity 7-2

1. b; 2. c; 3. d; 4. a; 5. c.

CHAPTER 9

Problem 9-1

The following approaches would help the team operate more smoothly:

◆ Strive for good cooperation and group planning among unit or team teachers. Each teacher must try to maintain the schedule. Have students watch the time. Post times for students to leave and list the materials they should take with them. Use a timer if necessary.

◆ Use established routines as much as possible for beginning and ending lessons; monitor the class to be sure students follow them.

◆ Teach students exactly what behaviors are expected during transitions; include expectations for voice level, use of the pencil sharpener, procedures for passing between classes, getting ready for the lesson, and so on.

◆ If early-arriving students are a problem, establish a "waiting area" where these students must wait quietly until the teacher can speak with them without interrupting the class.

◆ Use a short review activity with the group while waiting for stragglers to arrive.

◆ Make sure students know what they are supposed to do when they return to the class. If they return while the teacher is conducting a lesson, give the group or the class a brief activity to do while making sure students coming in get settled.

CHAPTER 9

Problem 9-2

Following are specific suggestions for Ms. Ortiz:

◆ Each day, plan assignments that all students can complete, then provide supplementary assignments at different levels: enrichment and extension for faster students, review and practice assignments for slower students.

◆ Find out if any students in the class qualify for special assistance (such as special education, resource room, or bilingual tutoring).

◆ Use some small-group instruction in both reading and (at least temporarily) in mathematics. Be sure to keep groups flexible, changing membership according to achievement.

◆ Consider whether it might be possible to team with one or more teachers so that students on similar levels can be grouped for basic skills instruction.

◆ Consider the use of peer tutoring for certain activities and assignments.

◆ Share materials with other teachers to build a collection of supplementary materials above and below your grade level.

◆ Arrange student seating so that you have easy access to lower-ability students and can monitor and help them readily during whole-class instruction.

◆ Be sure to include all students in class discussions and recitations. Do not let faster students answer most of the questions.

◆ After giving assignment directions to the whole class, check the lower-ability students first to make sure they understand directions and are beginning work. If more than two or three students need further directions, meet with them immediately as a small group.

◆ When instructing the lower-level students, break assignments and lessons into small segments and check frequently for understanding. Follow the suggestions for basic skill instruction presented in the section on teaching low ability students in Chapter 9.

◆ Consider using heterogeneous cooperative groups for activities and long-term projects.

References and Further Readings

Readers interested in other publications on classroom management by this book's authors and other writers in the field may choose from the following references.

Alberti, R. L., Ed. (1977). *Assertiveness: Innovations, applications, issues.* San Luis Obispo, CA: Impact Publishers.

Alvermann, D. E., O'Brien, D. G., & Dillon, D. R. (1990). What teachers do when they say they're having discussions of content area reading assignments: A qualitative analysis. *Reading Research Quarterly, 25,* 296–322.

Anderson, L. M. (1985). What are students doing when they do all that seatwork? In C. W. Fisher & D. C. Berliner (Eds.), *Perspectives on instructional time* (pp. 189–202), White Plains, NY: Longman.

Bandura, A. (1986). *Social foundations of thought and action.* Englewood Cliffs, NJ: Prentice-Hall, Inc.

Bassin, A., Bratter, E., & Rachin, R., Eds. (1976). *The Reality Therapy reader: A survey of the works of William Glasser.* New York: Harper & Row.

Bennett, N., & Dunne, E. (1992). *Managing classroom groups.* London: Simon & Schuster.

Berger, E. H. (1995). *Parents as partners in education: Families and schools working together* (4th ed.), Englewood Cliffs, NJ: Merrill/Prentice-Hall.

Brophy, J. (1981). Teacher praise: A functional analysis. *Review of Educational Research, 51,* 5–32.

Brophy, J. E., & Alleman, J. (1991). Activities as instructional tools: A framework for analysis and evaluation. *Educational Researcher, 20*(4), 9–23.

Burns, M. (1995). The 8 most important lessons I've learned about organizing my teaching year. *Instructor, 105*(2), 86–88.

Buzzell, J. G., & Piazza, R. (1994, October). *Case studies for teaching special needs and at-risk students.* Albany, NY: Delmar Publishers Inc.

Casey, M. B., & Tucker, E. C. (1994, October). Problem-centered classrooms: Creating lifelong learners. *Phi Delta Kappan,* 139–143.

Castle, K., & Rogers, K. (1994). Rule-creating in a constructivist classroom community. *Childhood Education, 70*(2), 77–80.

Cohen, E. G. (1994). Restructuring the classroom: Conditions for productive small groups. *Review of Educational Research, 64,* 1–36.

Cooperative learning [Special issue]. (1989/90). *Educational Leadership, 47*(4).

Crook, T. J. (1988). The impact of classroom evaluation practices on students. *Review of Educational Research, 58,* 438–481.

Curwin, R. L. (1995). A humane approach to reducing violence in schools. *Educational Leadership, 52*(5), 72–75.

Cutona, C., & Guerin, D. (1994). Confronting conflict peacefully: Peer mediation in schools. *Educational Horizons, 72*(2), 95–104.

Deci, E. L., & Ryan, R. M. (1985). *Intrinsic motivation and self-determination in human behavior.* New York: Plenum Press.

Doyle, W. (1983). Academic work. *Review of Educational Research, 53,* 159–199.

Doyle, W. (1986). Classroom management and organization. In M. Wittrock, Ed. *Handbook of research on teaching* (3rd ed., pp. 392–431). New York: Macmillan.

Dreikurs, R., Grunwald, B., & Pepper, F. (1982). *Maintaining sanity in the classroom: Classroom management techniques* (2nd ed.). New York: Harper & Row.

Duke, D. L., Ed. (1979). *Classroom management. The 78th Yearbook of the National Society for the Study of Education, Part II.* Chicago: University of Chicago Press.

Duke, D. L., Ed. (1982). *Helping teachers manage classrooms.* Alexandria, VA: Association for Supervision and Curriculum Development.

Edwards, C., & Stout, J. (1990). Cooperative learning: The first year. *Educational Leadership, 47* (4), 38–43.

Emmer, E. T. (1986). Academic activities and tasks in first-year teachers' classes. *Teaching and Teacher Education, 2,* 229–244.

Emmer, E. T. (1988). Classroom management and discipline. In V. Richardson-Koehler, Ed. *Educator's handbook: A research perspective* (pp. 233–258). New York: Longman.

Emmer, E. T. (1988). Praise and the instructional process. *Journal of Classroom Interaction, 23,* 32–39.

Emmer, E., & Aussiker, A. (1990). School and classroom discipline programs: How well do they work? In O. Moles, Ed. *Student discipline strategies: Research and practice* (pp. 129–165). Albany, NY: SUNY Press.

Emmer, E. T., & Evertson, C. M. (1981). Synthesis of research on classroom management. *Educational Leadership, 38,* 342–347.

Emmer, E. T., Evertson, C. M., & Anderson, L. M. (1980). Effective classroom management at the beginning of the school year. *The Elementary School Journal, 80,* 219–231.

Emmer, E. T., Evertson, C. M., Clements, B. S., & Worsham, M. E. (1994). *Classroom management for secondary teachers* (3rd ed.). Boston: Allyn & Bacon.

Evertson, C. M. (1982). Differences in instructional activities in higher- and lower-achieving junior high English and math classes. *The Elementary School Journal, 82,* 329–350.

Evertson, C. M. (1985). Training teachers in classroom management: An experimental study in secondary school classrooms. *Journal of Educational Research, 79,* 51–58.

Evertson, C. M. (1987). Managing classrooms: A framework for teachers. In D. Berliner & B. Rosenshine, Eds. *Talks to teachers* (pp. 54–74). New York: Random House.

Evertson, C. M. (1989). Improving elementary classroom management: A school-based training program for beginning the year. *Journal of Educational Research, 83*(2), 82–90.

Evertson, C. M. (1994). Classroom rules and routines. In T. Husen and T. N. Postlewaite (Eds.) *The International Encyclopedia of Education* (2nd ed.) Vol. 2, 816–820. Oxford: Pergamon Press.

Evertson, C. M., & Emmer, E. T. (1982). Effective management at the beginning of the school year in junior high classes. *Journal of Educational Psychology, 74,* 485–498.

Evertson, C. M., Emmer, E. T., Sanford, J. P., & Clements, B. S. (1983). Improving classroom management: An experiment in elementary school classrooms. *Elementary School Journal, 84*(2), 173–188.

Evertson, C. M., & Harris, A. H. (1992). What we know about managing classrooms. *Educational Leadership, 47*(7), 74–78.

Evertson, C. M., Sanford, J. P., & Emmer, E. T. (1981). Effects of class heterogeneity in junior high school. *American Educational Research Journal, 18,* 219–232.

Evertson, C. M., & Weade, R. (1989). Classroom management and teaching style: Instructional stability and variability in two junior high English classrooms. *The Elementary School Journal, 89,* 379–393.

Foster, H. L. (1986). *Ribbin', jivin', and playin' the dozens: The persistent dilemma in our schools* (2nd ed.). Cambridge, MA: Ballinger Publishing Co.

Gazda, G. et al. (1991). *Human relations development: A manual for educators* (4th ed.). Boston: Allyn & Bacon.

Glasser, W. (1975). *Reality Therapy: A new approach to psychiatry.* New York: Harper & Row.

Glasser, W. (1977). 10 steps to good discipline. *Today's Education, 66,* 60–63.

Glasser, W. (1986). *Control theory in the classroom.* New York: Harper & Row.

Good, T. L., & Brophy, J. E. (1994). *Looking in classrooms* (5th ed.). New York: Harper & Row.

Goodman, K. S. (1991). Yippie-aye-ay: Planning and organizing holistically. In Y. M. Goodman, W. J. Hood, & K. S. Goodman (Eds.), *Organizing for Whole Language* (pp. 3–17). Portsmouth, NH: Heinemann.

Gordon, T. (1974). *Teacher Effectiveness Training.* New York: Peter H. Wyden.

Holubec, E. J. (1992). How do you get there from here? Getting started with Cooperative Learning. *Contemporary Education, 63*(3), 181–184.

Johnson, D. W., & Johnson, R. T. (1994). Constructive conflict in the schools. *Journal of Social Issues, 50*(1), 117–137.

Johnson, D. W., & Johnson, R. T. (1991). *Learning together and alone: Cooperative, competitive, and individualistic learning* (3rd ed.). Boston: Allyn & Bacon.

Jones, V., & Jones, L. (1995). *Comprehensive classroom management: Motivating and managing students* (4th ed.). Boston: Allyn & Bacon.

Kagan, S. (1992). *Cooperative Learning Resources for Teachers.* San Juan Capistrano, CA: Resources for Teachers.

Kounin, J. S. (1970). *Discipline and group management in classrooms.* New York: Holt, Rinehart & Winston.

Kounin, J. S., & Gump, P. (1974). Signal systems of lesson settings and the task related behavior of preschool children. *Journal of Educational Psychology, 66,* 554–562.

Kounin, J. S., & Obradovic, S. (1968). Managing emotionally disturbed children in regular classrooms: A replication and extension. *Journal of Special Education, 2,* 129–135.

Kronberg, R., Jackson, L., Sheets, G., & Rogers-Connolly, T. (1995). A toolbox for supporting integrated education. *Teaching Exceptional Children, 27*(4), 54–58.

Lambert, N. M. (1994). Seating arrangements in classrooms. In T. Husen and T. N. Postlewaite (Eds.), *The International Encyclopedia of Education* (2nd ed.), Vol. 9, 5355–5359. Oxford: Pergamon Press.

Leinhardt, G., Weidman, C., & Hammond, K. M. (1987). Introduction and integration of classroom routines by expert teachers. *Curriculum Inquiry, 17*(2), 135–176.

Lepper, M. R., & Greene, D., Eds. (1978). *The hidden costs of reward: New perspectives on the psychology of human motivation.* Hillsdale, NJ: Erlbaum.

Maehr, M., & Midgley, C. (1991). Enhancing student motivation: A schoolwide approach. *Educational Psychologist, 26,* 399–427.

Marshall, H. H. (1987). Motivation strategies of three fifth-grade teachers. *The Elementary School Journal, 88*(2), 135–150.

Miller, P. W. (1981). Silent messages. *Childhood Education, 58*(1), 20–24.

Pitcher, G., & Poland, S. (1992). *Crisis intervention in the schools.* New York: Guilford Press.

Puro, P., & Bloome, D. (1987). Understanding classroom communication. *Theory into Practice, 26*(1), 26–31.

Raffini, J. P. (1996). *150 ways to increase intrinsic motivation in the classroom.* Boston: Allyn & Bacon.

Randolph, C. H., & Evertson, C. M. (1995). Managing for learning: Rules, roles, and meanings in a writing class. *Journal of Classroom Interaction, 30*(2), 17–25.

Rosenfield, P., Lambert, N. M., & Black, A. (1985). Desk arrangement effects on pupil classroom behavior. *Journal of Educational Psychology, 77*, 101–108.

Sanford, J. P., Clements, B. S., & Emmer, E. T. (1983). Improving classroom management. *Educational Leadership, 40*, 56–61.

Sanford, J. P., & Emmer, E. T. (1988). *Understanding classroom management: An observation guide.* Englewood Cliffs, NJ: Prentice-Hall.

Sanford, J., & Evertson, C. (1980). Classroom management in a low SES junior high: Three case studies. *Journal of Teacher Education, 32*(1), 34–38.

Schwarz, S., & Pollishuke, M. (1991). *Creating the child-centered classroom.* Katonah, NY: Richard Owen Publishers.

Short, K. G. (1992). Creating a community of learners. In K. Short & K. M. Pierce (Eds.), *Talking about books: Creating literate communities* (pp. 33–52). Portsmouth, NH: Heinemann.

Shrigley, R. L. (1985). Curbing disruption in the classroom—Teachers need intervention skills. *NASSP Bulletin, 69*(479), 26–32.

Slavin, R. (1995). *Cooperative learning: Theory, research, and practice* (2nd ed.). Boston: Allyn & Bacon.

Slavin, R., Sharan, S., Kagan, S., Hertz-Lazarowitz, R., Webb, C., & Schmuck, R., Eds. (1985). *Learning to cooperate, cooperating to learn.* New York: Plenum Press.

Solomon, D., Watson, M., Delucchi, K., Schaps, E., & Battistich, V. (1988). Enhancing children's prosocial behavior in the classroom. *American Educational Research Journal, 25*(4), 527–554.

Stigler, J. W., & Stevenson, H. W. (1991). How Asian teachers polish each lesson to perfection. *American Educator, 15*(1), 12–20, 43–47.

Stomfay & Stitz (1994). Pathways to Safer Schools. *Childhood Education, 70*(5), 279–282.

Stoner, G., Shinn, M., & Walker, H. (1991). *Interventions for achievement and behavior problems.* Silver Spring, MD: National Association of School Psychologists.

Strengthening Student Engagement [Special issue]. (1995). *Educational Leadership, 53*(1), 1–69.

Students with Special Needs [Special issue]. (1996). *Educational Leadership, 53*(5), 4–74.

Tomlinson, C. A. (1995). *How to differentiate instruction in mixed-ability classrooms.* Alexandria, VA: Association for Supervision and Curriculum Development.

Weade, R., & Evertson, C. (1988). The construction of lessons in effective and less effective classrooms. *Teaching and Teacher Education, 4*, 189–213.

Weinstein, C. S. (1979). The physical environment of the school: A review of research. *Review of Educational Research, 49*, 577–610.

Wiske, M. S. (1994). How teaching for understanding changes the rules in the classroom. *Educational Leadership, 51*(5), 19–21.

Wolfgang, C., & Glickman, C. (1986). *Solving discipline problems* (2nd ed.). Boston: Allyn & Bacon.

Woolfolk, A. E., & Galloway, C. M. (1985). Nonverbal communication and the study of teaching. *Theory into Practice, 24*(1), 77–84.

Zakariya, S. B. (1987). Fair, unfailing discipline is the least schools owe to delinquent kids. *American School Board Journal, 174*(2), 23–29.

Zucker, E. (1983). *Mastering assertiveness skills: Power and positive influence at work.* New York: AMACON.

Index